Beyond Token Change

Beyond Token Change

Breaking the Cycle of Oppression in Institutions

Anne Bishop

Fernwood Publishing • Halifax, Nova Scotia

Editing: Brenda Conroy
Printed and bound in Canada by Hignell Printing Limited

Every reasonable effort has been made to acquire permission for copyright material used in this book and to acknowledge such indebtedness accordingly. Any errors called to the publisher's attention will be corrected in future editions.

A publication of
Fernwood Publishing
Site 2A, Box 5, 32 Oceanvista Lane
Black Point, Nova Scotia, B0J 1B0
and 324 Clare Avenue
Winnipeg, Manitoba, R3L 1S3
www.fernwoodbooks.ca

Fernwood Publishing Company Limited gratefully acknowledges the financial support of the Department of Canadian Heritage, the Nova Scotia Department of Tourism and Culture and the Canada Council for the Arts for our publishing program.

Library and Archives Canada Cataloguing in Publication

Bishop, Anne, 1950-
Beyond token change : breaking the cycle of oppression in
institutions / Anne Bishop.

Includes bibliographical references and index.
ISBN 1-55266-163-6

1. Oppression (Psychology) 2. Organizational behavior. 3.Organizational change. 4. Discrimination in higher education. I. Title.

LC212.43.C3B58 2005   302.3'5   C2005-901066-5

Contents

This book is dedicated

*to the five strong women at the centre of "The Story"
and everyone caught in similar situations;*

*and to the memory of Barbara Rumscheidt, friend,
woman of both heart and mind, ally of gay and lesbian
people and many others. Barbara died the same day
the bits and pieces of this book finally came together
into a single first draft, January 20, 2003.*

Acknowledgements

I cannot name all the people who participated in the writing of this book, but here are a few of them:

The five women who survived the experiences recounted in "The Story" and re-lived them several times so that I could record them on paper. My deepest gratitude to Beth, Hannah, Laura, Lillian and Yuen.

I wish to recognize all the dedicated allies who sacrifice their time, energy, health and careers to support people caught in situations like that described in "The Story," especially Jennifer Bankier, Rosemary McKenzie and Madeleine Parent.

Wanda Walker, artist and designer, who worked hard to understand my complicated scribbles and record them in clear, understandable illustrations. She was full of life and creativity. Within days of finishing the task, she was killed by a man who should never have been released on parole, and wouldn't have been if the Parole Board had listened to Wanda.

I am deeply grateful to my thesis supervisors, Shelley Finson and Chris Levan, who spent a great deal of time and energy working with me on this project, over a long period of time.

The analysis in this book began to fall into shape during a research course taught by Pamela Brink in 1995. Her clarity, her book and her availability as an advisor ever since have been important to this project and several others.

My gratitude to the Coalition of Black and First Nations Faculty and Staff at Canadian University. I learned a great deal from my time with this group.

Several dedicated and knowledgeable human rights activists have contributed much to my thinking about institutional racism through the years that I have worked on this project, including Peter Englemann, Mike Dunphy, Maureen Webb, Maureen Shebib and Mary Margaret Dauphinee.

I am grateful to those who read the second-last draft of the book and gave me many excellent comments and references: Angela Freeman, Michael Hart, Les Jesudason, Charlotte Keen, Jan Morrell, Philippa Pictou, Maureen Shebib and Verna Thomas.

Particular thanks are due to Charlotte Keen, who helps me when I get stuck in my explorations of twentieth-century physics, Rieky Stuart, for our many conversations about institutional patterns of oppression, and

Robert Wright, for his exciting insights into the anti-racism learning process.

I also want to express my gratitude to the good people at Fernwood Publishing, Beverley Rach, Brenda Conroy, Errol Sharpe, Larissa Holman and Lindsay Sharpe. I am constantly reminded of how fortunate I am to be associated with a publisher as respectful of authors and grassroots communities as you are. I wouldn't even be an author without you.

And Jan, for everything.

Introduction

Over a period of many years, I came to understand that there are extra hurdles I must jump in my life because I am a woman and a lesbian. I found literature on oppression and liberation and explored these processes in my practice as an adult educator and community development worker. I also became involved in work against poverty and racism and discovered my role in the oppression of others. I found literature written by and about allies; for example, men working against sexism, white people opposing racism, able-bodied people supporting those with disabilities, people from more privileged classes striving to end poverty and straight people working on behalf of those who are gay, lesbian, bisexual and transgendered.

I often experienced people putting different forms of oppression in competition with one another, mostly in the form of "our oppression is worse than yours." This disturbed me because I found my parallel journeys of learning about myself as both oppressor and oppressed to be complementary. When I looked for literature on the larger jigsaw puzzle of oppression, I found very little. I began to write about it myself. It started as a journal but, over a period of years, became a book-length manuscript. In May of 1994, Fernwood Publishing published *Becoming an Ally: Breaking the Cycle of Oppression*, followed by a second edition, *Becoming an Ally: Breaking the Cycle of Oppression in People*, in 2002.

In the opening chapter I summarized my argument against competition among those who experience different forms of oppression:

> When I see people competing, claiming their own oppression as the "worst," or attacking the gains made by other oppressed groups, I see us all running on a treadmill. As long as we try to end our oppression by rising above others, we are reinforcing each other's oppression, and eventually our own. We are fighting over who has more value, who has less, instead of asking why we must be valued as more or less. We are investing energy in the source of all our oppressions, which is competition itself.
>
> The truth is that each form of oppression is part of a single, complex, interrelated, self-perpetuating system. The whole thing rests on a worldview that says we must constantly strive to be better than someone else. Competition assumes that we are separate beings—separate from each other, from other species,

from the earth. If we believe we are separate, then we are able to believe we can hurt another being and not suffer ourselves.

Competition also assumes that there is a hierarchy of beings. Those who "win" can take a "higher" position, one with more power and value than those who "lose." It is a short step from accepting hierarchy as natural to assuming that exploitation is just. It becomes right, even admirable, for those who have more power and value to help themselves to the labour, land, resources, culture, possessions, even the bodies, of those who have less power and value. The result is a class system, where power and privilege increase as you go up the ladder, and those standing on each rung take for granted their right to benefit from the labour and resources of those below them.

As long as we who are fighting oppression continue to play the game of competition with one another, all forms of oppression will continue to exist. No one oppression can be ended without them all ending, and this can only happen when we succeed in replacing the assumptions of competition, hierarchy and separation with cooperation, an understanding that each being has value beyond measure and the knowledge that we cannot harm anyone or anything without harming ourselves.

The connection between different forms of oppression is often seen in the liberal sense which denies differences, ignores the continuing presence of history and blames individuals: "We're all the same, all equal, everyone has problems, let's just decide to get along." I have found it difficult, when speaking in public, to say that all oppressions have one root without my audience hearing me say that all oppressions are the same, or equal. People often feel that their oppression has been belittled. But I am not saying that all oppressions are the same or equal; equality means nothing in this context, for how would you measure? I certainly am not saying that we all have problems and should just learn to get along; this denies a long, complicated history and all the terrible scars that need healing, collectively, before we can live together in peace. What I am saying is that all oppressions are interdependent, they all come from the same worldview, and none can be solved in isolation. We can either perpetuate a society based on competition, where some win and some lose, or we can work toward a society based on cooperation, where winning and losing become irrelevant. In the first scenario, oppression will continue to exist for almost everyone. In the second, it will fade away, because it serves no purpose.

The idea that one form of oppression, or even one person's oppression, can be solved independently, is of great benefit to the rich and powerful. This belief is enough to keep oppressed people fighting and jostling in competition with each other, never reaching a point of unity where we can successfully challenge those with more than their share.

In other chapters of *Becoming an Ally*, I analyzed how oppression came about and how it is maintained. I reflected on how the oppression we experience becomes internalized, so that we reproduce it in situations where we have a degree of power. I did a comparison of the similarities and differences among different forms of oppression, and I defined some steps for breaking the cycle of oppression in individuals: breaking the silence, consciousness and healing, becoming a worker in your own liberation and becoming an ally. I wrote guidelines for becoming an ally and a chapter on education of allies. Finally, I wrote a chapter on maintaining hope.

In the process of condensing my experience into *Becoming an Ally*, I developed an understanding of the patterns of oppression as they exist in, and are reproduced by, individuals. I answered my own questions as far as those questions went at the time.

When *Becoming an Ally* was published, I was working at a Canadian university. Because of my practice of acting as an ally, I became known as a supporter of Black, Native and gay/lesbian students and faculty on campus. This led to my involvement in a difficult and painful situation in one of the university's departments. At one point, I sat in a room of people deeply embroiled in conflict. We were discussing the possibility of asking a mediator to work with both sides. I looked around me, thought about my own experience in facilitating conflict resolution and thought, "Where would I start?" The sides were very far apart and their power in the institution was very unequal. Also, the dynamics of oppression as they function in and through individuals did not fully explain what was happening. I began to see that institutions have patterns resistant to change despite the will of the individuals that live or work in them.

I knew then that I needed to examine institutional oppression beyond the "sum of the parts" of the individuals within them. Because the situation at the university involved allegations of racism, I began to study the particular dynamics that come into play when an institution is accused of racism, the processes it uses to protect its interests and return life to "normal."

I am not abandoning the analysis I wrote about in *Becoming an Ally*. I believe that as individuals we unconsciously internalize the injuries done to us, both personally and as a result of belonging to oppressed groups. As long as the damage is unhealed and unconscious, it comes back into play when we achieve a measure of power. We sometimes project what we have experienced onto others and then act on it, behaving oppressively towards them.

Beyond this, however, there are patterns that belong to the institutions in which we participate. I can imagine them as accumulations of all the individual decisions and actions that have ever taken place within that institution since its founding, but it is even more than that. The institution itself takes on a character. It is not a living being, but it can sometimes behave as if it is one. It is, in the words of theologian Walter Wink, an "entity" (Wink 1992). It can put pressure on individuals—choosing, forming, punishing and rewarding them, shaping their attitudes and framework of understanding. As a result, certain patterns tend strongly to hold true, even when many individuals within the institution want them to change.

If individuals wish to change an institution, they must work together, taking action aimed at gaining power and influence over those basic patterns, and they must plan to work at it for a very long time. Too brief or shallow an effort to change an institution can act as a "vaccine," serving only to teach the oppressive elements in the institution how to resist real transformation, triggering defensiveness and making the situation worse than it was to begin with. Change strategies aimed at individuals can go only so far. The strategies required for institutional change must be directed toward transforming the institution itself.

An institution is like an elastic band. When people take collective action to change the basic patterns, the institution has a powerful tendency to snap back into its original shape. At this level there is another set of patterns, the strategies institutions use to return to "normal." We must understand and expect these "second level" patterns, often called "backlash," and prepare from the beginning to counter them.

Most of our methods of dealing with discrimination in institutions are modelled after our court system. They involve accusations, investigations and trial-like hearings where it is determined whether or not discrimination occurred. If the hearing finds that, on a "balance of probabilities," discrimination occurred, a remedy is ordered. These procedures, typically focussed on the behaviour of individuals, mask the characteristic patterns of the institution's behaviour and its power to shape the behaviour of the individuals within it.

This book begins with the story of how I learned that being an ally as an individual isn't enough. The account is based on interviews with the four students and one faculty member who were at the heart of the events. After transcribing the interviews, I wrote a draft of the story. That first draft was shallow and disconnected. I realized that I couldn't base my account on the interviews alone, because I was the one writing the story and it was my own experience that tied everything together. I re-wrote it with my own account as the central thread. Once the second draft was written, I began a process of negotiation. Drafts went back and forth with the interviewees. I incorporated their edits and suggestions, and tested my own, until I had an account that we could all live with.

I would love to have also included the viewpoints of those who became the "other side" in the conflict. Curious about how they perceived the events and particularly their reasons for their actions, I tried to talk with three of them. One had played only a peripheral role. For the other two, the situation had become so polarized and I was so clearly identified with the "other side," that they didn't want to speak with me about it. As a result, the story is told from one side only.

I have tried my best to be disciplined about simply telling the story. I have included as much detail as possible about what happened with as few general labels and judgements as I could. I have tried to avoid language that implies judgement. However, this is, in part, my own story. I could not be objective, even if I believed objectivity is possible, which I don't.

There is precedent and reason for telling a story about oppression from the point of view of those who are targeted by that form of oppression. Those with less power can usually see the situation more accurately than those with more power, because their survival depends on understanding and being able to predict the situation. Power and privilege obscure the view of those who benefit from them. I quote from *Becoming an Ally*:

> Part of the oppression is that we are cut off from our ability to empathize with the oppressed. If we are aware of it at all, we tend to get defensive or write it off as not very serious—"They are just whining." For another thing, the privileges that we obtain from oppressing others are invisible to us. For a third thing, oppression is structural. We derive benefits from being male or white or straight or able-bodied without taking any personal action against a woman, a person of colour, a gay/lesbian/bisexual person, or a person with a disability. (Bishop 2002: 128)

In her book *Is Nothing Sacred? When Sex Invades the Pastoral Relationship* (1989), Marie Fortune explains her choice to tell a story of sexual abuse from the point of view of the victims. She says:

> I will tell this story as truthfully and carefully as I can. I will tell it from the perspective of the women, because when considering the question of whose perspective should be taken as definitive in an ethical situation, "the one against whom power is used has the more accurate perspective on the situation." (xvi–xvii)

Fortune's internal quote is from *Professional Ethics: Power and Paradox* by Karen Lebacqz. Here is the full quote:

> All of this suggests that ethical issues related to the existence, use and abuse of power should be at the core of an analysis of professional ethics. Yet while sociologists have long touted the autonomy and power of the professions, most ethical analyses have

ignored this dimension and focused more narrowly on issues of trust. For instance, Sissela Bok argues that deception is akin to force or violence. She thus hints that analyses of power would be relevant for making decisions about truth telling. Yet in presenting and refuting arguments for lying, she fails to develop any explicit norms in response to the implications of this kinship between deception and power.

Nonetheless, Bok does give us a helpful beginning point. She suggests that we should look at lies from the perspective of the one who is deceived rather than from the perspective of the one who tells the lie. This focuses attention on the question of whose perspective on the situation should be taken as definitive. It suggests that the one against whom power is used has the more accurate perspective on the situation.

Now this is a startling suggestion in a professional context. Since professionals profess—that is, claim to know what is wrong and what to do about it—to suggest that someone else's perspective is more accurate is to turn the tables upside down. Yet this may be precisely what we need if we are to take seriously the questions of power that arise in a professional setting. (1985: 128–129, citing Bok 1982: 214)

As someone involved in these events but not central, hurt but not incapacitated, connected by friendship and common values with those whose stories I felt should not be lost, witness to much of what happened and holder of a great deal of information, I was, I felt, in as good a position as anyone to figure out what happened, why it happened and propose a model for institutions to deal with conflicts of this nature. Others involved in these events have written and published their perspectives on it, of course different from mine. I can't provide references because of the need to protect anonymity, but their work forms part of a growing literature on issues of institutional injustice and change.

The five women interviewed for the story chose pseudonyms. All other actors are identified by their institutional title or role. As part of my responsibility to make the story as anonymous as possible, I have changed the years in which it happened. I have, however, preserved the internal chronology of events.

In the chapters that follow the story, I give my own analysis of what happened, in terms of the institutional patterns displayed. I explore other writers to find documentation of other institutional patterns in circumstances like these. Finally, I propose some methods that I think will improve the way we go about solving the problem of oppression in institutions. Like *Becoming an Ally* before it, this book is part of an ongoing conversation. May it lead us towards justice.

Part 1

The Story

Chapter One

The Students' Story

Background

For ten years I was employed by a Canadian university. For the purpose of telling this story, I shall call it "Canadian University." My work involved outreach to organizations of marginalized people, including those in the Black and Native communities. Because of my work, I often knew members of these communities who studied or worked at the University. The location of my office also reinforced my contact with this group of workers and students; it was right above the Native Student Centre, a place where Native students and their friends gathered for mutual support. Their friends included Native employees of the University as well as Black employees and students. I stopped in for tea there once or twice a week. I heard their stories and did what I could to support them.

This is the story of my experience supporting two Native students, a Black student and a Native faculty member. I came to know all four through my work in the community and my contact with the Native Student Centre. Later I met another student involved in the same situation, an international student who, at the time of these events, was dependent on a student visa to stay in Canada. The Native students have chosen to be called "Beth" and "Laura," the Native faculty member "Lillian," the Black student "Hannah," and the international student "Yuen." I will use titles for everyone else in the story. The titles, along with the names of committees, departments and other bodies, and the years in which these events took place, have been changed to protect the identities of the participants as far as possible.

All four students and the faculty member were associated with a department of Canadian University that trains students to work in health-related settings. Students can choose to be trained for institutional positions, in hospitals for example, or for community-based research and service delivery.

At the time of this story, the Department officially took a "structuralist" approach to social issues. This means that, in theory at least, all course content included an analysis of the broad social context of health. Students were encouraged to organize people for empowerment and build strategies for change to benefit the least powerful sectors of society. In the courses for community-based work, this approach was the central focus.

The Department was a pioneer in affirmative action. There had been a special effort to admit Black, Aboriginal and ethnic minority candidates since the early 1970s. During the 1980s, the Department had conducted a bachelor's degree program designed specifically for Native students studying in their home communities. In later years, affirmative action was formally extended to include students with disabilities and, informally, gay, lesbian, bisexual and transgendered students.

Another aspect of the policy was the search for faculty from the affirmative action groups. The Department had had at least one faculty member with a disability since the 1960s. The first Black professor joined the faculty in the late1980s. Lillian, the first Native professor, was hired as a sessional lecturer in 1991 and promoted to the tenure stream in 1992. Her experiences are central to this account. The Black professor was away on a study leave during the time this story took place.

The Department's main structural mechanism for accommodating the needs of affirmative action students was a committee called the Equality Committee. It grew from the Equality Task Force, the original group that recommended an affirmative action admission policy. Later it became a standing committee of the Department. The Equality Committee was made up of three faculty members, two graduates, representatives from Black, Native and minority ethnic organizations in the community, three students, including "minority students from the region," and the Head of the Department. The committee was co-chaired by one faculty member and one community representative. In theory, it assigned a member to each of the Department's other committees—the Bachelor's Degree Committee, Master's Degree Committee and the Department's overall policy body, the Executive Committee. The Equality Committee's mandate included:

- to recruit students in [ethnic], Black and Native communities in the [region];
- to assist in admission procedures for minority applicants,
- development of means of implementing the [Department's] policy with respect to minority groups;
- to maintain liaison with other [Department] committees (by providing [Equality Committee] representatives) to promote the interests of minorities;
- to promote knowledge of minority concerns within the [Department's] personnel and curriculum;
- to counsel minority students as required regarding their individual concerns, including admissions, academic or department governance matters; and
- to suggest solutions concerning problems and issues associated

with the [Department's] policy of affirmative action and prefer-
ential admissions of specified disadvantaged groups, both on
and off campus.

A former Department professor and long-time Equality Committee
member explained to me that in practice it was difficult to make the
Equality Committee work as it was designed to. Except for a loyal few,
most faculty members did not participate in the Equality Committee.
Often there were not enough members to have a representative on each of
the other committees. Above all, the Equality Committee's original mandate
to handle complaints and carry out student advocacy was removed from
the Department's Constitution around 1980, after the Committee brought
forward a charge of discrimination from five minority students against a
faculty member.

Faculty members of the Department were also active in establishing
affirmative action principles in the national accreditation criteria for their
field. The accreditation manual in place at the time of these events required
admission procedures, curriculum, administration, faculty selection, faculty
self-awareness and education, and external relationships to fill the needs of
Aboriginal and "multicultural/multiracial" students and their communities.
These communities were to have a role in planning and evaluating academic
programs.

A separate section on Aboriginal peoples of the accreditation manual
required:

- support for Aboriginal peoples to maintain their "distinctive, cultur-
  ally-based helping systems,"
- incorporation of "the lifeways, languages, history, culture, and values"
  of Aboriginal people into the curriculum,
- facilitation of "access to traditional knowledge" along with a "critical
  analysis of interaction between Aboriginal and non-Aboriginal
  societies,"
- accommodation of the family and community responsibilities of mature
  Aboriginal students,
- recognition of traditional Aboriginal ways of learning when making
  faculty appointments,
- involvement of Aboriginal communities in initiating, managing and
  evaluating programs, and
- respect for the cultural differences reflected in Aboriginal peoples'
  ways of learning.

Proposed additions to the manual at that time required university
departments to recognize "the knowledge and life experiences of diverse
ethnic, cultural and racial communities, reflect ethnic, racial and cultural

diversity in student admission, curriculum, selection of field supervisors, and faculty composition, educate students to be aware of the impact on diverse communities of the cultural biases that have shaped [the field's] theory and practice models" and be able to "negotiate effective working relationships with clients of diverse ethnic, cultural and racial backgrounds." Also, "[departments] shall recognize a responsibility to acknowledge the existence of racism, and to deal with its affects (sic) on programs, faculty, staff, students and clients."

Field Placements

My involvement in this story began during the spring of 1993. I had met Beth in the Native Student Centre during the years she was working on her bachelor's degree, and then encountered her again when she was employed at a community agency where I was a member of the board. She is a Native mother, foster-mother and grandmother, with experience as a community activist and leader. At that time, I co-taught an active, experiential program designed to develop the skills and analysis of leaders in marginalized communities. We had offered to provide two field placements in this program for students in community-related academic programs. During the spring of 1993, Beth asked if she could do her master's level field placement with us during the coming academic year. We said that we would be delighted to have her as long as the Department would accept the placement. We felt she would be a great asset to our program.

During the summer, she planned to complete her bachelor's degree field placement, which was incorporated into her paid work at the community agency. Before the end of the summer, however, she became involved in a conflict between the staff and director of the agency. She explained to me that the staff had asked to see the agency's personnel policy, and the director had said she didn't know where it was. When the director went away for a few days, she left Beth the task of cleaning out the shelves in her office. Beth was coordinating an evaluation of the agency and was told to photocopy any documents that might be useful in writing a history of the agency that would form part of the evaluation document. While cleaning the shelves, Beth found the personnel policy and, while copying the other material, made copies for the staff. The director accused her of theft.

Shortly afterward, Beth's field placement at the agency was cancelled, and later she was fired. She found another placement, completed her degree and was accepted into the master's program, but the summer's experience followed her. The Bachelor's Field Coordinator met with the director of the agency and recorded everything she had to say about Beth in a set of notes. Without any attempt to speak with Beth or Lillian, who was her Faculty Field Supervisor, she gave the notes to the Community Specialty Coordinator, who would be Beth's professor and Faculty Field Coordinator in the master's program.

At this point it might be helpful to describe the structure of the Department's master's program when these events took place. Each specialty, institutional and community, had two core courses. One of these was intended to have a more theoretical orientation. The major paper for this course became the literature review for the student's final project. The other core course was intended to focus on practical skills and incorporated the student's 400-hour field placement. The teacher of this more practical core course located and coordinated the students' field placements. In the Community Specialty, the practical core course was called "The Practice of Community Work." According to the course description, "this course privileges the experience of 'systematically disadvantaged' members of our society as starting points for our course investigations. How knowledge and analysis informs community action and how community work is related to social movements is considered through the voices of women, minorities and people who are labelled as 'other.'"

Along with the two core courses, students had other required and elective courses. The choice of elective courses was meant to complement the student's choice of final project. For full-time students, the courses and field placement continued from September to April, and the final project was normally completed under a faculty member's supervision by the end of July. Graduation took place the following October.

Beth began her field placement with us in late September. We had proposed that the two instructors in our community leadership course act as a supervision team. We had both worked with master's students in their field placements before. On October 3rd, the Community Specialty Coordinator wrote a memo saying that my co-instructor could not be a supervisor because she was a master's student herself at the time. The memo went on to discuss other arrangements concerning the field placement without raising any question about my qualifications, so we assumed the placement had been accepted. Although we would both take part in the actual supervision, I would be the official Field Supervisor.

The next week I received a call from Hannah, a Black student also taking the Community Specialty. I knew her from several activities in the community and on campus. She was also a mother, grandmother and mature student with lengthy community experience. She had originally proposed a field placement in the setting of her paid work. She had been told that this cannot be done, although she knew of several students who had had workplace field placements accepted, including the one white student in the current year's Community Specialty class. She had then proposed a series of possible field placements, but each, in turn, was disqualified by the Community Specialty Coordinator. She asked the

Coordinator to suggest possible placements. The first agency already had a bachelor's student and couldn't supervise two placements. They referred her to another agency, where she got the same answer. The Coordinator then suggested another three possibilities. Hannah was turned down by two of them. Our program was the third. She was immensely relieved when we said we would be happy to have her.

Downstairs from my office, in the Native Student Centre, Laura, another Native student in the Community Specialty program, had begun work on her field placement in early August. The Native Student Counsellor was confirmed as Laura's supervisor, and since she had not done field work supervision before, I agreed to give her some support in the task.

Shortly after accepting Hannah as a field placement student, and a week after the October 3rd memo, the Community Specialty Coordinator raised questions about my qualifications. She said she would have to take my resume to the Master's Committee for consideration. I gave it to her. On October 18th, she reported that the Master's Committee had ruled that I was not qualified to supervise because I did not have a master's degree myself. The same day she told the Native Student Counsellor that she was not qualified for the same reason. She told us we could still supervise the students' work, but we could not be officially counted as supervisors or paid the honorarium that normally came with the position. The students would each have to have a "technical supervisor," someone with a master's degree.

The three students and three disqualified supervisors discussed the situation. The students were all established in their placements and had written more than one draft of the learning contract that must be signed by the student, field supervisor and Community Specialty Coordinator. We all wanted to challenge this abrupt change in policy, but not at the cost of delaying the students' placements. Over the next few days, we found a recent Master's Community Specialty graduate who was ready to take on the position of "technical supervisor" for all three students. The Coordinator accepted this proposal for Beth and Hannah, but wanted to supervise Laura herself. Laura resisted this suggestion, and finally the Community Specialty Coordinator accepted the students' choice of "technical supervisor" for all three placements. Soon after this, my co-instructor and I organized a meeting of all Community Specialty Field Supervisors to discuss the change in policy. This story will be picked up again later.

The next problem emerged over the learning contracts. The second draft of Beth's and Hannah's contracts incorporated the supervision team's suggestions, and we were ready to sign them. The Community Specialty Coordinator, however, continued to suggest changes. Both students continued to write drafts.

Beth's contract was the first to be signed, on November 9th. At the Community Specialty Coordinator's urging, the wording of her final draft had been modelled closely on sample wording presented in the Field Placement Manual. At the end of the meeting the contract was signed, and the Community Specialty Coordinator asked to see Beth alone. The three supervisors withdrew to my office to talk. Eventually we realized that Beth and the Community Specialty Coordinator had been together for a long time. I walked into the hallway to see if they were still talking. I could hear Beth sobbing. I opened the door and Beth used the opportunity to run from the room.

Back in my office, Beth told us that the Community Specialty Coordinator had asked her to write a personal statement to go with the learning contract. Beth objected for two reasons. First, the personal statement, as it is described in the Field Placement Manual, is something the student writes for the field placement agency at the time the field placement is proposed in order to help the agency make its decision, not when the placement is well established. Second, Beth knew that faculty at the Department had tried to convince several former Native students that they were not "healed enough" from childhood abuse to be appropriate candidates for a health-related profession. The information about their past abuse had come from their written personal statements. Because Beth is also a survivor of abuse, she was reluctant to put such personal information on paper. She wanted to know who would be allowed to see it. She told us that the Community Specialty Coordinator insisted, specifying what should be in the statement, including the childhood abuse. Finally she said that Beth must write the statement because, "I'm your professor and I say so." She told Beth if she didn't write it, her field placement would be invalid. Beth later wrote a very brief and impersonal personal statement.

The day after the signing and the argument over the personal statement, the Community Specialty Coordinator wrote a letter to the Department Head saying that my co-teacher and I had intimidated her into signing Beth's contract. She withdrew her signature and, despite having urged Beth to use the sample wording in the Field Placement Manual as her model, accused Beth of plagiarism because some phrases in Beth's contract were too close to the model contract in the Manual. If she caught Beth plagiarizing anything again, she said, she would report it and have her expelled from the University.

After this incident, Beth and Hannah began to have trouble arranging for us to meet with the Community Specialty Coordinator. The Coordinator would cancel meetings at the last minute or not call back in response to their messages. Downstairs in the Native Student Centre, Laura and her Field Supervisor reported having the same problem.

Even without the Community Specialty Coordinator's participation, Beth, Hannah and their Field Supervisors decided to sign the most recent draft of their learning contracts. This gave us some basis for proceeding with the field placements until a learning contract that satisfied the

Community Specialty Coordinator could be completed and signed. We met every week to discuss the students' experience in the placement. During these sessions, we also heard the unfolding story of what was happening in the Practice of Community Work classroom.

Tension in the Classroom

Beth and Hannah told us that there was tension as soon as the class began in mid-September. According to Beth, "From the start [the Community Specialty Coordinator] picked on Hannah, and that started up the whole dynamic." Hannah said: "From the time I went into that class it was pure hell." The two Native students protested Hannah's treatment by the Community Specialty Coordinator and tried to protect her.

The Black and Native students also noticed what appeared to be different treatment between themselves and the one white student in the class. They told us that the white student was frequently late because of the long drive from the city where she worked. The Community Specialty Coordinator always waited for her, told her how nice it was that she had come and took time to catch her up on anything she had missed. Once the Community Specialty Coordinator held up the class for forty-five minutes because a message from the white student saying she was not coming had not been conveyed from the office. When the other students were late, they said the Community Specialty Coordinator would look obviously at her watch or remark that it was about time they decided to come to class.

A third problem had to do with workload. The Practice of Community Work course was unusually heavy, with seven major papers—one to be written first as a draft, then in publishable form—a five-part field journal and shorter assignments every week on the topic of that week's class. Beth, Hannah and Laura had been encouraged by the Community Specialty Coordinator to take an elective course in qualitative research, a course that was also famous among the students for the amount of written work required. All three students saw right away that they could not do it.

In previous courses at the Department, they had successfully negotiated workload with professors. They approached both the Community Specialty Coordinator and the professor teaching the qualitative research course. Neither were willing to negotiate. As a result, Beth dropped the research course late in September, and Laura dropped it in October, after a family crisis began to claim much of her time. According to the students, the Community Specialty Coordinator reacted with anger. They said she felt that both students needed the qualitative research course for their projects. Both held firm, however, and insisted on dropping the course.

In place of the qualitative research course, Beth and Laura spoke to a professor of anthropology with a specialty in Native peoples about doing an independent reading course designed to help them obtain the background they required for their projects, both of which were in the field of Native education. He agreed. The two students met with him several times during the fall to work on a course outline and asked the Master's Degree Coordinator and the Registrar what the application process was for an independent study course. They were told to write the proposal, including a bibliography, and give it to the Master's Committee for approval. They did this; it was given back to them for re-writing. This process was repeated several times. At one point the Master's Committee rejected the proposal because the two students wanted to take the course together. By their definition an independent study could only involve one student. The Community Specialty Coordinator was a member of the Master's Committee and the person with the final power to accept or reject an independent study proposal from students in the Community Specialty.

When they wrote the list of books for the study, Beth and Laura used several books from a previous annotated bibliography written by Laura as an assignment for the Practice of Community Work course. When these same books appeared in the reading list for the independent study course, the Community Specialty Coordinator rejected it, accusing Beth of plagiarizing Laura's work and Laura of self-plagiarism; that is, submitting work for credit twice.

The tension in the class grew, reaching an explosion point in mid-October. During the September 26th class, the students brought drafts of a book review assignment. The drafts were read by all of the students and the Coordinator and comments were exchanged. The two Native students were impressed with Hannah's draft. They had written theirs quickly, just before class, but Hannah had worked hard on hers and brought it to class quite complete. She was working with a tutor, who had also gone over it and approved it. The other students praised her for it, and it appeared to them that the Coordinator agreed. At least, she raised no objections to Hannah's paper. When the final papers were marked, the Native students had A's, while Hannah had failed. All three students objected to this as unfair. The Coordinator criticized them for comparing marks, claiming this was too competitive, but agreed to re-mark the paper if Hannah re-wrote it. Hannah did this, but it came back with a note saying that the paper was much better now, written at an acceptable level, but the failing mark would remain. After this incident, the Community Specialty Coordinator wrote a letter about Hannah to the Dean of Graduate Studies. Hannah went to the Dean with her point of view and also contacted the University's Black Student Counsellor, who took up her case with the Dean of Graduate Studies as well.

Meeting alone with the Community Specialty Coordinator had become a major issue among the students. According to Beth,

> She started calling us into her office and ... really putting us down,

and yelling at us. She would tell us we were incompetent and we should quit, that we were troublemakers. She would give us more assignments. She would corner us, and pressure us, and yell at us.

One example was the meeting recounted earlier, where Beth was reduced to tears over the issue of writing a personal statement for her field placement. During another one-on-one meeting, Hannah said the Community Specialty Coordinator accused her of lying about the hours she spent at her field placement. When she suggested that the Community Specialty Coordinator check with the Field Supervisors, Hannah reported that the Community Specialty Coordinator said the Field Supervisors would lie on Hannah's behalf.

The students told us that after every class the Community Specialty Coordinator would try to take one or other of them into her office. When they said they didn't want to, she would insist. If they tried to leave the door open, she would close it. During a one-on-one meeting with Beth, she revealed that she was keeping two sets of files, an official file on each student and a private one, containing all her personal notes on what they said and did in class and in their meetings with her.

The growing tension came to a head in class on December 5th, when the students complained that the exercise of rewriting assignments for publication, when they had no intention of publishing, was not teaching them anything. They had previously taken this issue to the Master's Program Coordinator and had been advised to raise it in class. In response, the Community Specialty Coordinator yelled at the students that she would only meet with them individually about this and left the room.

Attempts to Negotiate Change

During our field supervision meetings we also heard how the students tried from the beginning to negotiate solutions to their problems with the Community Specialty Coordinator. At first they approached her directly, without success. Several times they went to the Master's Program Coordinator with their complaints, only to be sent back to the Community Specialty Coordinator. In November they asked to meet with the Department Head, a meeting that resulted in promises, but no changes.

Hannah had been accepted into the program on a probationary basis, with the conditions of her study directly supervised by the Dean of Graduate Studies. She kept the Dean informed of her progress and received a measure of protection as long as the Dean felt she was meeting her commitments. When Beth and Laura approached the Dean, however, she did not feel it would be appropriate for her to take on an advocacy role for them as well.

The students approached the Black Student Counsellor and Native

Student Counsellor, the University's Equity Committee for Black and Native Students and the Provincial Human Rights Commission. The Human Rights Commission process would have been too slow to be of use in the immediate situation. The Black and Native Student Counsellors and the Equity Committee tried to intervene but had no impact on the conditions the students were experiencing within the Department.

Lillian, the Department's one Native faculty member, was chair of the Equality Committee that year. Beth, Hannah and Laura were also members, along with other Native and Black students and community members. They had re-vitalized the Equality Committee, making sure they had active representatives on all of the Department's governing bodies, including the Bachelor's Committee, the Master's Committee and the Executive Committee.

The Master's Committee is responsible for overseeing graduate programs and had a mandate to act on problems in master's level courses. The student members of the Master's Committee asked the faculty members of this Committee for information about the process for complaints. They were told that they should go first to the Master's Program Coordinator. If they could not achieve resolution at that level, they should go to the Department Head. The students pushed for the step beyond that. They were told it would be the Dean of Graduate Studies, but they were asked not to put that in the minutes.

The student members of the Master's Committee also raised the issue of disqualification of their field supervisors. They were told that the decision to require a master's degree for field supervisors in the Community Specialty had been made September 15th, but there were no minutes for that meeting. This raised questions for the students, who had not been told that their supervisors must have a master's degree until late October. Beth and I had received a memo from the Community Specialty Coordinator written on October 3rd expressing an understanding that I would be Beth's supervisor, although she knew that I did not have a master's degree. I hadn't been asked for my resume until October 12th, and I was told I would not qualify because I lacked a master's degree on October 18th. The Native Student Counsellor had not been disqualified for her lack of a master's degree until November 8th, after supervising her student since August.

At this same meeting of the Master's Committee, the student representatives were told that they could not be present for any discussion of student matters. They objected, since they had understood that student matters were the reason for their presence on the Committee, but to no avail.

That same fall, the Native students re-convened a group they had started the year before, called the Native Support Circle. This group wrote a brief describing the treatment they experienced in their bachelor's level field placements, suggesting policy and practice changes to make the field placement system more equitable. The problems discussed in the brief included some students feeling pushed into field placements in Native organizations where they felt they could not accomplish their learning goals and others being denied Native placements or supervisors even when these were available and desirable. They also discussed the Department's procedures when there is conflict in a field placement, using the examples of Beth and Laura's field placements when they were bachelor's level students. In both cases the Bachelor's Field Coordinator had met with the members of the field agency who were in conflict with the students, wrote up their point of view, placed it in the students' files and distributed it without informing or involving the students or their Field Supervisors. The Department's field placement policy states that she should have met with both sides to resolve the conflict.

The brief also expressed the Native students' perception that the problems they had had in recent placements came about because they had worked toward justice for the dispossessed in their field agencies, exactly as they were taught to do. The Native Support Circle distributed the brief widely within the Department and University and sent it to two external Native organizations as well.

Lillian tried to speak to other professors about the students' concerns. In doing this, she was taking seriously her understanding of her role as chair of the Equality Committee. Its mandate, after all, included "to promote knowledge of minority concerns within the [Department's] personnel and curriculum."

When one-on-one meetings with the Community Specialty Coordinator became an issue, Lillian offered to accompany the students to meetings. Hannah accepted the offer, and Lillian accompanied her to a meeting in early November. As Hannah told the story, the Community Specialty Coordinator reacted to Lillian's presence in an angry fashion and asked her to leave. Feeling she had no choice, Hannah let her go.

After this incident, in mid-November, the Equality Committee wrote a brief suggesting that the Department grant students the right to take a support person to meetings. In this document they explained that there was often fear on the part of minority students facing professors and administrators alone and the possibility of reacting so emotionally that they could not remember the contents of the meeting afterwards. They wanted a Department policy stating that students always have the right to take a witness or support person to meetings with them. It was not adopted. Later, they discovered that a long-standing University policy gave all students the right to be accompanied at meetings.

When Christmas break arrived, it was a great relief to the students. Three of them still did not have their learning contracts signed. Beth had written four drafts; Laura had written six; Hannah had written seven. They were feeling anxious about it, since the deadline for having a learning contract in place is January 16th. However, the work in all three field placements was going well, and the team of Field Supervisors was working out well. They felt that they could make a new start after Christmas.

Winter Term

Hannah and Beth arrived at their first supervision session of the winter term in tears. The Practice of Community Work class had met that morning, with the tension heightened even further by the subject matter—race and racism. According to the students, Hannah had challenged the Community Specialty Coordinator's understanding of racism. The Community Specialty Coordinator told her that racism is a matter of perception and she, Hannah, did not know what racism is. Even the white student in the class objected to this, Hannah and Beth told us, saying that when it came to understanding racism, she would take Hannah's word over the Community Specialty Coordinator's.

Less than two weeks later, the deadline arrived for field learning contracts and independent study applications. On that day, the Community Specialty Coordinator cancelled Hannah's field placement because there was no signed contract, threatened to cancel Beth's and Laura's placements and rejected their independent study proposal once again. According to the students, their independent study proposal was turned down because it wasn't on the right form. In all the previous revisions of the independent study proposal, no one had mentioned that there was a form. These actions meant that all three students would have to repeat their year and pay another year's tuition, something none of them could afford.

The students had continued their efforts to have someone pay attention to their problems after Christmas, speaking to the University's Employment Equity Committee on January 13th. After the cancellation of Hannah's field placement and the Native students' independent study, there was an explosion of activity. Beth and Laura told their story to the Academic Vice-President on January 19th and to the university's Access Committee for Black and Native Students on January 24th. Hannah went to the Dean of Graduate Studies. There was also an outcry from the Field Supervisors, who had not been told, let alone consulted, about the cancellation of Hannah's field placement and the threat of cancelling Beth's and Laura's.

On January 23rd, the Department Head issued an invitation to all five students in the Practice of Community Work course. Their class on January 30th would be cancelled. Instead they would meet with her, the Community Specialty Coordinator, the Dean of Graduate Studies and the Dean of the Faculty of Health. The Dean of the Faculty of Health would facilitate the meeting, and they would try and settle the differences between the three students and the Community Specialty Coordinator. The Community Specialty Coordinator would be allowed to bring a representative from the Faculty Association.

The students refused to face such an array of powerful people without support of their own and asked if they could bring their Field Supervisors. The Department Head refused the request. The students asked the university's Employment Equity Officer to intercede for them. The Department still refused. The Employment Equity Officer checked with the Vice-President of Student Services. This is when the students discovered that the University had a policy of allowing students to take support people with them to any meeting with faculty or administration. The Employment Equity Officer took this information to the Department Head. A few days later, the Department Head said that three of the four field supervisors would be allowed to come, but they would not accept my presence at the meeting. After another consultation with the Vice-President of Student Services, the Employment Equity Officer insisted that the students could bring as many people as they wished. This issue was settled less than an hour before the meeting. By now the students had invited the Black Student Counsellor as well.

While the discussions went on about who would be allowed to come, the three students met for a day and a half with their Field Supervisors to organize the points they wished to make. They asked us to make the presentation for them.

In the end so many people were involved in the meeting that it had to be moved to another room. Present were all five Community Specialty students, Laura, Beth and Hannah's Field Supervisors, the Community Specialty Coordinator with her Faculty Association support person, the Black Student Counsellor, the Employment Equity Officer, the Department Head, the Deans of Graduate Studies and the Faculty of Health, and a note-taker for the students. The meeting began with the Field Supervisors speaking for Laura, Beth and Hannah, listing off the problems they had discussed during their planning meeting. The list included their treatment in class and one-on-one meetings, the problems over the learning contracts, the disqualification of the Field Supervisors in mid-term, the issue of personal statements, the personal and academic accusations, the difficulties getting the independent study course approved, inconsistent and changing rules, the contents of the students' files and the double files.

The Field Supervisors had also prepared their own statement objecting to several aspects of the field placement system. The list began with the fact that the students were responsible for finding their own placements and faced a series of rejections from faculty. We thought there should be a continuing Department-agency relationship to provide and supervise field work. We objected to the disqualification of supervisors in mid-term and the requirement that students replace their own supervisors, again facing a series of rejections. We spoke about the long and difficult process for approving learning contracts and the fact that the delays and problems were all blamed on the students. We also spoke about the stereotypical accusations that Native and Black students are lazy, lie, plagiarize and lack initiative; the accusation that the Field Supervisors pressured the Community Specialty Coordinator to sign contracts and would back up students' alleged lies about the hours spent in the field placement; and, finally, the cancellation of field placements without the Supervisors being consulted, or even notified.

In response, the Department Head and the Dean of the Faculty of Health said that procedure was being followed in the case of the independent study course—the Community Specialty Coordinator is the one who approves it and it simply didn't meet the standard. The Community Specialty Coordinator's responsibility is to see that academic and professional standards are met in every aspect of the course. She also has rights under the Collective Agreement.

The students raised the issue of Lillian, the Native faculty member and Chair of the Equality Committee, suffering because they had channeled their complaints through the Equality Committee. The Dean of the Faculty of Health and the Department Head told them that they should go to white faculty members for support. They said that the Department's student body had been diverse for many years, and therefore white faculty had experience in supporting Black and Native students. In addition, they said that there were many channels that the majority of students were using to resolve their problems, including the Black and Native Student Counsellors, the Vice-President of Student Services and the Deans. Also, the Department's Black professor would be returning the next fall, and she would help sort some of these issues out. The students objected that they had tried all of these channels, to no avail. The Black Student Counsellor said that when she took issues forward to University administrators, nothing happened. Several people present objected to the assumption that the Department's one Black faculty member should be responsible for sorting out the problems.

The Dean of Health and the Department Head repeated that their main concerns are maintaining academic standards and making affirmative action work. The Dean referred to the Department as "the flagship of affirmative action in the Faculty" and asked why the students weren't complaining about other departments that had not even begun to deal with issues of access for minority students.

In the end the Dean of Graduate Studies asked the Field Supervisors if they were satisfied with the students' performance in their field placements. After receiving an affirmative answer, she asked each of the five students in turn if they wanted to stay in the Community Specialty Coordinator's class or have another teacher for the remainder of the term. Hannah, Beth and Laura responded that they wanted another teacher. The white student said that she had no trouble with the Community Specialty Coordinator and would stay with her.

The attention then fell on Yuen, the international student. She objected that she was being put in a difficult spot, having to choose between her teacher and her classmates. She expressed her desire to remain silent. Everyone present had also agreed to a guideline at the beginning of the meeting that everyone had the right to refuse to comment. However, the Dean pushed her for an answer. She finally elected to stay with the Community Specialty Coordinator. The Dean of Graduate Studies then approved a budget to hire someone else to teach the three students who wanted to leave. She also made a commitment to see that Beth and Laura had another chance to get their independent study course approved in spite of the passed deadline.

On February 6th, the Community Specialty Coordinator met with her two remaining students. The Department Head barred Beth, Hannah and Laura from entering the building on class days. By the next week, space had been found in a different building and two instructors had been engaged to teach them. The remainder of the term did not go smoothly. One of the new instructors questioned Beth's and Laura's desire to study the experience of Native people in the education system; he did not view this as a subject related to community health. The result was a strained relationship and extra work for the students, as they were required to write additional material and participate in a meeting to defend their view of the relationship between formal education and community development for Native people. All three students also had their lives disrupted by family crises during the spring. Everyone concerned, however, simply wanted to finish out the remaining ten weeks of the course with as little disturbance as possible. Students and professors alike did their work, and all of the students passed. The students also finished their field placements.

With the support of the Dean of Graduate Studies, Beth and Laura rewrote their independent study and put it on the correct form. By the time it finished going through the approval process, however, the professor who had agreed to guide the work had gone on leave. The students found another professor to supervise the study. At last, they went into the Department office to register for the course. When the Registrar opened the file, however, there was nothing in it but the first draft of the independent study with the Community Specialty Coordinator's comments on it. All the subsequent drafts and all the correspondence with the Dean of Graduate Studies, along with the notification of the change of professor, were missing. The Registrar could not register them for the course under those conditions. That afternoon Beth and Laura dropped a letter off at the Graduate Studies office for the Dean. By the next morning, all documents had been returned to the file, and they registered for the course.

Laura completed the course during the summer, putting off her project until the fall. She missed her normal graduation time in October, but completed her project by the end of February and graduated at the following Spring Convocation.

Beth did not complete the course. She left her studies altogether, exhausted from family crises and her experience in the Department. The master's degree was so degraded in her estimation that her motivation to go on and finish it was very low. Three years later, when the Community Specialty Coordinator no longer taught there, Beth returned to the Department and finished her master's degree.

Another Charge of Plagiarism

Hannah worked through the summer completing her project under Lillian's supervision. She re-wrote her work four times before Lillian was happy with it. Hannah was put on the graduation list for October Convocation. She described her relief to me as "having the weight of the world removed from her shoulders."

A few days later, however, I received a call from her, very upset. She had just been informed that she had been removed from the graduation list and referred to the Senate Discipline Committee. As explained earlier in this story, the paper for the first core course is expected to be the literature review for the student's final project. However, Hannah was accused of self-plagiarism because of the similarity between these two documents. Self-plagiarism was defined in the university's graduate calendar as submitting work for credit in more than one course without the professor's knowledge or permission. It was a very serious charge; if the student was found guilty, Senate could require that courses be taken again or take away the degree altogether.

The University's Senate had just met for the first time that fall. The Discipline Committee had not yet been struck, and for a time it looked as though Hannah would not graduate in October simply because a Committee could not be formed in time to hear the case. Hannah's support person all along had been the Dean of Graduate Studies, but she had left that position and gone on sabbatical leave. Hannah contacted the Vice-President of Student Services and even the President of the University. Once a matter is before Senate, neither of them can do anything about it; however, someone saw to it that a Disciplinary Committee was struck quickly enough to hear Hannah's case before graduation. The hearing date was set just four days before Convocation.

Hannah had hired a lawyer who did some research on the procedure and collected several witnesses, all former master's students ready to testify that they were told to write their literature review as part of their core master's course. The lawyer tried to get a faculty member to testify about the structure of the program. She called the Professor who had taught the theoretical core course where the literature reviews were written. It was he who had told Hannah and her classmates, verbally and on the course description, that their paper would serve as the literature review for their project. He would not testify. The other faculty members approached by Hannah's lawyer refused as well. At the last minute, just a day before the hearing, one of Hannah's former professors came forward to testify concerning the structure of the program. She had just retired from the Department in the spring.

The Department Head arrived at the hearing to present the self-plagiarism charge. Another professor from the Department came with her for support. Hannah arrived with over twenty witnesses and supporters, including her family, friends, fellow students and former Field Supervisors. Lillian also came, since as supervising professor on the project, the hearing had implications for her. She was accompanied by her Faculty Association Representative.

The first discussion took place in the hallway. At the request of the Department Head, the Chair of the Discipline Committee asked all of Hannah's supporters to stay outside. The whole group objected, and Lillian's Faculty Association Representative, a lawyer herself, stepped forward to make the argument that the confidentiality of Disciplinary Committee proceedings existed for the protection of the student. If the student waived that right, she should be able to bring in as many support people as she chose. The Chair disappeared inside to consult with the Committee and the Department Head. The Committee decided that everyone could come in.

Upon this decision, the Department Head decided to leave. She made the argument that if Hannah had twenty support people, so should she. She wanted the hearing cancelled until she could organize more support for herself. The Committee discussed this and decided that because Graduation was only four days away, they would hear the case whether the Department Head presented it verbally or not. They could use the written charges as the basis for the hearing. At this point, the Department Head decided to stay, everyone but the witnesses entered the room, and the hearing began.

The Department Head outlined the case against Hannah; that is, that her literature review paper for her first core course and the literature review in her project were essentially the same. Hannah's lawyer made the case that students were expected to use the paper in this course to write the literature review for their project, backing up her arguments with excerpts from the course description and a memo from the course professor to the Dean of Graduate Studies.

Hannah's witnesses were brought in to speak one by one. First a fellow student from the same class testified that they were told that this paper would be the literature review for their project. Then a student from the Institutional Specialty course said that the same policy applies there. Finally, the retired professor that agreed to testify confirmed that this process was intended in the original design of the master's program.

The Committee questioned the Department Head on how she came to have the paper in her possession as well as the project and why she had compared the two—did she have reason to believe there would be self-plagiarism? She claimed that she reads all student projects to "be sure they are up to standard." The Committee then asked if she had compared all of the students' projects with the papers they had written for their courses. She responded: "I suppose I did."

The Committee deliberated for only five minutes before calling in their next case. The next day word quickly spread among those of us who attended that the Committee had decided in Hannah's favour and she would graduate.

On Convocation day, Hannah's trials were not quite over. Because her name did not appear on the graduation list, the ushers tried to prevent her family from entering the auditorium. Hannah had a last-minute scramble to get authorization for them to come in. By then they had to sit in a back corner. However, she settled the issue in time to take part in the academic procession and receive her degree.

Field Supervisors

In October 1994, when the Native Student Counsellor and I were disqualified as Field Supervisors because we lacked a master's degree, the students and Field Supervisors decided to separate this issue from the progress of the students in their field placements. We found a Technical Supervisor as quickly as possible. The three disqualified supervisors, however, called a meeting of all Master's Community Specialty supervisors, past and present, for the third week in January. This group raised many concerns, with three rising to the surface as the most pressing. The first of these was the impact on Black and Native students of needing a supervisor with a master's degree. Black and Native students can often pursue their particular learning goals only in their own communities and want the supervision of experienced practitioners from among their own people. However, master's degrees are not common in these communities.

The second concern had to do with the process. A Department-community committee had re-written the field manual just a few months before these events took place and specifically decided that experience was an appropriate substitute for a master's degree in the case of Community Specialty supervisors. They had checked to be sure this was within the criteria for accreditation of the Department. The group was concerned that this policy had been changed abruptly, in mid-term, when students were in supervision, and with no written documentation, not even a set of minutes from the meeting where the decision was made.

The third concern had to do with the emerging practice of having a community worker do the actual supervision, while another individual with a master's degree was named as Technical Supervisor, given the official responsibility and paid for the supervision. The group felt that this practice "leads to exploitation of community practitioners and a de-valuing of the work we do."

On February 2nd, the group sent a letter to the Department Head raising these concerns and requesting a meeting to discuss them. The Department Head responded on March 20th: "I am clear on the thinking of the community workers who have written and I will talk with faculty at the earliest opportunity, not likely before planning meetings in May or early June. Once we have had a chance to review our own thinking on supervision policies and practices, we will be in touch with you and other colleagues to arrange a meeting."

When we had not heard from her by late summer, a representative of the Field Supervisors' group called her. She claimed that the change in policy had simply been a matter of the Master's Coordinator misunderstanding the Field Placement Manual. During the next fall, on October 4th, the Field Supervisors' group received a letter from the Department Head saying that "the qualifications for field supervisor in the [Master's] Program remain as outlined in the [master's] field manual, that is, field supervisors may hold a [master's] degree, or its academic equivalent, or in the case of community practitioners, an equivalency reflected in an advanced level of practice activities."

Chapter Two

Lillian's Story

Cross-Cultural Practice

In November 1993, while I and the other field supervisors were supporting the students in their struggle to have their learning contracts accepted, Lillian also asked me for support. What follows is a summary of what she told me about her experiences during this difficult fall term.

Lillian had started working in the Department as a sessional instructor during the 1991–92 academic year. During the 1990–91 academic year, in cooperation with the Department, she had developed a curriculum for teaching the Department's Cross-Cultural Practice course. It used the traditional Talking Circle of the Aboriginal Nations as the basis of an experiential, student-centred, action-oriented pedagogy. The Black faculty member who usually taught the Cross-Cultural Practice course was away on a sabbatical leave, and Lillian was hired to teach the course in her stead. The course had gone well. There were discontented students, but for the most part student response was enthusiastic and the evaluation scores were high. When the Black professor decided to stay away another year, Lillian was asked to continue. She was given a full-time, tenure-track contract.

During her first year in the Department, Lillian had started doing some advocacy on behalf of Native and Black students. During the second year she began challenging the negative attitudes her fellow faculty held toward students from affirmative action groups.

Attendance Policy

In the summer of 1992, the Department faculty decided to introduce an attendance policy. According to the policy, students who missed more than two classes in a half-credit course, or three in a full-credit course, would be given a mark of "incomplete" on the course. Lillian objected to this change because she thought it would have a discriminatory impact on Aboriginal students. Student funding from the Department of Indian Affairs is dependent on attendance. If the Department began to keep attendance records, Indian Affairs could ask to see them, and students would lose their education funding for missing a few classes, no matter what the reason. This degree of punishment would not be hovering over the heads of students from any other group. Lillian also felt taking attendance in class would remind Aboriginal students of the patronizing manner of the Department of Indian Affairs and before that, the Residential Schools. A third point she raised was the fact that many Native students place a higher value on their community responsibilities than other students and refuse to miss events such as funerals, assemblies, elections and Treaty Day celebrations. Finally, the sense of time in Aboriginal culture is different from that of the mainstream. In spite of Lillian's objections, the policy was passed.

When the term began, the Aboriginal students, along with many others, objected strongly to the policy. A meeting of all students and faculty was called to discuss it. The professor conducting the meeting was doing most of the talking, preventing the students from having a voice. Since the chairs were already arranged in a circle, Lillian suggested that the meeting be conducted according to the principles of a Talking Circle, where each person has an opportunity to speak their mind and heart on the issue. It took two efforts to control the chairperson's domination of the conversation, but eventually, with the aid of a stone passed from hand to hand, the meeting became a Circle. The Native students were not the only ones opposed to the policy; in fact, almost no one supported it. Over the next few weeks, the policy was defeated in all of the Department's committees.

Shortly after the attendance policy meeting, Lillian's teaching methods were questioned by the Department's Executive Committee. However, she continued to teach the course, using Talking Circles and an action-oriented pedagogy.

Open Talking Circle on Discriminatory Harassment

During the spring term in 1993, Lillian told me she found herself again in conflict with other faculty in the Department. In March, the whole campus was involved in discussion of a proposed policy to deal with discriminatory harassment. Canadian University had policies, procedures and an officer in place for dealing with sexual harassment, but there was no recourse for harassment based on any other form of discrimination. The debate over the proposed discriminatory harassment policy brought out arguments becoming familiar all over North America during that decade—freedom of speech versus the right of all students to an atmosphere conducive to learning, academic freedom versus excluded groups' access to a university education. There were also many problems involved in working out a fair and practical mechanism for dealing with harassment.

The proposed policy passed in the University's Senate, but on March 20, the day before the International Day for the Elimination of Racism, the policy was defeated by the Board of Governors. In the meantime, Lillian's Cross-Cultural Practice class had been discussing it and for the action component of the course, decided to hold an Open Talking Circle on Discriminatory Harassment. They invited everyone in the Department. The day they had chosen was March 21, the International Day for the Elimination of Racism.

Lillian told me the Circle was well attended, including several faculty members and the Vice-President of Student Services. The students, now accustomed to speaking their minds and hearts in the Circle format, did so, with the Black and Native students in particular giving emotional descriptions of their experiences of racial harassment in the Department and in other locations on campus. They mentioned no names, but many of the incidents were recognizable to anyone directly involved in them, including some of the faculty involved in the Circle. The coincidental timing of the Circle, the day after the defeat of the policy, gave an added degree of passion to the participants' contributions.

The Circle had progressed most of the way around when the feather was passed to a professor who, instead of accepting it, rose and left the room, gathering up the notes she had been taking. No one had noticed her notes before. Note-taking is a major breach of the structure that gives the Circle its safety as a place to speak. Leaving is another breach. The students who had shared their experiences of harassment felt vulnerable and fearful of retribution.

After the Circle, several of the students spoke with Lillian about their concerns. She, along with the Black and Native Student Counsellors, who were also present at the Circle, issued a joint memo to everyone who took part, recognizing that the principles of the Circle had been breached. They promised that the rules would be made clearer in the future and asked that anyone who experienced retribution from what they had said in the Circle come to them and they would do what they could. They had a commitment from the Vice-President of Student Services to back them in their efforts.

The concerns about the Circle were also brought to the next meeting of the Equality Committee. Lillian reported that this meeting was dominated by the anger of the Committee's Chairperson, a senior Department professor, in reaction to the Circle. The Chairperson questioned the honesty of the students who spoke, saying they could not be believed if they would not name names. In her opinion, people were slandered by hearsay. She also accused Lillian of coercing the students to speak, putting words in their mouths. She claimed that the Department had never had any problems with Black and Native students before Lillian came, so she must be inciting them, a statement she repeated to another faculty member at the University Faculty Club. This remark was overheard by Lillian's Faculty Association Representative.

At the meeting, the Chairperson was confronted by several of the community members of the Equality Committee. The Native Student Counsellor, an Elder, told the Chair that her problem, and that of the whole Department, was denial. They refused to see the racism in their own Department. At that point the Chairperson resigned from the Committee and left the room.

This was the final Equality Committee meeting of the year. Within two weeks, Lillian said, she was called to the Department Head's office and accused of intimidating the Chair of the Equality Committee. The Department Head also told her that the joint memo regarding the Open Circle was not acceptable—it was "too negative."

The Department Head raised one more matter with Lillian at that meeting. Laura was Lillian's partner. The day before, Lillian had attended Laura's final bachelor's degree field presentation. It was a last-minute decision to do so, made possible by the cancellation of another meeting. The field placement had not gone smoothly; Laura was nervous about the presentation and had asked her partner to attend for personal support. She was careful to say at the beginning of the presentation that Lillian was there in a personal support capacity, had no role in the placement and would not be saying anything in the discussion. In the meeting the next day, however, the Department Head told Lillian that her attendance at the presentation was unprofessional behaviour and by her presence she had intimidated the Faculty Supervisor involved in the placement.

Equality Committee

During the following summer, at the Department's annual faculty retreat, the Department Head proposed that since the Equality Committee had lost its chairperson and no one else was willing to chair, the committee should simply be closed down. Lillian immediately offered to chair the committee and the topic was dropped. In late September the committee started up again, with Lillian in the chair. She expanded and re-organized the Committee, making sure that there were representatives on every other committee in the Department.

The newly re-organized and more active Equality Committee soon ran into conflict. The first incident came when the Equality Committee wanted to have an Honouring Ceremony for Affirmative Action graduates. The Department's faculty objected to this, because it would leave out the white students. In the end, it was decided to have a reception for all graduating students.

The next major conflict arose over the re-appointment of two faculty members. Re-appointments are normally done in promotion and tenure committees set up by departments specifically for that purpose. In the Department, re-appointment, promotion, and tenure decisions were made by the Executive Committee, on which Lillian sat as the Equality Committee representative.

At this particular meeting two re-appointments were up for consideration, the Bachelor's Field Coordinator and the Master's Community Specialty

Coordinator. It was Lillian's first experience with re-appointment decisions. She came into the meeting having just returned from a family crisis in another province. She was exhausted and had not seen the agenda for the meeting. When the re-appointments came up, she felt obliged, as the Equality Committee representative, to raise the fact that the Native and Black students were having difficulty with both of the professors being considered for re-appointment. In the case of the Community Specialty Coordinator, she described some of the problems but did not vote against her re-appointment. In the case of the Bachelor's Field Coordinator, she did. She expressed her uncertainty about the procedure, wondering if this was the time and place to raise these points. No one responded to her at the meeting, although under the collective agreement between Canadian University and its Faculty Association, voting against a candidate on the basis of information that had not come before the committee previously for consideration was considered a breach of natural justice. Lillian did not know this, nor did the Department Head suggest that the committee consider Lillian's information and vote at a later date.

The Letter

Four days later, on October 18th, the Department Head wrote a long letter to Lillian about her "negative ways of working on issues related to race and racism." A list of accusations followed. Concerning the Cross-Cultural Practice class, she said white students complained of feeling intimidated by the atmosphere in Lillian's classes. On the subject of the Equality Committee, she said that the committee put a "negative spin ... on every issue," was "badmouthing the [Department]," and was not "constructive in its approach to difficult and painful issues." In the matter of her advocacy for the students in the Community Specialty, she said that Lillian had been "undermin[ing] other faculty and interfering with the academic freedom of faculty members in their duly constituted workloads" by "interfer[ing] with the requirements of other faculty with respect to the amount and standard of work required for credit." Concerning the relationship between Lillian and Laura, she said that "the onus is on faculty to be impeccable in her or his conduct to prevent situations or actions that would be or appear to be biased" and "this standard is not being maintained in your case." She said that she was hearing "frequent and serious concerns about some of your actions." She concluded with these sentences:

> This is disappointing, especially when I hoped and many of us hoped, that your appointment to faculty would help us build on what has been accomplished and move forward in the area of cross-cultural and anti-discriminatory theory and practice. We have talked about most of these issues on more than one occasion and I am willing to do so again. If, however, I cannot soon see

progress, then I will have [to] consider referring these matters to the Dean for disciplinary action.

The Equality Committee meeting discussed the letter at their October meeting. Members felt that Lillian was experiencing a backlash for raising student concerns through what they had understood to be the designated channels. The group was also concerned that some of the issues raised by the committee were Laura's and therefore could be seen as a conflict of interest because of Lillian and Laura's relationship. They decided to divide tasks in a way that would make conditions safer for Lillian or any other faculty member who chose to back the students in their concerns. They divided the functions of the committee between two co-chairs, with Lillian overseeing the internal functioning of the committee and a community member from outside the University carrying forward student concerns. There was also a sub-committee of community members formed to hear student concerns and decide how to carry them forward, thus removing this responsibility from faculty members.

Lillian wrote a long and detailed response to the Department Head's October 18th letter. In it she stated her desire to "clarify my positive intentions, and to dispel any negative perceptions of me and my efforts which appear to be producing and sustaining barriers to healthful growth for both of us and for the [Department] community." In response to the Director's allegations, she pointed out that it is harassment and discrimination that are negative, not efforts to raise them for discussion. She also made it clear that the issues raised by the Equality Committee were coming not from her, but from the experience of Native, Black and ethnic minority students dealing with discrimination and harassment in a "deeply euro-centric" setting; the Equality Committee's mandate was to bring forward these concerns as a service to the Department in the context of its affirmative action commitment.

The Department Head's request that no academic issues be brought forward, she said, seems to contradict the Equality Committee's mandate to address the concerns of minority students. The issues brought forward at the Executive meeting were Lillian's attempt to fulfil this mandate as it seems to be expressed in the Department's governance document, since there was no other place to raise affirmative action students' concerns.

Concerning the Cross-Cultural Practice course, she referred back to an understanding she and the Director had already achieved about the reactions of a small minority of white students, particularly white male students, to a female, Native professor teaching an anti-racist, social change oriented course.

Concerning her attendance at Laura's final field presentation she said it was "well within protocol, as students can invite who they choose to their presentations ... I identified myself as her friend, and that I was not in my role as a Department faculty member at the meeting," and as the only Native faculty member in the Department, there is no one else she could ask for support. She claimed that she had been open about the cultural requirement to respond to Native students' need for support, whether it was included in her work or not, and open about her prior relationship with Laura. She had never taught or advised Laura as a credit student.

At the end of the letter, Lillian expressed her sadness that the Department Head could not sit down and deal with these concerns on a face to face basis first, nor could the others who, according to the letter, had presented "frequent and serious concerns" to the Director. She was unclear on the progress the Department Head desired, but hoped that removing herself from the student advocacy function of the Equality Committee would be seen as a positive step.

On November 9th, the Department Head referred Lillian's case to the Dean of the Faculty of Health. The Dean asked to meet with Lillian and the Department Head. Realising that she was in serious trouble, Lillian contacted the Faculty Association, which provided her with a Representative, and invited the Dean of Graduate Studies, who had been open to supporting Hannah and knew some of the story. It was at this point that she came to me as well, asking me to accompany her, monitor the issues having to do with sexual orientation, give her personal support and take notes.

First Meeting

The first meeting was held on November 28th. The Dean and Department Head insisted that it was not a disciplinary meeting, thus leaving everyone unsure of whether or not the protections provided by the Collective Agreement in a disciplinary action applied. The meeting followed the format of a disciplinary action, with the Dean and Department Head stating their complaints, and Lillian, along with her Faculty Association Representative and support person taking notes.

The complaints discussed at the meeting were those enumerated in the October 18th letter. According to a confirming letter written after the meeting, the Dean and Department Head were asking Lillian to "make a genuine dissociation between your academic and personal affairs with respect to your partner. This would be applied whenever [Laura] is in the role of a student and you are in the role of a faculty member. You are a faculty member in any activity related to the Department." They asked Lillian to stop student advocacy "at the point of interference with other faculty or with students' academic programs" and "not express any opinion of any other faculty member's work or any opinion on students' academic progress." They added that "it would perhaps be more helpful in the future if this advocacy were done in a more constructive fashion." Although early in the meeting the Department Head seemed to be demanding that Lillian resign from the chair of the Equality Committee, later this was amended to be simply that she "would accept [Lillian's] resignation."

The requirement that Lillian dissociate from Laura immediately began to be a problem, since they were two of only three people on campus studying Native learning and education. The third person was Beth. As a precaution, Lillian stopped attending gatherings related to her academic pursuits, including a colloquium at the Department on Native community healing. Lillian and Laura both felt that they should not be seen in the same room together while the situation remained unresolved, even though it limited their ability to pursue their academic interests and could be defined as a denial of their academic freedom.

Lillian reported one more small incident before Christmas. On December 6th there was no one around the Department office except the clerical staff decorating the Christmas tree. Lillian had some work to do, so did it on the office computer. The next day a memo was issued to all faculty reminding everyone that "the computer in the main office … is for everyone's use … please, then, try not to sit the whole morning or afternoon or day working at the computer."

Second Meeting

Lillian's second meeting with the Department Head and the Deans was set for February 9th. Two days before the scheduled date, she opened her mail to find four extremely critical student evaluations and a note from the Department Head saying that she wanted to talk about them. The documents were all anonymous, all written more than a month after the end of the course and all typed on the same typewriter. All said prominently on the front page "Please submit this page separately from the others, as only your instructor will receive these written comments."

In preparation for the February 9th meeting, Lillian went to the person responsible for tabulating teaching evaluations to get copies of all of her evaluations to date and some help with interpreting the statistics. The evaluations given to her on February 7th were all from one class, a master's level class where she had met major resistance. Her average evaluation rating from that class was 3 out of 5. However, the rest of her ratings ranged from 4.3 to 4.8 out of 5. In each case, the average was pulled down by one or two low ratings, but most students had given her remarkably high evaluation scores. The person who tabulates the ratings pointed out that hers were the highest in the Department and among the highest in undergraduate teaching in the University.

The same people who were present on November 28th gathered on February 9th—both Deans, the Department Head, Lillian, her Faculty Association Representative and myself. The Dean of the Faculty of Health and the Department Head wanted to raise the matter of the student evaluations. The Faculty Association Representative immediately put that issue to rest, referring to a clause in the Collective Agreement that forbids the use of anonymous student comments in faculty evaluation unless specifically approved by Senate or the Faculty.

Lillian and the two of us who were supporting her had decided before the meeting that the best strategy would be to try to avoid a formal disciplinary procedure, suggesting an external mediator to resolve the conflict. The first mediator suggested was the Employment Equity Officer. We had invited her to the meeting to discuss the possible mediation. The Dean of Health, however, when asked if the Employment Equity Officer could come to the meeting, called up the Employment Equity Officer and told her that if she came at Lillian and the Faculty Association's invitation, she would automatically be seen as biased and associated with Lillian's side of the case. The Employment Equity Officer stayed away from the meeting to preserve her neutrality as a possible mediator. All that was agreed to during the meeting was that the Dean and Department Head would consider mediation. There was never any further response on the matter.

The day after the meeting there was a faculty meeting at the Department. Recent events were discussed and, according to Lillian, some faculty members expressed the opinion that there was no racism in the Department. One, a white male, claimed that if he cannot see racism, it doesn't exist.

A Series of Letters

During the last week of February, the Department Head wrote to Lillian asking her to meet about the student evaluations. Lillian, who by now was not at all inclined to meet with the Department Head, or anyone else, without a witness, asked her Faculty Association Representative to come with her. This was not acceptable to the Department Head and a series of letters ensued:

On February 28th, the Department Head wrote:

> I believe that I can and must be able to talk with faculty members about the ordinary work of the ... [Department] ... I have asked to talk about feedback on your teaching and you are not willing to meet. I will, therefore, refer the matter of feedback on your teaching to [the] Dean [of the Faculty of Health] and ask that this item be taken up in any future meeting.

On March 6th, Lillian's Faculty Association Representative wrote to the Department Head requesting clarification of the reasons for attempting to use anonymous student evaluations for faculty evaluation and why forms clearly marked as for the instructor's eyes only were in the hands of the Department Head.

On March 9th, the Dean of Health wrote to Lillian:

It is normal practice for a faculty member to meet with his/her Department Head on matters related to the [Department] in a timely fashion. The matter of teaching is an appropriate point of discussion for a faculty member and Department Head. The concerns expressed by students with regard to your teaching are serious ones which must be addressed. I, therefore, suggest that you arrange a meeting between yourself and [the Department Head] to discuss this matter as soon as possible.

Lillian's Faculty Association Representative responded to the Dean on March 27th, enclosing a copy of her letter to the Department Head clarifying the use of anonymous student comments. She said:

As you can see, there are serious issues surrounding the procedures to be employed regarding teaching evaluations. To date I have received no reply from [the Department Head] on this matter. Therefore, in my view your suggestion that [Lillian] meet with [the Department Head] is premature.

On April 25th, the Dean terminated the quasi-disciplinary process. She wrote to Lillian:

It is my impression that the informal meeting process begun in November 1994 with you has provided an opportunity for the airing of views but that it has not been a forum in which these issues have been satisfactorily addressed. There is now correspondence between yourself and the Department Head regarding the Department Head's desire to meet with you to discuss serious concerns with respect to your teaching. It may be that our meetings have inhibited you from meeting with your Department Head. I feel it is, therefore, in the best interest of all concerned that we close the informal meeting process at this time. I would urge you to meet with your Department Head directly and to begin a one-on-one dialogue with her to discuss these teaching-related issues.

On May 5th, Lillian wrote to the Department Head, saying:

I am prepared to have these discussions, along with discussion of other and more recent course evaluations which are positive. I would also like to discuss the deployment issue for the Cross Cultural [Practice] course for next year.... Because part of this discussion is about student evaluations and the legal and proper use of them under the Collective Agreement, I would like to include [my Faculty Association Representative] in these discussions.

On May 10th, the Department Head responded:

> I have asked many times to talk with you, [Lillian], about the student feedback on your teaching and I ask again in this letter. As you know, I have a right and a duty to talk with faculty members about their teaching and all aspects of their work as faculty members in this [Department]. I must insist that you and I meet in the normal Department Head and faculty member way.

On May 12th, the Faculty Association Representative responded:

> Please be advised that it is the advice of the [Faculty Association] personnel counselling [Lillian] that she should not meet with you unless a [Faculty Association] representative is present, in the light of the sensitive state of affairs that exists in respect to a variety of matters at the present time. Our advice to [Lillian] was that I should accompany her to this meeting because of my familiarity both with respect to the present controversy and with respect to the significance of teaching evaluations under the Collective Agreement, and in the context of equity disputes.

On May 19th, the Department Head again wrote directly to Lillian:

> I am writing again to ask to meet with you concerning issues raised about your teaching in Cross-Cultural [Practice] courses. As I have already said on many occasions, I am entitled as Department Head to have such a meeting with a faculty member. I believe that the presence of representatives on one or both sides will alter the nature and purposes of our meeting and will not facilitate a genuine discussion of the serious matters raised by students. If your position remains that which was expressed in [the Faculty Association Representative's] letter of May 12, 1995, then I have to conclude that you refuse to meet with me to discuss in a collegial fashion the concerns expressed to me. I am giving you one further opportunity to reconsider your position. If I do not hear from you by or on May 25, 1995, then I will have to act upon the information I have without the benefit of your input.

On May 24th, Lillian's Faculty Association Representative wrote back to the Department Head:

> Your letter appears to be taking the position that if [Lillian] does not disregard the advice that the [Faculty Association] has given her, and meet with you alone, that this will violate some unspecified

managerial right, and give you cause to take disciplinary action that will have an adverse impact on our Member.... In [the Faculty Association's] view, it is neither fair nor reasonable to assert that a [Faculty Association] member should be deemed uncollegial, denied an opportunity to share her views of facts that are in controversy, or subjected to disciplinary action because she accepted the advice of her Faculty Association on the handling of a sensitive and difficult matter, where there is a history of serious disagreement over both issues of fact and legal interpretation of the provisions of the Collective Agreement. The right of a Member to have a [Faculty Association] representative attend meetings that address these kinds of matters is clear in other parts of the Collective Agreement, and we believe that such a right exists in the present situation. Moreover, [the Faculty Association] is frequently invited by Members to attend discussions of the significance of student reactions to courses, and the other administrators that we have dealt with on such matters have not objected to our presence at such meetings. Accordingly, I would suggest that we proceed to schedule a meeting to be attended by yourself, [Lillian], myself, and any advisor that you wish to bring.

On June 18th, the Department Head responded:

I have expressed my position many times, that is, that I have the right and the duty to talk with faculty members about their teaching and related work at the [Department] and that direct discussion between me and a faculty member is the best way to address and try to solve any concerns or problems. I regret that meeting with me is not acceptable to [Lillian] or to you. Should [Lillian] decide to meet with me, she can call me.

In a letter written in August 16th, the Dean closed this series of letters with this statement:

I am aware that students have expressed concerns to the Department Head and in teaching evaluations about the Cross Cultural [Practice] courses.... You have yet to meet with your Department Head on these serious criticisms and I continue to urge you to do so.

During the Summer

In July, the Dean asked for Lillian's annual report early. The faculty of Canadian University were at that time restricted by a provincial government wage freeze, but one small annual increase was still allowed, the

Career Development Increment (CDI), a recognition of increasing experience at the University. Under certain circumstances, the CDI can be denied as a disciplinary action, with the Dean's recommendation and the President's approval. The Dean wanted Lillian's annual report early because she was making a decision on whether or not to grant her CDI in the light of "the serious concerns raised by some of your students and your Director with respect to your teaching performance." Lillian worked quickly and submitted her annual report about ten days later. There were a few changes in details but, in substance, the report was identical to her report of the previous year. The previous year's report had earned specific praise from the Dean for being "appropriate and informative;" this report earned three pages of critique, particularly concerning the ongoing problems over the student evaluations given to Lillian in February and the amount of her administrative work that had been "self-assigned, and difficult to receive credit for without evaluation through the normal routes, such as accountability for a committee's work or assisting with the achievement of the objectives of the Unit." She did not, however, continue with the process to deny the CDI.

Two other decisions were made during the summer. Lillian had discovered that the Department was planning a course in health and the law and went to the Bachelor's Degree Coordinator and offered to teach it. She had taught this course for several years at another university. The Department decided to have the course taught by a variety of guest instructors and never responded to Lillian's offer. Also, the assignment of teaching assistants was reviewed. The Cross-Cultural Practice course and the Equality Committee were both cut from a full-time to a half-time teaching assistant.

Also in mid-August the Department Head stopped insisting on meeting alone with Lillian. She assigned work for the coming year without consultation, giving her a double load of field supervision, mostly outside of her area of expertise, and geographically widely scattered. She also removed the master's level of the Cross-Cultural Practice course from her workload and took her off of the Equality Committee.

During the summer, Lillian stopped going to faculty meetings. She said that even the sight of them marked in her calendar made her physically sick.

Proposal to Replace the Equality Committee

During June 1994, the Department Head indicated that race issues would be discussed at the annual staff retreat. Lillian put in a request for vacation from June 2nd to 22nd and indicated that she had booked flights to visit her family in another province. Shortly afterwards, the Director announced that the staff retreats would be held on June 2nd and 22nd. At these meetings a decision was made to abolish the Equality Committee and replace it with a body chaired by the Department Head and composed of a single student representative of every affirmative action group in the Department.

On October 4th, the Department's Annual Meeting was asked to vote on this motion. A large group of Black and Native students, graduates, community members, present and former Equality Committee members and their allies, including myself, gathered for the meeting. The professor who had chaired the Equality Committee before Lillian, who walked out during the discussion of the Open Circle on Discriminatory Harassment, presented the motion. She spoke on behalf of disabled people at the Department, saying that they have felt left out by the Equality Committee structure and without a voice of their own. Members of the Black and Native communities and student bodies spoke to their need for the Equality Committee, even if there was another body formed to allow for representation of other groups. Lillian, in her last act as chair of the Equality Committee, pointed out that she and the other current members of the Committee had not been consulted on this decision.

The Annual Meeting decided to continue the Equality Committee and to strike a Task Force with the mandate of proposing a new structure to provide representation for all affirmative action groups in the Department. Later, in a faculty meeting, the decision was made to elect faculty to the Committee rather than appointing volunteers as had been done in the past. Two professors were elected, including the Bachelor's Field Coordinator who had been the subject of several complaints by the Native students.

Investigation and Report

In March of 1994 another process had begun, involving the Black students. A former student and member of the provincial association for Black members of the profession chaired a meeting in which the students aired their grievances. These were communicated to the Department Head in a letter. This led to a process in the Black community, resulting in the Department Head being asked to come to a meeting with representatives of some of the Black community's major organizations.

The community leaders present at the meeting asked for an investigation into the Department's treatment of Black and Native students, carried out by members of both communities. This request went forward to the President of the University, who decided to investigate, but not to involve anyone outside of the University. He appointed a Professor from another department to carry out the investigation. Several people involved in the events, along with community members present at the August meeting, objected to the decision to keep the investigation internal, but the President went ahead.

There was also some protest over the mandate of the investigation. It was defined as examining the "effectiveness of the Department's affirmative action policy in the light of academic standards." Those who had requested the investigation in the first place had no complaints about the affirmative action policy, which is limited to admission, but with the treatment of students once they have been admitted. Again, the President stood firm.

Those who were invited to be interviewed debated among themselves whether to participate in a flawed process or stay away. There was a high risk either way. In the end, most decided to participate. The professor assigned to the task interviewed dozens of people during October and November. Hannah, Laura and Lillian told her their stories. I took notes while Lillian talked to her for six hours.

As the time for presentation of the report approached, the President announced that it would be given orally only, and those present would be restricted to himself, the Dean of the Faculty of Health and the Department Head. Later, under pressure, he admitted the President of the Faculty Association, along with the Association's lawyer. The oral nature of the report increased the vulnerability of those that had given information in the process. Some who had taken part said they regretted their decision to participate.

The report was delivered on December 14th. With the President's agreement, the professor who did the investigation then produced a written report as well, which was widely distributed during January. Lillian and the students from the previous year's Master's Community Specialty felt betrayed by the report. Their stories were absent from the text, while stories from white participants' point of view were included. The pain on both sides was portrayed as equal, with no mention of the fact that with unequal power and security, the losses were much greater for those with less power. Also, the discomfort of some white students in the Cross-Cultural Practice class was featured, while the discomfort of most Black and Native students in other classes was not mentioned.

Re-appointment

Lillian's three-year contract with the Department was due to expire on June 30, 1995. By now the Department had created a Promotion and Tenure Committee to deal with faculty contracts. One member of the Committee was the former chair of the Equality Committee, who had said to that Committee that she believed Lillian was coercing the Black and Native students.

The normal process would have been for Lillian to apply for re-appointment and prepare a dossier of her teaching and scholarly work for the committee. According to the Collective Agreement, she had to state her intention to stand for re-appointment by October 31, 1994. On Friday, September 13th, 1994, she received a memo from the Department's

Promotion and Tenure Committee asking her to state her intentions by Monday, September 16th. By Monday she still had not decided whether to go ahead. The chair of the Promotion and Tenure Committee came to her office door while she was on the phone informing a very upset Hannah about her referral to the Senate Discipline Committee for self-plagiarism. He waited at the door for the full fifteen or twenty minutes that it took to finish the conversation. Lillian reports that by the time she hung up the phone, she was very annoyed with him. He asked her if she was planning to apply for re-appointment. She said she was not sure if she wanted the job when the working conditions were so bad. The next day he circulated a memo saying she was not a candidate for re-appointment.

Lillian told me she panicked at this—suddenly the full reality of unemployment sunk in. She called her Faculty Association Representative, who told her she legally had until October 31 to apply, but considering that there were major concerns about conflict of interest on the Department's Promotion and Tenure Committee, she should apply for a year's extension while a fair way of evaluating her work could be worked out. Lillian made the application as suggested.

Both the Department Head and the Dean of the Faculty of Health turned down the application by the end of October. With the support of the Faculty Association, Lillian appealed the decision to the Academic Vice-President. The Vice-President consulted with the Dean and Department Head and turned the application down as well. The application was then appealed at the level of the President. He referred it back to the Vice-President Academic again.

In April 1995, Lillian, her Faculty Association Representative and I met with the Vice-President Academic. Two weeks later, the President made a final rejection of Lillian's appeal. His reasons were: he felt Lillian had had sufficient time to state her intention to apply for re-appointment before the September 18th deadline; the Department Head and Dean said that Lillian's allegations of bias in the process were unfounded; "your unilateral decision not to participate in collegial processes, and your repeated refusal to meet with the Department Head contributed to the very circumstance you allege was created by others," and finally, because the internal investigation, "in which you participated," did not give "any grounds to warrant extension of your appointment."

Several months later I talked with the professor who had done the internal investigation. The President had sent her a copy of his letter at the time. She was angry that her report had been misused in this way and showed me her letter back to the President. In this letter, she pointed out that "the suggestion that my Report could be the basis for either denying or extending someone's appointment is completely at odds with the mandate I was given or could properly have been given." She also objected to the President's statement that the Report provided no basis for finding extenuating circumstances explaining why Lillian missed the September 18th deadline. "I find that contradicted ... by my Report. I made clear to you my premise that the ordinary processes were unworkable in the circumstances.... My understanding at the end of our conversation was that ... there would be some sort of substitute process to deal with the merits of [Lillian's] case. Moreover, this all had to be on the assumption that the missed deadline was not determinative. I was very surprised, therefore, when the next thing I heard was that [Lillian] was not being renewed, without there having been any further process to consider the merits of her case beyond the issue of the missed deadline."

Grievance

Following the final rejection, the Faculty Association launched a grievance. In early May, Lillian, her Faculty Association Representative and I met with the President for the informal first stage of the grievance. At the end of the month, he again rejected the request for an extension to allow a fair way of evaluating Lillian's work to be developed. At the end of June, the Faculty Association presented the written formal grievance, and again, on July 10th, the President rejected it. In this letter he said "[T]here are numerous allegations of fact and alleged breaches of the Collective Agreement with which we take strong exception. The tone of the grievance is in our view irregular and inappropriate. My decision in relation to the grievance is that it is without merit."

On July 11, the Executive of the Faculty Association decided to carry the case forward to arbitration with a lawyer from the Canadian Association of University Teachers (CAUT) who had experience with systemic discrimination cases in University settings. Lillian, however, lost her job on June 30th, 1994, and put her house up for sale. She was still supervising the project and thesis work of three students, one of whom had just submitted her second last draft and was trying to meet a deadline at the end of July. This student had used Lillian's personal contacts in the Native community to do her research and was depending heavily on Lillian to be sure she wrote up this material in a respectful way. During the formal stage of the grievance, Lillian appealed to the President to be able to finish her work with at least this student and possibly all three. The President referred her back to the Department Head, where he "believ[ed] the [Department] has the ability to address the matter of student supervision to the benefit of all concerned." Meanwhile, the Department Head had written to Lillian asking her to report on the progress of her students in preparation for handing them over to another supervisor. Rather than enter yet another battle over whether or not she would meet alone with the Department Head, Lillian saw no option but to allow the Department to assign the three students to new supervisors.

The "Smudge Memo"

Before leaving Lillian's story, there is one more incident to report. Because Lillian's teaching was based in Native traditions, a key feature of her classes was the smudge. This is an herb, such as sage or sweetgrass, burned to purify the room and participants in the Circle. Smudging is also part of Lillian's personal spiritual practice as a Traditional Native person. During a difficult time in April 1995, Lillian retreated to her office with Laura to talk and smudge themselves before going on to other commitments. As they left the room, they told me, they overheard the Community Specialty Coordinator in conversation with another faculty member across the hall. The two of them commented on the smell and joked about marijuana. The next day the Department Head issued a memo to all faculty and staff asking that no substances be burned or smoked in Department buildings in consideration of people with sensitivities and allergies.

Thesis Proposal: How Did This Happen?

As mentioned in the Introduction, during the meeting on February 9th, 1994, when Lillian and her two supporters unsuccessfully proposed mediation to resolve the situation, I asked myself what I would do if I were ever asked to mediate a situation such as this one. In spite of ten years of professional conflict resolution experience, I didn't know. Also, in spite of fifteen years of teaching and writing about the dynamics of sexism, racism and other forms of oppression, I couldn't say how or why this situation escalated the way it did. I had been looking for a thesis topic; I had found it. I began to search the literature for others who had studied similar situations, and I spoke about it to Lillian and the students who were at the centre of the story. Word began to spread, bringing both encouraging and discouraging responses.

The peak of the discouraging response was a summons from my own Dean to discuss the matter. She had a copy of the collective agreement opened to the conflict of interest clause. This clause forbids teachers in my faculty from "engag[ing] in any professional activity, paid or unpaid, which competes or conflicts with [faculty] activities." The Dean said that she felt I was destroying my faculty's relationship with the Department, and since my faculty's survival depends on good relationships with the rest of the university, I was in conflict of interest. She wanted me to change my thesis topic. After some discussion, she admitted that she was doing this under pressure from the Dean of the Faculty of Health. A consultation with the Faculty Association assured me that in this case the conflict of interest clause would probably not stand up against the academic freedom clauses that give all faculty the right to criticize our own institution. Perhaps the University's lawyer had the same opinion, for nothing was done to discipline me under the conflict of interest clause.

The encouraging side of the response brought me supportive comments and many powerful stories from other Black and Native students and graduates of the Department. Given the carefully drawn boundaries of my study, I could not use most of them, but they gave me more motivation to go on and attempt to solve the riddle of what happened and how it could have been done differently.

One story given to me, however, was directly related and added a new dimension to my picture of what happened in the Master's Community Specialty class during the 1993–94 academic year. This is the story of Yuen, the international student who was in the course that year. At the time the events were happening, she felt she had to separate herself from her Native and Black classmates, although her sympathies lay with them, and she felt she could not seek out potential allies like myself, because she was afraid of losing her student visa. For various reasons, that would have been a personal disaster. By the time she talked to me, she had temporary immigrant status and, soon afterward, achieved landed immigrant status. This gave her enough security to tell her story.

Chapter Three

Yuen's Story

Studying in Canada

Yuen had trained in her profession in her home country and had worked at it there for seven years. When she came to Canada, she did not have enough mastery of the language and culture to work in the profession here without further training. She completed a bachelor's degree at another university. She came to Canadian University to complete a qualifying year and a master's degree.

Yuen found she had to coach the Department carefully through the immigration bureaucracy. She wrote the letters from the Department affirming that she was a student there to avoid any error that might cause her to be sent back to her country of origin. She found the help she needed with writing in English at the University's Writing Centre, a service that provides writing tutors to help students with their papers. She was bored during her qualifying year, because most of the work was a repeat of her undergraduate degree and her previous training.

Between the qualifying year and her master's year, Yuen asked if she could register for a summer course. This would save paperwork with the Immigration Office, the fare for a return flight to her country and allow her to keep her medical benefits, which would be lost if there were an interruption in her studies. She knew of other students who were taking courses in the summer. Her request was refused for reasons she did not understand, forcing her to scrape together enough money to fly home for the summer, as well as lose her medical benefits. In the fall she returned, successfully renewed her student visa and began her master's program. She chose the Community Specialty because she had had a good experience with the Community Specialty Coordinator during her qualifying year.

Practice of Community Work Class

The tensions in the Practice of Community Work class during the fall immediately affected her, but she didn't know exactly what was happening. She told me:

> Sometimes [Hannah's] eyes are wet and they never tell me what's going on, but I feel it, and I don't feel comfortable to attend the

class, and sometimes the dialogue between [the Community Specialty Coordinator] and them, it's misplaced, I can feel it, but I have nobody that I can talk to.

Yuen was part of the group trying to negotiate workload, but when it became obvious that the Community Specialty Coordinator was angry about the other students dropping their elective research course, she was too frightened to join them. She knew she must get a letter from the Department to maintain her student visa. In her words: "[The Community Specialty Coordinator] knew my whole situation; so, in fact, she has this card in her hand. She knows she can control me ... so I am under her mercy.... So even though [the Native students] and all of them say, 'Oh change your professor, change this, change that,' they forgot she had the last card in her hand."

She restricted her sleep to four hours a night in order to complete both courses. The white student in the class, she told me, was never put under pressure to take the research course. Later, when the white student was working on her project, she told Yuen that she was having difficulty doing her research, but the Community Specialty Coordinator coached her through it.

While the Native and Black students struggled to get Field Supervisors and learning contracts in place, Yuen took the only field placement available that would allow her to pursue her interests. The Community Specialty Coordinator suggested that she be Yuen's Field Supervisor herself. After beginning her placement, Yuen discovered that the Community Specialty Coordinator was a former board member of the agency and had considerable power there. The Community Specialty Coordinator was now her Field Supervisor and her Faculty Field Supervisor, as well as her Specialty Coordinator and Professor, and later would supervise her final project as well. Yuen wrote more drafts of her learning contract than anyone else through the fall, adding the extra work to her night-time load. Her contract was signed by the end of the fall term.

After a month in her placement, the Community Specialty Coordinator asked her, too, to write a personal statement. Yuen objected because neither the Field Placement Manual nor the agency required it. The Coordinator responded that she must write one because "I am your supervisor and I say so." Only later did Yuen realize the problems that could arise from revealing too much information about her personal history.

The Meeting

On January 23rd the Community Specialty students were invited to the January 30th meeting with the Community Specialty Coordinator, Department Head and Deans. While the other students negotiated who would be allowed in to support them and prepared their presentation,

Yuen went through an agonizing week. She understood that it was a very serious event, but could not figure out what the politics of the situation were and wondered if she should or shouldn't be involved. She tried to get advice from the International Student Counsellor, who simply dismissed the problem as not serious. She made two appointments to talk with the Department Head. Both were cancelled, the second one after she had waited in the Department Head's outer office for an hour and a half. After the January 30th meeting, the one white student in the class told Yuen that as soon as the meeting was called, she had received a call from the Community Specialty Coordinator explaining the situation to her.

Yuen finally went to the Student Counselling Service and asked one of the counsellors to help her sort out the situation. He told her she had the right not to go to the meeting, but his advice was to attend, observe, learn, but don't say anything. This proved impossible, since the Dean of Graduate Studies asked each student individually whether they wanted to stay with the Community Specialty Coordinator or have another teacher. Yuen objected that it put her in the difficult position of having to choose between the Community Specialty Coordinator and her classmates. However, the Dean pushed her to make a choice. Given her complete dependence on the Community Specialty Coordinator, she felt she had to stay in her part of the class.

The next week, the Community Specialty Coordinator met with her remaining two students. She asked Yuen if she wanted the situation explained to her. Yuen said no, she just wanted to get on with the work. She told me that the Community Specialty Coordinator spent half of the class explaining the situation to her regardless. According to Yuen, she said:

> Those students will be penalized ... they may not graduate on time, and the ... Department will not let them do it so easily.... They are not the victim, they just manipulate the power ... including [Lillian] ... [Lillian, Beth], and those people have bitter lives and they have some issues outside the [Department], so they just vent it on me.

Before the Community Specialty Coordinator's comments, Yuen did not know that Lillian was part of the situation at all. Yuen said that she worked persistently to steer the Community Specialty Coordinator back to the content of the course, an effort she had to keep up for the rest of the term, although she felt very vulnerable herself. She told me:

> But for me, I feel she is threatening me also. I don't know, this is my interpretation. "If you don't co-operate with me, you will be the next person to be penalized, and you will have trouble to

graduate." That's the message I get, although maybe she doesn't have this intention. And after that class I was horrified ... because if anything happened in the [Department], if they deal with the immigration officer and they terminate my student visa, I would disappear in this country forever.

The Rumour

Over the Christmas vacation, Yuen accompanied the Community Specialty Coordinator on a visit to friends in another city. Between Christmas and February, Yuen told me, a rumour started, somewhere in either the Department or Yuen's field placement, that the Community Specialty Coordinator was having a lesbian relationship with Yuen, or sexually harassing her. The rumour was strengthened when Yuen sat with the Community Specialty Coordinator and her friends at an evening of International Women's Day celebrations, although Yuen says that she was never under any pressure to take part in social activities with the Coordinator.

After hearing the rumours, both in the Department and in her field placement, Yuen went to the Community Specialty Coordinator to suggest that they shouldn't spend time together outside of class. A few days later, Yuen received a call from the Community Specialty Coordinator, who was with the University's Sexual Harassment Officer. She asked Yuen to come to the Sexual Harassment Office and talk about the rumours. Yuen did not want to go, but felt she had little choice. "I felt it's another thing of this disempowerment. I am scared to say no by having witnessed how [Beth, Laura and Hannah] were suffering. What if I say no? What will happen?"

The three of them talked about the rumours, then the Community Specialty Coordinator left and the Sexual Harassment Officer talked to Yuen alone, then the Community Specialty Coordinator was invited back in to talk about a strategy to counter the rumours. Both with the Community Specialty Coordinator present and alone, Yuen was asked if she thought the rumours were coming from Beth, Laura and Hannah. She was also asked for the names of those who had brought the rumours to her attention. She insisted that she did not know where the rumours came from in the beginning and she would not give the names of those who passed them on to her.

Shortly after this, the Department Head called Yuen to her office and asked her for the names of those who told her about the rumours and also asked her if she thought they were started by the three students who had left the Community Specialty Coordinator's class. Again she resisted implicating the others or giving information.

During the following weeks, the Community Specialty Coordinator put Yuen under, in Yuen's words, "extremely high pressure," calling her repeatedly at home to ask who had told her about the rumour. Finally bending under the pressure, Yuen told her the names of three white students who had mentioned the rumours to her. She told one of the students that she had given her name to the Community Specialty Coordinator; the student was extremely angry with her. She decided not to tell the other students, but simply hope they could take care of themselves.

In February and March, the Community Specialty Coordinator made calls to Yuen's other professors asking them how she was doing and suggesting that she be protected from Laura. She implied that Laura was intimidating Yuen. Yuen and Laura both told me they heard about the phone calls when one of their professors checked the story out with them. Laura said the Department Head also stopped her one day and told her that she must stop intimidating other students.

Graduation

Yuen completed her project over the summer, under the Community Specialty Coordinator's supervision, and graduated at fall convocation. At the end of the process, the Coordinator asked Yuen for a letter of reference implying that it would say she was a good teacher. Yuen asked if this was required and was told it was "general practice ... it's the Canadian system." Later Yuen's Student Counsellor told her there was no requirement to do this.

At that point Yuen began doing everything possible to avoid the Community Specialty Coordinator. This proved to be difficult. Several professors in the Department, including the Community Specialty Coordinator, are active in the community. They sometimes ran into each other. Yuen says she wondered how much she would suffer if she revealed what had happened to her and the poor treatment Black, Native and ethnic minority students receive in the Department. Perhaps she already had suffered in her professional life, she told me, particularly in her difficulties finding a job in the community.

Chapter Four

The Story Continues

More Delays

From 1994 to 1997, I wrote the account you have just read (Chapters One to Three), based on my own experience and interviews with Beth, Hannah, Laura, Lillian and Yuen. By April 1998, we had negotiated changes to the draft until we had a version we all agreed with.

Lillian had been waiting for her grievance to come to arbitration for three years, but by then the process had very little to do with her. It had become a struggle between the Board of Governors of Canadian University, represented by an outside lawyer, and the Faculty Association, represented by the legal staff of the Canadian Association of University Teachers (CAUT). Few Canadian lawyers have experience with systemic discrimination cases. Even fewer have experience with such cases in academic settings, where academic freedom and collegiality are issues. The CAUT legal staff had this experience and had been consulted when the grievance was first written in 1995. Because they saw Lillian's case as precedent-setting, they became directly involved.

The delays went on and on. There were changes in the CAUT legal staff, discussions about hiring and payment of outside lawyers and complicated maneuvering over the choice of arbitrators. At one point the lawyer for the Board of Governors didn't return telephone calls for four months. In February 1998, the Board of Governors' lawyer raised objections about the validity of the process. This led to a preliminary hearing where the Arbitrator would decide if the case should be heard at all. A week before the scheduled dates in May the Arbitrator resigned from the case, causing another cancellation, a new search for a suitable arbitrator and a great deal of pain and confusion.

Preliminary Hearing

Finally, on August 9, 1998, the preliminary hearing got underway. Because it was concerned with the validity of the grievance rather than its content, Lillian was not present.

The Board of Governor's lawyer claimed that the grievance was not valid because of missed deadlines—the Department's deadline for Lillian's re-appointment application and the collective agreement's deadline for submitting a grievance—and because too much time had passed and Lillian had found another job. He also claimed that it was not valid to use an individual's situation to remedy what the Faculty Association saw as a University-wide problem. His final argument was that the Arbitrator had no jurisdiction in this case because an allegation of systemic discrimination belongs in a Human Rights Tribunal, not a labour arbitration.

The Faculty Association was, in the end, represented by an outside lawyer. He argued that the case was much broader than the technical matter of Lillian's re-appointment because of the context of that event within the climate of the Department at the time. He defined the case as one of constructive dismissal; that is, one where an employee is forced to resign by the conditions of the workplace.

He presented several legal precedents for labour arbitrators hearing systemic discrimination cases when the collective agreement includes a broad discrimination clause. In previous cases senior managers have been held responsible for discrimination because of their failure to deal with incidents that have taken place in their institutions. In this case, he argued, the University President decided without any investigation that the grievance had no merit and the Faculty Association had good reason to ask that he be held accountable under the collective agreement for his responsibility to investigate and act on systemic discrimination.

He brought forward precedents for an arbitrator ruling that, in a case like this, timelines and deadlines cannot be applied in the ordinary manner because of the continuing nature of systemic discrimination. Systemic discrimination is gradually revealed through many individual incidents, sometimes over many years. Previous arbitrators have ruled that it is proper to ask for broad systemic relief in cases brought forward by an individual because systemic discrimination in an institutional pattern.

Another reason for making an exception from the usual time limits, the Faculty Association's lawyer argued, was that it is in the interests of everyone involved if informal channels for resolution are tried first, making it difficult to file grievances within a certain brief time after each incident. He made a final major point: that the grievance was still relevant because others continue to suffer from the systemic discrimination Lillian experienced and it is important to her and the Faculty Association to see that situation addressed.

Only two witnesses were called—for the Board of Governors, the Department Head, and for the Association, Lillian's Faculty Association Representative. The Faculty Association's lawyer carried out his role in the hearing in a business-like and civil manner, but the Administration's lawyer chose to use a nasty tone, particularly with the Association's witness. My task was to take notes for Lillian, and I had borrowed a friend's laptop so that I could record the discussion almost verbatim. Throughout my notes I tried to add comments on the tone of the hearing as well as its content. When the Board of Governors' lawyer was questioning the Association's witness, my notes were filled with bracketed words and phrases such as "(snarky)" or "(mimics her voice)." For example:

> [Board of Governors Lawyer]: (Cuts off witness's explanation, nasty tone) "You understand the question. It's a simple question. You're a lawyer. Surely you can answer a simple question."

There is one more element of the hearing I wish to note because it becomes important in the analysis later in this book. Part of the Board of Governors' case was to argue that it was impossible for the Department to discriminate because it had taken steps against racism, steps such as the affirmative action admittance policy and the hiring of a Black faculty member.

The Board of Governors' lawyer referred to "the ridiculous allegations that this [Department], which is the opposite of racist, be accused of these things." He also accused the Association lawyer of wanting "to suffocate the facts because it is obvious that the allegations in this grievance are ridiculous, affirmed by senior faculty," and argued that "this [grievance] was considered a bogus issue in the most senior levels of the [Department]."

During her testimony, the Department Head was asked to comment on the systemic remedies suggested in the grievance. She replied: "I don't think they have any relevance to the [Department]. I would argue instead that the [Department] has had a long record of affirmative action, staff training in regard to minority groups, and has tried to develop its curriculum to include women and minorities. I would argue that we have a long list of accomplishments. I don't think this has any relevance to the [Department]."

The Board of Governors assumption seemed to me to be that an organization is either racist or not, so that some steps taken against racism prove that no further discrimination is possible. Put another way, good intentions can be used to prove absence of racism or other forms of oppression. This observation became an important part of my later analysis of what happened (see Part Two of this book).

The Arbitration That Wasn't

In October 1998 the Arbitrator ruled in favour of the Association on all points. He would hear the case, but it took until October 1999 to find dates suitable for everyone involved. In the meantime, a new President of the Faculty Association had opened discussions with the Board of Governors aimed at finding a mutual settlement. On October 17, 1999, when the arbitration was scheduled to begin, he had not succeeded, but wanted to make one more attempt. The arbitration hearing was put off until the next day to discuss the proposed settlement. It included some networking with minority communities, education for senior management and a complaint process with no external investigation and the possibility of discipline for complaining "in bad faith." Those who experience discrimination do not trust such complaint processes because the result is often that they are found to be complaining "in bad faith." Lillian's case is an example. The agreement also contained a small financial award for Lillian and an order that she never talk or write about what happened to her. Lillian and her Faculty Association Representative made it clear that the settlement was not acceptable for several reasons:

- the money offered was too low;
- an issue of academic freedom had been turned into a human rights accommodation issue;
- there were no changes to the tenure and promotion process to allow for cases like Lillian's;
- the settlement would force Lillian to declare the University innocent of any wrongdoing in her case;
- it would imply her agreement with a proposed complaint process that included no external investigation and a "bad faith" clause allowing discipline of the complainant if the complaint was not upheld; and
- it would require Lillian to agree to silence on all the events of the past years, both for herself and anyone else speaking or writing on her behalf.

Lillian and her Faculty Association Representative expressed the fear that the Association would not take the grievance forward to arbitration even if Lillian did not accept the settlement. The President of the Association gave his absolute promise, in no uncertain terms, that the arbitration would go ahead if Lillian wanted it.

There were also some issues concerning Lillian's legal representation. The CAUT lawyer had been given the file only two weeks before the arbitration and had not been told that the outside lawyer who argued the preliminary hearing would be ready to act as a consultant on the case. Lillian and her Faculty Association Representative wanted clarification of the CAUT lawyer's mandate. She informed them that the President of CAUT told her to take her instructions from the President of the Faculty Association.

The two groups broke up for separate meetings, Lillian with her Faculty Association Representative, Grievance Committee Chair and supporters, the Faculty Association group with the CAUT lawyer. Lillian considered her options in that meeting and decided to go ahead with arbitration. Meanwhile, the Faculty Association/CAUT group had been working on new wording for the silence agreement in the settlement. When the two groups got back together, Lillian rejected the new wording and asked for the arbitration to go ahead.

The next day the arbitration was scheduled to begin, but was put off once more because the Faculty Association/CAUT group wanted to meet with Lillian and her supporters again. This time the Faculty Association President put pressure on Lillian to sign the agreement. He said that in all their opinions and that of CAUT's senior lawyer, she couldn't do better than the currently proposed settlement. To ask for more would damage their credibility with the Arbitrator. The Faculty Association President claimed they could get the other measures Lillian wanted through contract negotiation. The Chair of the Grievance Committee challenged that statement. She pointed out that there is always a long list of requests for negotiation and those that do not have strong majority support fall off of the table.

The meeting fell apart. Lillian's Faculty Association Representative walked out rather than be party to the Faculty Association's pressure to force Lillian to sign the agreement. One of Lillian's supporters expressed her anger over the process and the Faculty Association President walked out. The meeting quickly broke up after that. Lillian and her supporters met again and decided that she should ask the Arbitrator for separate legal representation since her interests were no longer being represented by the Faculty Association.

The next morning, October 19, all the parties finally sat down with the Arbitrator. The Arbitrator sat at a table at one end of the room with the University's Personnel Director, the Board of Governors' Lawyer, the Faculty Association President and Lawyer and the CAUT Lawyer sitting at a long table to his right. Lillian, her Faculty Association Representative, Grievance Committee Chair and two supporters (including me) sat at a shorter table on his left. There was some joking about the Faculty Association/CAUT contingent and the University Board of Governors' group sitting at one table facing Lillian and her supporters. The tables were re-arranged: the Faculty Association/CAUT table was turned sideways to face the Arbitrator.

Lillian's Faculty Association Representative put forward Lillian's request for a separate lawyer, but the President of the Faculty Association told her that it was too late. The Faculty Association and the Board of Governors had come to an agreement and Lillian had until the following week to sign it.

Lillian's Faculty Association Representative argued that the grievor has standing regardless and the agreement is meaningless without her signature. The Arbitrator, she said, gets his mandate from labour and human rights law as well as from the Collective Agreement. The Board of Governors' lawyer responded that the arbitration process was finished because the University and the Faculty Association had come to an agreement. Lillian refused to sign it, forgoing her financial settlement and avoiding the silencing clause.

Lillian had no standing in the process and no power to force either body to take part in a hearing. The Canadian University Board of Governors and Faculty Association groups left the room along with the Arbitrator. Lillian and her supporters were left to grieve in another sense.

Later Lillian wrote about the experience, including these words:

I sit in silence
        tears creep down
                my finger covered face.
Women run to get tissues
                to squeeze my shoulders.
A wail rises up my body
        lodges in my throat.
                It is not safe to release here....
In this moment
                        I have failed.
                        Fires of my Hopes
                                Desires for Justice
                                have been Extinguished.

I feel
        I have lost the battle....
I am truly Grievor.
                Solitary.
                Alone
                        with the magnitude
                                of my losses.

Loss of hope
Loss of trust
Loss of opportunity
        to make 6 years
                of pain
                oppression
                tonguelessness
        count for something
                        to set clear precedent
                        vindicate my reality
                change inequities
                remediate unjust systems
        to support Aboriginal
                                African-Canadian
                                Asian
                                Anti-racist
                                Lesbian and Gay
                                Colleagues
                                across Canada ...

Lillian's Faculty Association Representative and the Grievance Committee Chair resigned from their positions in the Faculty Association. Lillian joined a human rights complaint made by a Black faculty member against the University for systemic discrimination and the Faculty Association for failure to represent minority members. The Black faculty member later lodged another human rights complaint against the new discrimination complaint procedure.

In July 2002, the Human Rights Commission negotiated a settlement between Lillian and Canadian University. Like all human rights settlements, the contents of the agreement are confidential. Lillian was not happy with its terms, but accepted it to finally bring closure to this long and painful conflict. In Lillian's poem about the experience she wrote:

I have Not lost my Soul.
My Spirit is intact.
I did Not sell out.
I preserved my integrity
    forced them to face their lack.
I will live on
        Limping
        still on my feet.

Part Two

Institutional Equity—Naming Patterns

Chapter Five

The Structural View

The Institution as a Player

In both the Introduction and "The Story," I described my experience during Lillian's second quasi-disciplinary meeting, when mediation was proposed to resolve the conflict. I had experience facilitating conflict resolution processes and tried to imagine myself attempting to mediate this conflict. I realized that a conflict resolution process would probably not be possible because of the degree of polarization and power inequality, as well as because the institution itself was an important player. The university not only granted power in an unequal fashion but, beyond that, had its own self-interest, its own desire to continue in its present form and its own methods of acting on and through the individuals in the room and many others who were playing a role in the conflict from beyond the walls.

The second time I thought about the role of the institution itself in the conflict came about because of a dream. After I interviewed Lillian, Beth, Laura, Hannah and Yuen and wrote "The Story" based on their accounts, I dreamt that I was standing at a blackboard drawing "The Story" in the form of a chart. The scale along the bottom represented time, and the scale along the side represented the hierarchy of the university. Later, I pulled out some sheets of scrap paper and drew the framework of time and hierarchy as they had appeared in the dream. I began to plot each incident in "The Story" on the resulting graph. My first version contained every detail. I hunted for a roll of scotch tape and more paper. When I finished, the chart was over six feet long.

Then I began a process of simplification, looking for patterns. Through seven drafts I pared "The Story" down to three types of interaction: requests for support, supportive or "ally" responses and blaming, punishing responses. I also identified the individual people on the chart as male or female. I don't like the duality of racial identification as white and "other," but on my chart it seemed helpful in identifying the dynamics around race. See Figure 1 for the simplified chart.

I will come back to this drawing and its further evolution in Chapter Seven. At this point, I want to talk about one important insight into the role of the institution itself as an actor in the conflict. When I started the chart, I gave a great deal of thought to what incident truly marked the

Figure 1: Personal and Institutional Dynamics in "The Story"

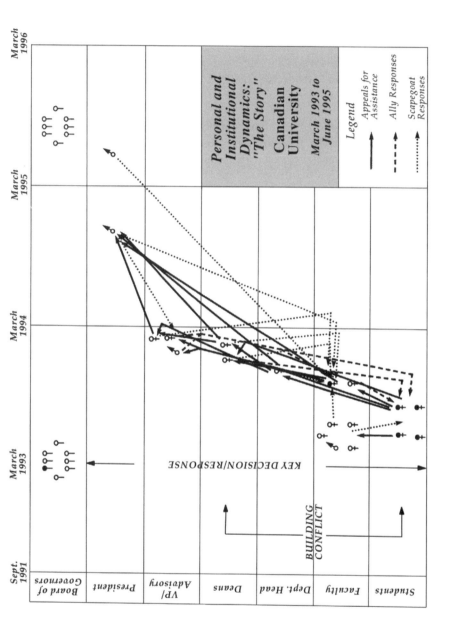

Personal and Institutional Dynamics: "The Story" Canadian University March 1993 to June 1995

Legend

Appeals for Assistance

Ally Responses

Scapegoat Responses

KEY DECISION/RESPONSE

BUILDING CONFLICT

March 1996 | March 1995 | March 1994 | March 1993 | Sept. 1991

Board of Governors | President | VP/ Advisory | Deans | Dept. Head | Faculty | Students beginning of the chain of events I wanted to study. I chose the Open Talking Circle on Discriminatory Harassment, March 21, 1993, but then realized that I should have gone back one day earlier. The reason the Talking Circle became such a powerful catalyst for conflict, I thought, was because the University's Board of Governors had rejected the Draft Policy on Discriminatory Harassment the day before. This was a decision on behalf of the whole institution. Most of the events recorded in the chart took place at the level of the Department, but the incident I selected as the end of the chain of events was also an institutional decision, when the President, on behalf of the Board, rejected Lillian's final request to have her work assessed by a tenure committee outside of her department. The chart now opened and closed with actions involving the whole institution; it took place within that frame. I realized that the story is, in fact, not only about individuals but about an institution acting in its own interests.

As individuals we have free will and are responsible for our actions, but we are powerfully shaped by larger structures, such as history, ideology, culture, institutions and power inequalities, like class and institutional hierarchies. These are all systems with their own built-in logic. Structures behave in certain ways and carry us with them, with our cooperation or not, and whether or not we are conscious of the process. However, it is difficult for mainstream North Americans to see these structures and systems because of the strong individualism of our culture.

Liberal Ideology: A Collection of Individuals

In Barbara Kingsolver's novel *The Bean Trees* (1988: 117), a young white woman apologizes to her friend, an illegal Guatemalan immigrant, for a neighbour's remark:

> "Really, I don't think she knew what she was saying, about how the woman and kid who got shot must have been drug dealers or whatever."
>
> "Oh, I believe she did. This is how Americans think" He was looking at me in a thoughtful way. "You believe that if something terrible happens to someone, they must have deserved it."
>
> I wanted to tell him this wasn't so, but I couldn't. "I guess you're right," I said. "I guess it makes us feel safe."

We, in mainstream United States and Canada, attribute almost everything to individuals. Any time you read through a newspaper, listen to daily conversation in a workplace or sit around a neighbour's kitchen table, you will hear it. If someone is poor, it is because they're lazy or a drinker. Someone who has lost a job is "hard to get along with." Whatever happens to a person, they must deserve it in some way. If a corporation has done something unethical, there must be a "bad actor" somewhere in management. If an organization makes a mistake, someone within its decision-making structure must have misjudged.

Every culture and society has an ideology—a collection of values, beliefs and ideas about how the world works, what is good and bad, right and wrong, worthy of attention or ridiculous. The dominant ideology of North American society is the one we generally call "liberal."

Liberal ideology has several variations because of its long history. It began in the French and U.S. revolutions, when monarchies were overthrown and the merchant "middle" class came to power. Originally it was an economic theory, defined by Adam Smith in *The Wealth of Nations*, published in 1776. The key principle was no government intervention in economic matters. Wealth, according to this theory, comes from "free" enterprise, "free" competition and "free" trade.

After 1870, liberalism was modified by thinkers who believed that it was appropriate for government to regulate economic matters to a certain degree and intervene in the social realm to prevent conflict. In the 1930s this form of modified liberalism, as defined by John Maynard Keynes (1935), inspired the "New Deal" of the Franklin Roosevelt government in the United States.

Since about 1975, however, many powerful political and economic players have returned liberalism to its roots. Generally called "neo-liberalism," this philosophy promotes a "free" market with no state intervention, minimal expenditures for social services, deregulation, privatization and the elimination of the concept of "the public good."

Because of the changes liberalism has gone through during its 250-year history, the term is now sometimes confusing, with different connotations in Europe, where it maintains its original meaning, and the United States, where the term refers to the type of programs put in place during the New Deal era. Canadian usage of the term falls somewhere between the two.

When I use the term in this book, I am referring to an ideological system defined primarily by its belief in the individual. Individuals are equal in this way of thinking, or can be with some reform. Liberalism believes that, because of people's essential equality, social problems are shared, affect all equally and can be solved by negotiation. There is little recognition of the unequal resources and power different parties bring to the negotiations. Liberal systems of thought put a great deal of emphasis on individual freedom. Class inequality thrives in liberal societies. Their public policy is shaped by those with power, money and historical advantage because it is assumed that they have their resources and position through merit. Liberals are reluctant to recognize historical and structural inequalities, particularly class.

For example, for decades Canada's wealthiest individuals and corporations have lobbied successfully for more tax cuts and loopholes. They benefit enormously from tax relief. It gives them more disposable income for luxuries and more money to invest in accumulating further wealth. Meanwhile people in lower income brackets actually suffer from tax relief. Lower taxes mean less money in the public realm, money for fixing roads, maintaining schools, funding health care and paying for other public services. Tax breaks may mean a small amount of money in ordinary people's pockets at tax time, but in the end costs them far more in damage to their cars, reduced access to quality education, more user fees, and privatization in health care and other services (McQuaig 1987, 1993; Kerstetter 2002; Janigan et al. 2000). However, tax cuts are a very popular campaign promise in Canada, popular across all class levels (Yalnizyan 1998: 30). The very people who will lose quality of life if money is removed from the public realm support cutting taxes. Liberal ideology prevents them from seeing the gap between wealthy people and themselves; in fact, most do not consider class structure at all when they think about taxes. This is an example of the way liberal ideology erases structural inequality and portrays all people as equal, with common problems.

Iris Marion Young summarized some of the key points of liberal ideology as they apply to an understanding of difference and oppression (1990: Chapter 5). According to her, liberalism includes the idea of impartiality, the exclusion of those identified with the body and feeling (that is, women, "feminine" men and people of colour), the elimination of forms of social equality that affirm difference, belief in merit and a hierarchical division of labour, the importance of intention and the depoliticization of public life.

Other assumptions of a liberal ideology include:

- an a-historical worldview, that is, a fresh start can always be made;
- an institution is made up of the individuals in it;
- institutions and the people in them are basically fair-minded, objective and free of discrimination;
- good intentions excuse bad behaviour;
- a positive attitude has almost limitless power to shape reality; that is, if you look "on the bright side" and expect the best of any person or situation, this will eliminate most problems;
- comfort is an important goal in human activities;
- conflict is undesirable;
- all voices carry equal weight, because all people are equal.

In a liberal democracy, decisions are made by majority vote in a system that ignores the impact of inequality; for example, who votes and who does not; who can purchase the means of influence and who cannot; who has historical reasons to believe they will be heard in the process if they take an active part and who has learned not to bother because they will not be heard anyway.

Liberals believe in tolerance of all differences, views and opinions, with no judgement. In fact, liberals often deny difference altogether. This makes liberals wonderful, kind, accepting friends and relatives, but it also means that the more powerful forces in a liberal society are free to increase their power without being limited or judged.

When injustice in an institution is examined through the "lens" of liberal ideology, the problem is interpreted as a search for "bad people," particularly people with bad intentions. As Iris Marion Young points out, intention counts strongly in a liberal worldview. If no "bad people" are found, those who express their experience of injustice are seen as overly sensitive, negative, suffering from poor mental health (depressed, paranoid, etc.) or using accusations to get attention or draw attention away from their own dishonesty, lack of intelligence or poor performance.

In *Case Critical* (1995), Ben Carniol talks about the liberal tendency to see class as a matter of individual illness:

> Despite the much-touted freedom of choice that we are supposed to enjoy, it is dramatic how un-free our thinking is, especially when we probe the causes behind the powerlessness and despair experienced by a large segment of the population. There is ample support for inquiries into the "pathologies" of the poor and the troubled, their personality deficits, their family stress, or their childhood traumas. Yet at the same time there is a strong taboo against asking: To what extent are unemployment, poverty, and basic inequalities directly or indirectly traceable to decisions made by a small group of people who possess the most power and wealth in the society? (6)

Liberalism helps keep oppressive systems in place by constantly directing our attention to the "good" and "bad" individuals in the system and, therefore, away from the systems and structures themselves. As I mentioned in "The Story," at one time I co-taught a course for leaders of low-income and marginalized communities. In one session, we taught students to distinguish among the viewpoints held by Canada's major ideologies. We divided the students into three groups and gave each a folder of research material. They were asked to prepare a presentation for an imaginary government committee studying the causes of and solutions to poverty.

One file contained material from a right-wing viewpoint, blaming poverty on the moral degeneration of the poor and advocating a tough, punishment-based approach. The second file represented a liberal point of view, looking at poverty as disadvantage and proposing ways to improve the life of the poor. The third file contained articles about Canada's wealthiest citizens and corporations, the proportion of the country's wealth they control, their power and the fact that they pay minimal taxes or none at all. The group with the third file would finish reading their material and then call us over, puzzled. "There is nothing in here about poverty," they would say. They were so accustomed to the conservative and liberal interpretations of poverty, focussed always on the poor, that they couldn't even see what information on the rich and powerful, their systems and structures, had to do with it.

Liberal ideology is the dominant one in Canada. To the right of liberal thought is the conservative (also called traditional or fundamentalist) minority, who believe in a God-given hierarchy that is the only "right" way to run a society. To the left is the progressive, or radical minority, who believe that equality is yet to be achieved and requires systemic change. Sometimes the conservative and radical minorities in Canada are more comfortable with each other than with the liberal majority, in spite of their opposed views—at least both groups have a sense of right and wrong that can be clearly defined. Liberals are much harder, if not impossible, to pin down. The experience of social justice activists in Canada has been likened to "trying to nail jelly to the wall."

The heart of liberal ideology, in all its variations, is the belief in the individual. In this worldview, events, technologies, decisions, systems, organizations and institutions boil down to the sum total of the individuals involved in them

Looking at Power: A Structural View

The alternatives to a liberal framework, both to the right and left, tend to look at individuals in their context in social systems or organizations, although for different reasons. A conservative or fundamentalist framework seeks to preserve the current structures, or go back to an idealized past, while a progressive or radical one seeks to change them. Our concern here is with efforts to change structures or systems, from the roots, toward more justice and equality. This way of thinking can be referred to as "structural."

A structural worldview assumes that human behaviour is shaped by the collective forces of history and the social/political/economic structures that make up the society. Its assumptions include:

- our history is always present, influencing our perceptions, behaviour and degree of social and economic power;
- an institution is a structural entity that functions to reinforce its traditional power relationships;
- all institutions and individuals in a discriminatory society reflect that discrimination;
- behaviour is not judged by intention but by impact;
- conflict is the means to growth and is therefore desirable;

- privilege is invisible; therefore, the word of those who experience a certain form of oppression should be given more weight than that of those who receive benefits from that form of oppression.

There is a story that has been used for years to describe the difference between a liberal and a structural view of assisting people in trouble. Two women are walking along a river and see a small child struggling in the current, calling for help. They plunge in and rescue her. They no sooner reach the bank than another child comes bobbing along. They put the first child down in the grass and rescue the second child. Before they even reach the bank, a third child comes down the river. One woman takes the second child to the bank while the other goes after the third child.

Soon dozens of children are coming down the river. The women are fully occupied pulling them to shore. Suddenly one woman looks as far as she can upstream. "What are you day-dreaming for?" calls out the other woman. "I can't save all these children alone!"

"Just a minute," says her friend, then climbs out of the river and disappears. With her friend shouting after her that she can't leave her to do it all, she walks upriver. Soon she comes to a wharf where there is a large crowd of children and several adults throwing them into the river.

At this point in the story she and her friend face a decision. If they take a liberal view of the situation, they will go downstream and rescue all the children, because without both of them there, some will slip by. If they take a structural view, they will go upriver to the wharf and stop the people there from throwing the children into the river.

Following are some further examples to illustrate the contrast between a liberal and structural worldview.

Example Number One: Twinning the Highway

There is a stretch of highway with exceptionally high rates of traffic accidents and fatalities. The debate about what to do with this road appears from time to time in letters to the editor. They demonstrate very well the difference between a structural and liberal approach. Those who take the liberal view argue that the problem is not the road, but rather the drivers. People drive too fast and are too impatient when they want to pass. What is needed is more admonitions to drivers in the media, higher fines for speeding and more police officers on the road to enforce traffic laws. These letters almost always talk about driving on that stretch of highway and seeing people going too fast.

On the other side, those with a structural viewpoint argue that there will always be people who drive too fast and pass other traffic carelessly. Especially with the pressures and technologies of the modern world teaching people to expect more speed in everything they do, people will be ever less likely to put up with patiently waiting for a passing lane. Also, parts of the road have four lanes, with speed limits of 100 or 110 kilometres per hour. People actually travel at 110 to 120 kilometres per hour on those portions of the road. They are not likely to be patient about slowing down for the two-lane segments of the road.

The solution, according to the structuralists, is to widen the road into a four-lane highway with wide medians and fully paved outside shoulders. This will allow people to travel at different speeds, pass safely and have some room to maneuver should something go wrong. Going even further into structuralist thinking, one could examine the reason for so much traffic in the first place and propose increased public transportation as a solution. One group places blame on the individual drivers, the other on the structure of the road or the lack of public transport.

Example Number Two: Technology

In our dominant liberal worldview we tend to think of technology as something neutral that we control, something that serves us in our individual lives. We fail to see the larger structural implications of our technologies and how they shape us. In his book, *In the Absence of the Sacred: The Failure of Technology and the Survival of the Indian Nations* (1991), Jerry Mander describes the structural or systemic nature of technology and our failure to see it:

> We think of [technology] in personal terms, based on our own interactions with it. We use machines in our lives and evaluate them in terms of their usefulness to us personally. The machine vacuums our carpets. The car drives easily and well. The television entertains us. The microwave cooks dinner in a flash. The computer helps us do our work. We make little attempt to fathom the multiplicity of effects that computers or television or microwave ovens or cars may have on society or on nature. Nor do we think about how the technological march is affecting the planet. As a result, we are left with a view of technology's impact that is much too personal and narrow. (32–33)

Contrary to our perception of technology, it does not provide more leisure time. Mander points to the research of Marshall Sahlins and others that have shown "stone-age societies had more than twice the amount of leisure time we do today, which they used to pursue spiritual matters, personal relationships, and pleasure" (26).

Mander also argues against the liberal notion that technology contains no inherent political bias:

> From the political Right and Left, from the corporate world and the world of community activism, one hears the same homily:

"The problem is not with the technology itself, but with how we use it, and who controls it." This idea would be merely preposterous if it were not so widely accepted, and so dangerous. In believing this, however, we allow technology to develop without analyzing its actual bias. And then we are surprised when certain technologies turn out to be useful or beneficial only for certain segments of society. (35)

Mander discusses nuclear versus solar power to illustrate his point:

Because it is so expensive and so dangerous, nuclear power must be under the direct control of centralized financial, governmental, and military institutions. A nuclear power plant is not something that a few neighbors can get together and build.... The existence of nuclear energy, and nuclear weaponry, in turn requires the existence of ... a technical and military elite capable of guarding nuclear waste products for the approximately 250,000 years that they remain dangerous. So if some future society, tiring of the present path, should determine to move away from a centralized technological society and toward, say, an agrarian society, it would be impossible. Solar energy, on the other hand, is intrinsically biased toward democratic use. It is buildable and operable by small groups, even by families. It does not require centralized control. It is most cost effective at a small scale of operations, a reason why big power companies oppose it. And solar energy requires no thousand-year commitment from society. So, where nuclear energy requires centralized control, solar energy functions best in a decentralized form. These attributes are inherent to the technologies and reflect the ideological bias of each. (35–36)

Mander argues against the liberal view of technology as a tool we control. Rather it is, he argues,

a worldwide technical creature that includes us in its functioning: the way our minds operate, the way we perceive alternatives, what we imagine are good and bad ideas. We have entered into a universe that has been re-formed by machines; we are a species that lives its life within mechanistic creations; our environment is a product of our minds. Locked inside our cities and suburbs, working in our offices, controlling and conceptualizing nature as a raw material for our consumption, and now even including ourselves as raw material suitable for redevelopment, we are at one with the process. (189–190)

Example Number Three: The Clock
Another example of the contrast between a liberal and structural view is the history of the clock. We tend to think of it, in liberal fashion, as a simple tool, at our service. Indeed it started out in the twelfth century as a simple tool for monasteries to regulate periods of work and worship during the day. In *Technopoly* (1992), Neil Postman describes how the clock became an institutional structure that in turn has shaped Western culture:

> Embedded in every tool is an ideological bias, a predisposition to construct the world as one thing rather than another, to value one thing over another, to amplify one sense or skill or attitude more loudly than another.... what the monks did not foresee was that the clock is a means not merely of keeping track of the hours but also of synchronizing and controlling the actions of men. And thus, by the middle of the fourteenth century, the clock had moved outside the walls of the monastery, and brought a new and precise regularity to the life of the workman and the merchant....
> "The mechanical clock," as Lewis Mumford wrote, "made possible the idea of regular production, regular working hours and a standardized product." In short, without the clock, capitalism would have been quite impossible. The paradox, the surprise, and the wonder are that the clock was invented by men who wanted to devote themselves more rigorously to God; it ended as the technology of greatest use to men who wished to devote themselves to the accumulation of money. (13–15, 27)

The clock has played such an important role in shaping Western culture that it became a key component of colonialism. One justification for oppressing indigenous peoples has been their flexible, subjective, nature-based—and therefore "primitive"—concept of time. Forcing other cultures to live by the Western concept of time became an important part of the task of assimilation and exploitation. A participant in an anti-oppression workshop I was leading once remarked that Native people would be "better off if they would just learn to be on time." Such a remark demonstrates how deeply and unconsciously we have internalized the mechanical clock.

A Structural View, Free Will and Moral Responsibility

During the 1970s, some leading civil rights activists like Charles Hamilton and Stokley Carmichael began to speak about structural inequality, using the term "institutional racism." Other civil rights leaders objected to the term on the grounds that it released individuals from their moral responsibility to fight racism. I believe that we are powerfully shaped by the structures, systems and institutions around us, but I also believe that we have individual free will and moral responsibility. Sometimes I find it difficult to explain to others how these concepts can co-exist. Sometimes I even lose my own hold on this intricate balance of ideas.

I think the problem is that I, like most North Americans, have deeply internalized Western culture's love of dualities—good or bad, healthy or ill, male or female, right or wrong, black or white, free and responsible for our own actions or bound by outside forces. Free will and moral responsibility are not in an either/or relationship with the influence of social structures on our actions. When it comes to responsibility for more justice and equity in our institutions, it is not helpful to think in terms of excusing either individuals or the institutional structure from responsibility. The two are knit together in a close and complex set of interactions.

A parallel example, I think, is the question of free will and moral responsibility in relation to addiction. It is not uncommon to hear comments that condemn people with addictions for moral weakness; for example: "No one raised the glass to his lips," or "In the end it's just a matter of saying no." However, most successful addiction programs treat addiction as a disease. This approach works, in part, because it releases the person with an addiction from a destructive, self-hating form of guilt that re-enforces the problem. It does not release them from the responsibility for recovery. On the contrary, release from destructive guilt allows the person to stop denying the problem and begin the healing process. "Which is responsible for the addiction, the person or the illness?" is not a useful question. It distracts attention from the healing process. In fact, it is not a question at all, because addiction and free will/moral responsibility are not in an either/or relationship.

Likewise, understanding that institutional structures can influence individual behaviour does not release us from responsibility for our actions. On the contrary, it is in the nature of institutions and systems to mask our responsibility for our own actions—to lull us, or push us, into following the norms of the institution or system. These larger structures do not encourage us to think for ourselves. By understanding the mechanisms institutional structures use to influence our behaviour, we are better equipped to take back our personal responsibility.

How Institutional Structures Shape Individual Behaviour

There is plenty of evidence that our behaviour as individuals is strongly shaped by institutional structures and large systems. We take on the roles assigned by these collective bodies, act them out and incorporate them deeply into our idea of who and what we are. In my opinion, institutional structures and systems use both conscious and unconscious mechanisms to influence individual behaviour.

On the conscious level, institutions offer us certain roles, and we take them on. There are those that seek out institutional leadership roles in order to attain or maintain their position in the elite class. They get status, wealth and power from the institutional structures, in their field, nation or even the world. People in the elite class or high-level positions in institutional structures can attain these things through their public role in the structure or through the loopholes they may find there. For example, a high-level leader may not be watched as closely as someone on a lower level of the organization and therefore may be able to get away with theft, kickbacks, conspiracy, fraud and other illegal acts.

On any class level, we may sign a contract that spells out our job, negotiate responsibilities with our spouse or understand clearly what it means to become treasurer of a voluntary organization. This can be a joyful transaction if we agree wholeheartedly with the goals and values of the company, organization or domestic partnership. It can be a voluntary commitment in the beginning and turn out to be not quite what we thought it was. As one of the readers of a draft of this book commented, it is easier to get into an institutional structure than it is to get out.

When there is disagreement between the individual and the institutional structure, the individual sometimes still does what the institution requires of them. There are many reasons for this. Perhaps the institution is the source of the person's living and there are few other options. The institution may provide status that the individual would find very difficult to abandon. The institutional role might be a means to an end for the individual, who decides that the longer-term purpose is worth some compromise. Individuals can also tire of resisting, give up or decide to fight only certain battles for the sake of physical and emotional survival.

Far more powerful, in my opinion, are the unconscious mechanisms by which institutional structures influence our behaviour. Institutional structures have internal cultures and ideologies, complete with goals, values and a range of acceptable behaviour. There are always rewards and punishments to encourage desirable actions and enforce limits. If an individual does not belong to a contrasting culture outside of the institution, it can be difficult to be conscious of these norms. Many are subtle, just "the way things are done."

Sometimes it is difficult to be aware of internal norms because they contrast with the institution's stated goals. The public vision might be to help and protect people, or even to bring about equity and social justice, but if the pursuit of the vision threatens the power structure of the institution in any way, a different set of actual values may be quietly shaping its everyday practices.

Anne Wilson Schaef and Diane Fassel (1988) describe a consulting contract with a national service organization in the United States. They were hired to examine the decision-making practices of the organization and see if they were helping the organization fulfil its vision of pluralism by including everyone. Their research showed that many members of the organization, especially women and minorities, were excluded from the decision-making process. The organization's leaders were not surprised by their findings and pleased with the practical recommendations in the report. However, the report was soon shelved. Despite the fact that the organization was going through a re-structuring process, the leadership decided that the report's recommendations would require too much change. They didn't want to risk the angry response they thought they would get from some powerful elements in the organization. Schaef and Fassel state that although the organization's "stated goal was to include all people in decision-making ... in fact, the unstated goals were, Don't rock the boat, Don't introduce wide change in the system, and Don't ask us to operate congruent with our stated principles of pluralism." They conclude that in a situation like this, the "employees become hooked on the promise of the mission and choose not to look at how the system is really operating.... Its actions are excused because it has a lofty mission" (123).

Those who cannot see how the actual practices of an institutional structure contradict its stated goals may excuse their own behaviour, or choose not to question it at all, because it is also excused by the organization's lofty mission. They may, however, experience confusion and frustration in their work. As Schaef and Fassel point out, "they join an organization to do one thing and spend most of their time doing another.... Frequently, the thing they end up doing is totally incongruent with the reasons they became helpers in the first place" (123).

In my search to understand what happened at Canadian University, I found several examples of research into the power of institutions to shape individual behaviour. Karen Lebacqz (1985) reviewed the work of several researchers who looked at the impact an organization can have on the behaviour of an individual professional. Gaye Tuchman studied female newspaper editors' attitudes toward women. Although not stereotypical women themselves, they continued to believe the culture's views about women: "While they were interested in politics, they thought of women in general as being interested only in fashion, clothing and food—typical 'woman's page' fare." Tuchman concluded "that the process of professionalization encountered in their work undermined their ability to identify with other women. 'It is difficult for women employees to resist ideas and attitudes associated with success in their profession even if those ideas disparage women'" (Tuchman 1979: 535, quoted in Lebasqz 1985: 137).

Lebascqz comments:

> Women who become executives and then perpetuate images deni-grating other women are not "bad" people. They are simply re-sponding to and exhibiting the sexism that is structured into their profession. The socialization process, both during professional training and also during the practice of the profession, provides a

powerful forum in which the profession as a whole impacts on the perspective of individual practitioners. Depending on the integrity of the individual practitioner to counter distortions in the social construction of reality is not sufficient, for these pressures can be structured in so subtly that most are not aware of their impact. (137)

Lebasqz describes research done by Eliot Freidson on medical professionals:

Work settings are very important determinants of behavior. He [Freidson] contends that there are organized pressures built into all situations and that what people do "is more an outcome of the pressures of the situation they are in than of what they have earlier 'internalized.'" Indeed, he suggests that "there is some very persuasive evidence that socialization does not explain some important elements of professional performance half so well as does the organization of the immediate work environment." (Freidson 1970, quoted in Lebasqz 1985: 138)

Lebasqz also notes a research project conducted with nurses working in different departments of a community hospital. The researcher was Rose Laub Coser, a sociologist at State University of New York:

[Coser] found that the immediate work environment effected serious differences in everything from behavior to professional self-image. She attributes these differences to the different structures in which the nurses worked. On one ward, the goal was to return patients to the community; hence, even small tasks such as filling out release forms could gain importance. On the other ward, that goal was lacking and the same chores were seen merely as bothersome. The group that was praised for not calling physicians learned not to call physicians!... Hence, though all had received the same professional training, the structures and settings in which they worked, including very specific factors such as systems of reward, led to very different self-images and very different behavior. (Coser 1963, quoted in Lebasqz 1985: 139–40)

Lebasqz concludes:

Professional training, images, and ideals therefore do not suffice to ensure professional performance in accord with norms and virtues written into codes. While the inside view of the professions might think personal integrity sufficient, the outside view demonstrates that it is not. Attention must also be paid to the work setting. This setting affects not only the power balance between professional and client, but also the way in which the professional will be likely to interpret events and respond to them....

Structures and systems have their own reality and they can limit what a person does. To put it starkly, being a "good" person does not change the system. (137, 140)

I found another description of the impact of institutional structures on individual behaviour in the work of Rosabeth Moss Kanter, a Harvard business professor and international consultant on organizational change. She wrote about NASA's first unsuccessful effort to establish the multi-million-dollar Hubble telescope in space: "Organizations, as is well known, are not neutral with respect to people's behavior. On the contrary, they exercise considerable and sometimes deterministic effects on the behavior of the people associated with them" (Kanter 1983).

Kanter and her consulting colleagues have noticed a tendency for organizations to have "habit patterns." They came to call these patterns organizational "character."

Character includes both structures—for example rewards, physical geography, and employee roles and responsibilities, and cultural features such as behavioral and social norms and informal relationships. We have described how character shapes behavior and its impact on both organizational and individual outcomes elsewhere. The important point to be made here is that the very powerful effects of organizational character on individuals are often unrecognized, even as they are experienced.

There are two fundamental lessons to be learned from the Hubble story—one at the level of the individual, the other at the organizational level. The individual lesson is this: the majority of those involved, most of the time, were almost certainly doing what they thought was best for NASA, for the project, for the telescope, for the mission, for science, for the USA. This is not, at its most fundamental level, a story about bad or even misguided people doing bad things; it's a story about good people doing bad things. Accordingly, the most important lesson to be learned at this level is about how easy it is for an organization to convert good intentions to bad results, how powerful and pervasive are the processes for effecting those conversions, and how common those effects are....

These lessons are not about weak managers and "soul-less" organizations; they're about the dangers of complex structures and the power of organizations and social systems to persuade well-meaning people to act in ultimately destructive ways.... This is not a story about unusual circumstances, rare events, peculiar effects or unpredictable outcomes. Rather, it's about perfectly banal organizational behavior. If it seems startling at all, it's because it is presented as if it were unusual since it had great importance and the consequences were so visible. (Kanter 1983)

Karen Franklin, an American forensic psychologist, examined a social institution that extends beyond the boundaries of any particular organization. By investigating the psychological roots of gay-bashing, she looked at a feature of the ideology and culture of North America and its ability to inspire individual action

Gay-bashing is, unfortunately, a fairly common form of hate-crime, known for its extreme levels of brutality. Most gay-bashing is done by young heterosexual men acting in groups. An individual or liberal view labels these young men as evil or sick. It tends to place the blame on their hatred of homosexuals, their desire to prove their masculinity or their need to fit into a peer group. Franklin did research with young men convicted of violent assault against gay men. She interviewed them to find out what they claim as the motivation for their violence. She found some evidence for individual motives, such as desire to prove toughness and heterosexuality to friends, and self-defence based on a belief that all homosexuals are predators. However, during the course of her research, she found herself shifting to a structural view of gay-bashing. She began to see this type of violent crime not as a personally motivated attack but as enforcement of the gender norms of the larger society. She says:

> Although their assaults fall within most legal definition of hate crime ... all insisted that their assaults were not motivated by hatred of homosexuals. To reconcile the apparent contradiction between the normative attitudes often held by assailants and the viciousness and brutality of their behavior toward gay men and lesbians, during the course of my research I came to conceptualize the violence not in terms of individual hatred, but as an extreme expression of American cultural stereotypes and expectations regarding male and female behavior. From this perspective, assaults on homosexuals and other individuals who deviate from sexual norms are viewed as a learned form of social control of deviance rather than a defensive response to personal threat. Thus, heterosexism is not just a personal value system, it is a tool in the maintenance of gender dichotomy. In other words, through heterosexism, any male who refuses to accept the dominant culture's assignment of appropriate masculine behavior is labeled

as a "sissy" or "fag" and then subjected to bullying. Similarly, any woman who opposes male dominance and control can be labeled a lesbian and attacked. The potential of being ostracized as a homosexual, regardless of actual sexual attractions and behaviors, puts pressure on all people to conform to a narrow standard of appropriate gender behavior, thereby maintaining and reinforcing our society's hierarchical gender structure. (1998)

In my earlier book, *Becoming an Ally* (1994, 2002), I explored the work of those who have written about the psychological roots of violence in unhealed childhood pain. A friend later brought to my attention that I had overlooked what she called the "ideological roots" of violence and abuse. A large part of it, she pointed out, has to do with cultural messages about who can do what to whom. Karen Franklin's work underlines this statement. The ideology of the society or a particular institutional structure sets strong norms about who is valuable and who is not, what actions are out of bounds and who can punish those that cross the lines or do not have the right to be where they are.

Another examination of a broad social institution and its power to influence individual behaviour was Stanley Milgram's research on obedience. It was inspired by Hannah Arendt's 1963 book about the trial of Adolph Eichmann for his role in the Holocaust. Eichmann's prosecutor and the public portrayed him as a sadistic monster, a twisted personality, evil incarnate. Arendt disagreed, describing him as an uninspired bureaucrat just doing his job. The book gave us a phrase that has been used often since, the "banality of evil."

Milgram, a social psychologist teaching at Yale, wanted to test Arendt's assertion that Eichmann and other architects of the Holocaust murdered millions simply in obedience to orders. He set up a series of experiments where the subjects came into the room in pairs. One was designated the "teacher," the other the "learner." They were told that the purpose of the experiment was to explore the effect of punishment on learning. The "learner" was seated in what looked like a small version of an electric chair, with his or her arms strapped down to electrodes on the arm of the chair, and given a list of word pairs to read. The "teacher" was instructed to test the "learner's" memory. The "teacher" would read the first word; the learner was required to repeat the second word of the pair.

The "teacher" was seated at a console with a set of thirty levers. Each lever was labelled with a voltage ranging from 15 to 450 volts. Each group of four switches had a label as well, ranging from "Slight Shock" at one end, through "Moderate Shock," to "Intense Shock," "Extreme Intensity Shock" and "Danger: Severe Shock." The last two switches were labelled "XXX." Each time the student made a mistake, the experimenter instructed the "teacher" to administer a shock, gradually increasing in intensity.

Unbeknownst to the "teachers," the "learners" were actors. They were not receiving any actual shock, but began to show distress with a grunt at 75 volts. At 120 volts, they complained loudly. At 150 they demanded to be released from the experiment. The protests became more vehement as the voltage increased, until at 285 volts their responses were only agonized screaming. Beyond that they did not respond at all. The purpose of the experiment was to see how far the real subjects, the "teachers," would go in obeying orders to inflict pain on another human being.

Before the experiments began, Milgram asked people from many walks of life to predict the response. They guessed that the subjects would not go past the point where the "learner" asked to be released from the experiment. They were very wrong. In the first experiment, twenty-five out of forty subjects pushed the "learner" to the maximum 450 volts. The "teachers" objected frequently to their orders and showed many signs of stress, but the experimenter told them to go on, that the experiment must be pushed through to conclusion, that the subject was in pain but would not be hurt. Most of them obeyed.

The first subjects were students, and the results were questioned on this basis. Milgram repeated the experiment with people drawn from different social classes and various occupations. The results were the same. Sixty percent of the subjects obeyed the experimenter completely. When the experiments were repeated in Princeton, Munich, Rome, South Africa and Australia, the obedience levels were even higher. The experimenter had no means of either rewarding or punishing the "teachers," but they obeyed regardless.

To be sure that what they were observing was obedience to authority and not innate cruelty, Milgram did another series of experiments where the "teachers" were allowed to choose for themselves the level of voltage administered. Most of the forty subjects in this version of the experiment went no higher than 60 volts, before the level where the "learner" expressed discomfort. Only two out of forty went beyond the first loud protest at 150 volts.

"This is, perhaps, the most fundamental lesson of our study," concluded Milgram. "Ordinary people, simply doing their jobs, and without any particular hostility on their part, can become agents in a terrible destructive process. Moreover, even when the destructive effects of their work become patently clear, and they are asked to carry out actions incompatible with fundamental standards of morality, relatively few people have the resources needed to resist authority"(Milgram 1973: 76).

One more variation of the research looked at what happened when the task was broken down into parts. The subjects did not pull the levers themselves, but only read out the words of the test to the "learner." Thirty-seven out of forty subjects continued to the highest level of shock. They excused their behaviour by claiming that the man who pulled the switch bore the responsibility. From this portion of the experiment, Milgram drew some conclusions about complex societies:

> The problem of obedience is not wholly psychological. The form and shape of society and the way it is developing have much to do with it. There was a time, perhaps, when people were able to give a fully human response to any situation because they were fully absorbed in it as human beings. But as soon as there was a division of labor things changed. Beyond a certain point, the breaking up of society into people carrying out narrow and very special jobs takes away from the human quality of work and life. A person does not get to see the whole situation but only a small part of it, and is thus unable to act without some kind of overall direction. He yields to authority but in doing so is alienated from his own actions.
>
> Even Eichmann was sickened when he toured the concentration camps, but he had only to sit at a desk and shuffle papers. At the same time the man in the camp who actually dropped Cyclon-b into the gas chambers was able to justify his behavior on the ground that he was only following orders from above. Thus there is a fragmentation of the total human act; no one is confronted with the consequences of his decision to carry out the evil act. The person who assumes responsibility has evaporated. Perhaps this is the most common characteristic of socially organized evil in modern society. (1973: 77)

Milgram was widely condemned for the ethics of this experiment because it was devastating for many of the subjects, some of whom suffered depression as a result. Professional standards for informed consent were tightened because of it (Donham 1997). However, Milgram's work stands as a powerful testament to the ability of institutional structures to influence the behaviour of individuals. They do not control our behaviour, as demonstrated by the three out of every forty experimental subjects that refused to go on with the experiment, but they influence our behaviour. We may object to the actions we are told to take, as many of Milgram's subjects resisted at each step. Many more took comfort from the fact that they had disagreed with the procedure in their minds, but, in the end, they pulled the levers they were told to pull, inflicting what they thought was extreme pain on an unwilling victim. Their internal resistance did not change their behaviour or the consequences for the "learner."

The ultimate example of how our behaviour is influenced by an institutional structure is the corporation. At this point in history, the market is the world's dominant organizing principle and the corporation is its dominant institution. Corporations are now the vehicle for the exercise of power and the organization of class in the way that monarchies and the church once were. They are so omnipresent, they have become the background of our lives, the pattern on our wallpaper. They are so visible, they are invisible.

Jerry Mander (1991) talks about the overwhelming power of corporations to shape the lives of people in the United States (and of course Canada as well)—through the jobs we work in, the machines that accomplish our tasks and shape our communication, the building of our homes, the manufacture of our cars, clothing, soap, appliances, the production of our information and entertainment, the ownership of vast areas of land, the backing of election campaigns and the influencing of public policy through lobbying and surrounding us with public relations and advertising. As he says, "Living in the United States today, there is scarcely a moment when you are not in contact with a corporation or its manifestation" (122). Yet in spite of this awesome power, we take corporations completely for granted, like background noise. We have no idea how or why they function. As a result of this failure to understand "the nature and inevitabilities of corporate structure" (121), we allow them to increase their power, influence and freedom from accountability.

Robert Monk, an economist and investment manager once employed by Ronald Reagan, and an insider when it comes to corporations, wrote in 1991 about the drive of corporations to "externalize" their costs by shifting them as much as possible to consumers and governments. He said that the corporation is:

> an externalizing machine, in the same way that a shark is a killing machine—no malevolence, no intentional harm, just something designed with sublime efficiency for self-preservation, which it accomplishes without any capacity to factor in the consequences to others. (quoted in Richardson 1997: 2)

Peter Montague, of the Environmental Research Foundation in Annapolis, Maryland, says:

> The corporation pretty much determines all the basics of modern life, just as the Church did in the Middle Ages.... Small corporate elites determine what most of us will read; what we will see in theatres and on TV; what subjects will become public issues permissible for discussion and debate; what ideas our children will absorb in the classroom; what modes of transportation will be available to us; how our food and fibre will be grown, processed, and marketed; what consumer products will be made by what technologies using what raw materials and which manufacturing techniques; whether we will have widely-available, affordable health

care; how work will be defined, organized, and compensated; how war will be waged and, generally, against whom; what forms of energy will be available to us; how much toxic contamination will be present in our air, water, soil, and food; who will have enough money to run an election campaign and who will not. (quoted in Richardson 1997: 1–2)

Montague refers to "small corporate elites" having the power to make these important decisions on behalf of all of us and, of course, they do. However, they also have to work within the limits of their role in the corporation. Mander says:

The most basic rule of corporate operation is that it must produce income, and (except for that special category of "nonprofit corporations") must show a profit over time. Among publicly held companies there is another basic rule: it must expand and grow, since growth is the standard by which the stock market judges a company. All other values are secondary: the welfare of the community, the happiness of workers, the health of the planet and even the general prosperity....

So human beings within the corporate structure, whatever their personal morals and feelings, are prevented from operating on their own standards. Like the assembly-line workers who must operate at the speed of the machine, corporate employees are strapped onto the apparatus of the corporation and operate by its rules....

In this sense a corporation is essentially a machine, a techno-logical structure, an organization that follows its own principles and its own morality, and in which human morality is anomalous. Because of this double standard—one for human beings and another for "fictitious persons" like corporations—we sometimes see bizarre behavior from executives who, though knowing what is right and moral, behave in a contrary fashion. (1991: 124–126)

Mander says he is waiting for the day when a corporation apologizes for damage to the environment or human health. That day, he points out, will never come. Even if a corporate executive might personally see the company as in the wrong, an admission of this opinion would open the corporation to legal action by all levels of government, damage suits by victims and lawsuits by shareholders. By law the managers of publicly traded companies must act in the financial interest of shareholders, so are obliged to ignore the welfare of the workers, the community and the environment if there is any conflict between these concerns and the profitability of the company. The result is case after case of corporations denying any responsibility for harmful products or manufacturing processes until a court case, an internal whistle-blower or a particularly determined investigative journalist reveals that the company's research warned it of the harm decades before the victims or the public caught on (123–124).

All human beings have choices to make, and we are accountable for our actions—this is free will and moral responsibility. There are many examples of individual resistance and courage in the face of oppression, individuals sacrificing status and income to "do the right thing" and whistle-blowing when an organization is doing something wrong. However, the systems and institutions around us have a powerful ability to shape our behaviour, by conscious and unconscious means. The individualistic ideology of mainstream North American culture tends to see only individual agency. We tend to look only for "good" and "bad" people in every scenario. A structural view of events sees a much more complex interaction between individuals and systems.

The university Department involved in "The Story" was made up of good people—sincere, intelligent and with a long history of taking action against discrimination. How, then, did it become the setting for what happened there? I don't think we can prevent or correct situations like that described in "The Story" without answering this question, and I don't think we can answer the question without looking at the institutional setting of "The Story" through a structural lens.

Institutions as Entities

We often speak of institutional structures as actors in events. We say: "The city has overspent its snow-removal budget," or "The university wants to raise tuition," or "The Anglican Church apologized for its role in the Residential Schools." Sometimes we are referring to the decision-making bodies of those institutions—the members of City Council, the Board of Governors of the University or the General Synod of the Anglican Church. Sometimes we really do mean "the city," "the university" or "the Anglican Church." Is this just a figure of speech?

Earlier I referred to the 1970s, when some leaders in the civil rights movement, such as Charles Hamilton and Stokley Carmichael, began to use the term "institutional racism." Other civil rights leaders objected. For example, John Sibley Butler wrote:

> It is important to view institutions not as things which take on a life of their own and account for inequality, but rather as labels which refer to abstractions invented by social scientists as a convenience for handling the data which they are trying to understand. Thus, when a statement is made, for example, that "educational institutions demand racist policies," it should be

viewed as a figure of speech or an abstraction, because institutions cannot demand anything. (1978: 6)

There have been other writers over the past few decades that believe it is important to recognize institutions not only as influential structures in society, but as entities in themselves, capable of action and reaction. Walter Wink, a theologian who has spent many years exploring the Biblical concept of "principalities and powers," says: "It is a virtue to disbelieve what does not exist. It is dangerous to disbelieve what exists outside our current limited categories" (1992: 4).

He goes on to say:

> The three volumes comprising this study are themselves the record of my own pilgrimage away from a rather naive assurance that the "principalities and powers" mentioned in the New Testament could be "demythologized"; that is, rendered without remainder into the categories of modern social, depth psychology, and general systems theory. (1984: 5)

The powers, according to Wink, are impersonal, but they seem to act wilfully and can replicate themselves. They have no body, but they can take action through people (1992: 8–9). They are not "beings," but "entities." "It is characteristic of the Powers," he says, "that, although they are established, staffed, and perpetuated by people, they are beyond merely human control" (1992: 41).

Anne Wilson Schaef defines a "system" as an entity, that is, with a life of its own:

> A system is a series of contents and processes that is larger than the sum of its parts. It has a life of its own, distinct from the lives of the individuals within it, and it calls forth certain characteristic behaviors and processes in those individuals. (1987: 25)

Jerry Mander describes corporations as entities:

> Though human beings work inside corporations, a corporation is not a person, and does not have feelings. In most senses a corporation is not even a "thing." It may have offices, and/or a factory or products, but a corporation does not have any physical existence or form—no corporality. So when conditions in a community or country become unfavorable—safety standards become too rigid, or workers are not submissive—a corporation can dematerialize and then rematerialize in another town or country.

> If a corporation is not a person or a thing, what is it? It is basically a concept that is given a name and a legal existence, on paper. Though there is no such actual creature, our laws recognize the corporation as an entity. So does the population. We think of corporations as having concrete form, but their true existence is only on paper and in our minds. (1991: 124)

Mander points out that although corporations are entities, they are recognized as "persons" in law. This gives them many of the rights of an actual person. For example, corporations can buy and sell property or sue for injury or libel. In the United States, corporate advertising is protected as "free speech" under the Bill of Rights.

However, because corporations are entities rather than persons, they cannot be held to human responsibilities. They can be fined, but not jailed. "[Their] structure is never altered; [their] 'life' is never threatened" (1991: 130).

Above all, unlike a person, an entity is not capable of morality:

> Lacking the sort of physical, organic reality that characterizes human existence, this entity, this concept, this collection of paperwork called a "corporation" is not capable of feelings such as shame or remorse.... Corporations cannot have morals or altruistic goals. Decisions that may be antithetical to community goals or environmental health are made without suffering misgivings....
>
> Corporations, however, seek to hide their amorality, and attempt to act as if they were altruistic. Lately there has been a concerted effort by American industry to seem concerned with contemporary social issues, such as environmental cleanups, community arts, or drug programs. The effort to exhibit social responsibility by corporations comes precisely because they are innately not responsible to the public; they have no interest in community goals except the ones that serve their purposes. This false altruism should not be confused with the genuine altruism human beings exhibit for one another when, for example, one goes for help on behalf of a sick neighbor, or takes care of the kids, or loans money. Corporate efforts that seem altruistic are really public relations ploys, or else are directly self-serving projects, such as providing schools with educational materials about nature. In other cases, apparent altruism is only "damage control" to offset public criticism....
>
> When corporations say "we care," it is almost always in response to the widespread perception that they do not care. And they don't. How could they? Corporations do not have feelings or morals. All acts are in service to profit. All apparent altruism is

measured against possible public relations benefit. If the benefits do not accrue, the altruistic pose is dropped. When Exxon realized that its cleanup of the Alaskan shores was not easing the public rage about the oil spill, it simply dropped all pretence of altruism and ceased working. (1991: 130–131)

Another writer who describes an institutional structure behaving as an entity is Marie Fortune. In her book, *Is Nothing Sacred: When Sex Invades the Pastoral Relationship* (1989), she characterized her church as an institution capable of preventing a just solution to the incidents she recounts, even though the individuals involved are capable of it:

> An institution acts first on what it perceives to be its self-interest. Seldom does it identify its self-interest to be the same as the interests of the people it is supposed to serve. Thus it tries to protect itself by preventing disclosure of professional misconduct. It prefers instead to shoot the messenger, that is, to denigrate whoever had the courage to tell the secret. (xiii)

Fortune also says that there are predictable patterns of behaviour in an institutional entity. We will return to this concept later:

> Although this is a story about a church, its pastor, and its laity, about a particular time and place and particular people, it is also a story about an institution. As such it could be a story about any institution.... Institutions ... share a pattern of response to the misconduct of an authorized representative and to the public disclosure of that misconduct. (xiii–xiv)

Walter Wink discusses the spiritual nature of institutional entities. In ancient times, he says, the peoples of the Middle East believed that every nation and institution on earth had a parallel "angel" or "demon" in heaven. When a war was fought on earth, the matching angels and demons were fighting in heaven as well. This is the medieval notion of "correspondences" ("As above, so below").

Later Western belief systems have either defined the spiritual world as imaginary, or seen it as existing but completely separate from physical reality. Wink, however, sees the two as one: an outer manifestation—institutions—and an inner spirit—the principalities and powers. He defines the principalities and powers as the "heart," the "interiority" or the spiritual force emanating from institutions (1992: 3–7). He describes an institution true to its beneficial calling of service to human society as having an "angel" spirit, and one that has betrayed its vocation has "fallen," and he describes its spirit as a "demon" (1992: 8–9).

He explains the concept further by using the example of a riot at a soccer game. Decent people are caught up in the crowd madness, acting in violent ways that they would never consider under normal circumstances. The spirituality of the situation could be described as a "riot demon," crystallized suddenly out of the conjunction of permissiveness, heavy drinking, the violent ethos of competitive sports, the inner violence in the fans and a triggering incident. Eventually the situation is subdued, and the demon disappears, not "rocketing back to heaven," but dissipating, going out of existence as its human participants are scattered (1992: 9).

Wink's thinking about the spirit of institutions stretches reality for someone who thinks in a typically Western way, but the traditional Native people I have talked to do not find it strange. In fact, Wink's description parallels a traditional concept of the Mi'kmaw First Nation, one of the indigenous people of the Atlantic Provinces and the State of Maine. "Beth" explained "*mindu*" to me as the belief that all things have a spirit, with the potential for good and evil. "Spirits contain energy, that can be fed and activated," she wrote. "When you put out positive energy it activates other positive energy, which cycles back to you, and when you activate negative energy, it also activates other negative energy, which also cycles back to you" (Personal communication, 2004).

Wink was not the first theologian to name institutions as entities with spirits. In fact, he was originally inspired in this line thinking by William Stringfellow. Addressing a conference on religion and race in 1963, Stringfellow defined racism as a "demonic power," one of the world's "principalities and powers." During his speech, he said:

> The drama of history takes place amongst God and humanity and the principalities and powers, the great institutions and ideologies active in the world. It is the corruption and shallowness of human-ism which beguiles Jew or Christian into believing that human beings are masters of institution or ideology. Or to put it differently, racism is not an evil in human hearts or minds; racism is a princi-pality, a demonic power, a representative image, an embodiment of death, over which human beings have little or no control, but which works its awful influence in their lives. (quoted in Wylie-Kellerman 1998: 16–17)

In my opinion Stringfellow goes too far in taking responsibility away from the individuals in institutions. We may not have control over institutional entities, but we have our own form of power and influence when we take responsibility and act collectively. However, Stringfellow's is a powerful description of the ability of an institution to act as an entity, with a will and spirit of its own.

Implications for Strategy

I have spent many pages describing institutions as structures, as entities, as having spirits. So what? Is this way of looking at institutions helpful to those of us who seek to make our institutions more just and equitable? I think it is, although I also think it is dangerous.

First, the danger: a structural view of institutions can be used to excuse the actions of individuals. I have said this already, but I think it is worth repeating: I am not suggesting that a structural view of institutions releases individual actors within institutions of moral responsibility. In fact, my intention is quite the opposite. One of the functions of the institutional entity is to separate individuals from their moral responsibility. Those who perceive the institution as an entity can help to re-unite us with our human moral principles. By making it clear that the institution is an entity that can act in its own interests by strongly influencing the individuals within it, I hope to make us all the more aware of our individual responsibility and the need to work actively for justice and equity in our institutions.

Now, the benefits. Earlier in the chapter I quoted Walter Wink saying: "It is a virtue to disbelieve what does not exist. It is dangerous to disbelieve what exists outside our current limited categories" (1992: 4). He has also said: "Any attempt to transform a social system without addressing both its spirituality and its outer form is doomed to failure" (1992: 10). I think that understanding institutions as structures and as entities with a spiritual nature affects our justice and equity strategies in three ways: First, it makes nourishing our own spirits, individually and collectively, not something we do in our spare time but a central piece of our strategies. Second, it can clear away the confusion, powerlessness and defensiveness that comes from seeing institutions as a collection of individuals. Third, it suggests some new questions and tactics in our strategies for justice and equity.

The first reason for social justice activists to learn to see institutions as structures and entities has to do with our own spirits. I define "spirit" broadly, as our connections: with our own deep nature, our feelings, our bodies, one another, our special places, our history, our people, our culture, all other histories, people and cultures in the world and with other species, with the earth, with the universe, with life. It includes terms like "compassion" and "solidarity." Others have more specific definitions of spirit or definitions that include beings outside of the universe. Whatever our definition, it usually includes the sense of connection among a group of people. If we understand that part of our strategy as social justice activists is to engage the spirits of the institutions around us, then nurturing our own spirits, however we understand them, and the spirit of connection among those who share our vision, becomes central to the task. Working for justice has to include engaging with one another, listening to one another, struggling with our conflicts until they are resolved, taking care of one another, developing compassion and having fun. To quote Walter Wink again: "This is the secret of social activists: they do not simply oppose evil because it is wrong, but also because the struggle is exciting and sometimes even fun"(1992: 321). Means and ends are not separate in social change work. We are creating a new way of doing things as we go, making a new reality real. Taking time to celebrate a friend's birthday, to reflect, meditate, talk, pray or sing together, to have coffee, is not time out of the struggle, it is the struggle!

The second point is that a structural view of institutions can clear away the confusion, powerlessness and defensiveness that are characteristic of an individualistic or liberal view of social change. We get confused by the liberal notion that we deserve what happens to us. As Walter Wink says: "The early Christians would never ask 'Why do bad things happen to good people?'" (1992: 316). In their day, the extreme individualism of Western culture did not yet exist. In mainstream Canada and the United States, we imagine that we are at the centre of the universe in a way that would be beyond their imagination and that of many other cultures in the world today.

We also get confused because we tend to believe that injustice comes about only because someone has that intention. The other side of that coin is that we get defensive when someone names an injustice perpetrated by our own group. When a woman describes the impact of sexism on her life, some men hear that as a personal accusation. Their response is: "Don't look at me; I've never hurt a woman." Likewise a story of racism or heterosexism can elicit a response such as: "I treat everyone the same," or even "I feel silenced," or the infamous "Some of my best friends are..." Individual defensiveness, as we will see later, can be the trigger for institutional backlash.

The other problem of liberal ideology for social change activists is that we get confused about our own power, seeing ourselves either as all-powerful, and therefore personally responsible for every injustice, or completely without power to make change.

I will return to these points, discussing defensiveness and institutional backlash in Chapter Seven and illusions about our own power in Chapter Eight.

My third point is that taking a structural view of institutions brings new questions to our strategies for social justice. Some of these questions concern the behaviour of institutions: If institutions are entities, capable of acting in their own self-interest apart from the individual interests of the people who work in them, are served by them or even lead them, how can we discover what the institution sees as its self-interest?

It is obvious to me that institutions will tolerate some kinds of change, but not others. What kinds of change will they tolerate? What kinds of change do they find threatening? How will an institution react to something it perceives as threatening? Is it possible to promote change in a way that moderates the threat or delays the reaction without compromising our desire to make real structural change in the institution? Are the reactions of an institution predictable?

When it comes to the point of building specific strategies for increasing justice and equity in institutions, there are more questions to ask: Which of our current equity tactics make change only at the individual level? Which are capable of making change at the institutional level? Which are capable only of reform? Which have the potential to bring about structural transformation? What new tactics do we need to develop, and what old ones can we revive, that would focus not just on individuals, but on the institution itself and its habitual, often unconscious, ways of doing things? I will return to these questions about strategy in Chapter Eight.

After reading all the literature I could find about a structural view of institutions, I feel I can answer my first question in general terms. I would say that an institution's self-interest lies in the preservation of its own essence, which comes from its history and is expressed in its deepest values and structures, particularly its methods of granting, maintaining and regulating power. Following from this definition, I would say that there is great scope for change that makes a difference in individuals' lives but is not threatening, because it does not touch the institution's essential values and structure. In structural terms, it is "token" change. When change does touch the institution's essence by challenging its deepest values and structure, the institution will defend itself.

Are the reactions of an institution predictable? Earlier I quoted Marie Fortune when she said: "Institutions ... share a pattern of response to the misconduct of an authorized representative and to the public disclosure that misconduct" (1989: xiv). I think this is what we must understand in order to say whether institutional reactions are predictable or not: are there certain patterns of behaviour shared by all institutions, or by all of a certain type of institution?

Chapter Six

The Quantum Universe, Chaos and Predictable Patterns

An Entity Is Not a Machine

After years of reading about struggles for equity in various institutions, I am convinced that there are recognizable patterns in institutional behaviour, but are they predictable? Although institutions exert a strong influence on individuals, human beings still have free will and are full of surprises. Individual behaviour will never be completely predictable.

Also, institutions are not machines, although our common speech about them often implies that they are. We speak of our organizations as if we can tinker with them, repair them, take them apart and put them back together. We often assume that we can understand each piece of them in isolation, and the whole is the sum of the parts. Machines are predictable, at least if you know enough about them.

If organizations are entities, however, they are not machines. What does "predictable" mean in the context of something as organic, multi-dimensional and complex as an entity? My search for answers to this question led me straight in chaos—chaos theory, that is—and the quantum universe within which chaos operates.

Just as we tend to think of organizations as machines, so did science, from the seventeenth to the nineteenth centuries, conceive of nature as a machine. In particular it assumed that one could understand each piece of the machine and move from there to understanding the whole machine, because the whole was the sum of the parts. The universe and all systems within it were thought of as pre-determined. If you knew the state of a system at a beginning point and the rules that guide its behaviour, you could predict what its state would be at any point in the future.

During the twentieth century the image of nature as a machine was blown completely away and replaced with a more complex and mysterious picture, where things cannot be predicted accurately, even though their state is determined by very simple rules; where understanding the part is misleading because it is interdependent with every other part and with the observer. This insight is not new to the world, of course. Indigenous peoples have seen nature this way for thousands of years. Within science, however, the re-discovery of nature as an irreducible whole changed scientists' understanding of everything—space, time, matter, cause and effect.

The Quantum Universe

During the twentieth century, physicists were working with electrons, the tiniest particles that make up matter. They discovered a surprising thing. The "building blocks of matter" are not matter at all, or rather, they are matter only under certain circumstances. In other contexts, observed in other ways, they are waves of energy. Huge implications came from this discovery. First, no tiny part of the universe can be understood out of context—because its behaviour, nature and even its existence depend on its relationships with the whole system and with the observer. This is the central feature of quantum theory (Peat 1994: 233).

When studying electrons in the form of laser photographs, called holograms, physicists made another discovery. Each particle of the hologram "contains the entire structure of the entire hologram; each piece is not just a part of the whole, it has the entire pattern and way of functioning of the whole embedded in it" (Schaef 1987: 37).

During the 1960s, physicist David Bohm began to conceive of reality not as a collection of material objects, but as a "holomovement," or movement of the whole. He began to speak of an "implicate" or "enfolded" order, one in which the whole is "enfolded" in each part. The "implicate" order, or flowing movement of reality, "throws out" "explicate" forms, which we can perceive through our senses; but these material things are only a small portion of reality (Peat 1994: 6, 140).

As physicists and other scientists began to understand reality as a single entity, other discoveries were emerging about the nature of order in the "movement of the whole."

Chaos Theory

At the beginning of the twentieth century, science itself was broken down into many parts, specialties with little communication between them. The profound shift from nature-as-machine, easily broken down into parts, to nature as a single living entity came about in several branches of science independently and simultaneously.

Ironically, in a world where indigenous people have understood nature as a living entity for thousands of years, the end of nature-as-machine in science came about, not by listening to this ancient wisdom, but because of a machine. The computer, with its ability to make thousands of calculations in fractions of a second, was at the heart of the conceptual revolution known as chaos theory.

Scientists use the language of mathematics to describe nature. Before the computer, scientists generally limited themselves to the mathematical equations they could solve. These are called "linear" equations. They are "proportional"—as one side changes, so does the other. They can be expressed by a straight line on a graph. You can take them apart and put them together again, and the pieces always add up. James Gleick gives the verbal example of "the more the merrier"(1987: 23).

Non-linear systems are not that simple. They can't be solved and don't add up the same way every time. Gleick gives this example of a calculation involving friction:

> Without friction a simple linear equation expresses the amount of energy you need to accelerate a hockey puck. With friction the relationship gets complicated, because the amount of energy changes depending on how fast the puck is already moving. Non-linearity means that the act of playing the game has a way of changing the rules. You cannot assign a constant importance to friction, because its importance depends on speed. Speed, in turn, depends on friction. That twisted changeability makes non-linearity hard to calculate, but it also creates rich kinds of behavior that never occur in linear systems. (23–24)

The massive ability of the computer to calculate made it possible to work with non-linear equations and create images of non-linear systems. While there is no simple solution, if you can make millions and millions of calculations, you can see how a non-linear system unfolds over time.

In 1960, Edward Lorenz, a meteorologist, created a computer model of the weather. Gleick describes the amazement of Lorenz's colleagues when they saw his simple deterministic system—twelve simple equations calculated over and over again—which produced chaotic and unpredictable results. It was a true model of the weather.

Lorenz meanwhile decided to see if he could produce unpredictable behaviour with an even simpler set of defining equations. He found he could create a system just as complex and chaotic as his weather system with only three equations—three *non-linear* equations. In 1961, he developed a computer program that would plot the movements of this system on a three-dimensional graph. Each time the computer completed another repetition of its calculations, it would mark the result with a dot in the three-dimensional space of the graph. At this point, Lorenz began to discover the order within chaos. The drawing that emerged on his computer screen never repeated itself and never crossed its own path. It was infinite in its complexity, and yet it created an orderly pattern contained within clear limits. Lorenz speculated that the pattern stayed within its bounds because of something that drew it toward the centre. He called this something a "strange attractor." The drawing is now famous as the Lorenz Attractor. It has become a symbol of the chaos that lies within order and

The Lorenz Attractor

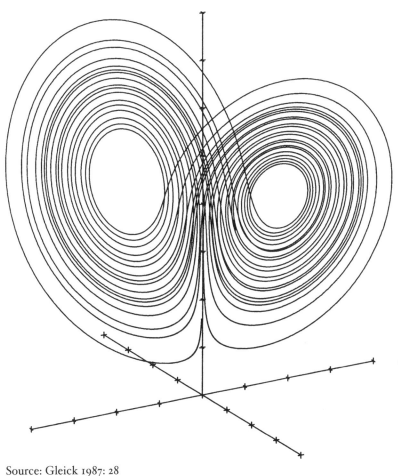

Source: Gleick 1987: 28

the order that lies within chaos. It was unpredictable in its details, but the overall system was stable (Gleick 1987: 48): "The system is deterministic, but you can't say what it's going to do next" (Gleick 1987: 251).

Fractal Geometry

Because of the separation between the various branches of science, few scientists outside of meteorology saw Lorenz's work. Instead, his discoveries about non-linear systems were repeated in field after field. Robert May, a biologist, found them in his study of the rise and fall of wildlife populations (Gleick 1987: 66). They were discovered by a French astronomer studying galactic orbits, a Japanese electrical engineer modelling electronic circuits, a mathematician studying oscillations (45) and a Dutch engineer studying electrical currents (49). The same principles of chaos and order emerged in economics, genetics, fluid dynamics (45) and epidemiology (79). Western scientists soon discovered that their Soviet counterparts had been working with these rules for complex systems since the 1950s (76).

During the 1960s, a mathematician named Benoit Mandelbrot had access to the most powerful computers of the day because he worked in the research branch of IBM. He found the same patterns in river flooding, electronic transmission noise and cotton prices (103). He worked with computerized graphics like the one Lorenz used, with more and more dimensions, to create pictures of systems ruled by non-linear equations. In the end, he developed a whole new type of geometry.

For centuries the geometry we had was that of Euclid, with its lines and shapes such as circles, squares and rectangles. Mandelbrot's geometry was much more complex, capable of describing the shapes that actually appear in nature, shapes that appear to be random and "chaotic." A question posed in one of his key papers was: "How long is the coastline of Britain?" The answer is: infinite, because the degree of detail depends on the distance between the observer and the boundary between land and water. From a satellite, the coast may appear to be a certain length, but if you look at it from an airplane, it becomes longer, because you can see more detail. If you stand and look at a piece of shore in front of your feet, it becomes longer still, because you can see every indentation in the beach. With a magnifying glass, you can see the shape of each grain of sand. In a microscope it becomes even longer, because you can see the rough shape of each grain of sand, and so on (Gleick 1987: 94–96). Mandelbrot added the concept of scale to the picture of complex systems and found that patterns repeat at every scale. If a system has a certain shape when seen from far away, that shape will appear again in the medium detail, in the fine detail, in the microscopic detail, and so on into infinity.

In 1975, Mandelbrot named his new geometry "fractal" after looking through his son's Latin dictionary and finding the word "*fractus*" from verb "*frangere*," meaning "to break" (98). Gleick says:

> In the end, the word fractal came to stand for a way of describing, calculating, and thinking about shapes that are irregular and fragmented, jagged and broken up—shapes from the crystalline curves of snowflakes to the discontinuous dust of galaxies. A fractal curve implies an organizing structure that lies hidden among the hideous complication of such shapes.... [P]atterns ... with ... complex boundaries between orderly and chaotic behavior, had unsuspected regularities that could only be described in terms of the relations of large scales to small. The structures that provided the key to non-linear dynamics proved to be fractal. (1987: 114)

Scale provided a key to the relationship between order and chaos in complex systems. As Gleick says: "In an apparently unruly system, scaling meant that some quality was being preserved while everything else changed. Some regularity lay beneath the turbulent surface of the equation"(172). Mandelbrot gave his name to a beautiful pattern called the "Mandelbrot Set." From a distance, the Mandelbrot Set looks like an oddly-shaped child's snowman with an antenna on its head. From a closer perspective, the outline of the "snowman" becomes a complicated set of spirals and whorls. Each piece of the pattern, from a closer perspective, reveals another set of spirals and whorls, just as complicated as the larger ones, and in the midst of them, here and there, is a repetition of the "snowman" (114–15, 221–26). It is a shape of extreme complexity and extreme simplicity at the same time (221).

Chaos Theory, Fractal Geometry and Institutional Change

Chaos theory and fractal geometry have spawned a whole new branch of material science, the study of patterns. It has one key guiding principle: at the point of change in a complex system, one can expect complex behaviour from simple causes and simple behaviour from complex causes, unpredictable freedom at the local level and a pre-determined pattern to the whole—a pattern that is repeated at every level. This principle can be applied to electricity, ice crystals and metals, but can it tell us anything about patterns in institutions at the point of change?

Gleick says the beautiful patterns revealed by the scientists and mathematicians working with chaos theory show us something universal; that is: "different systems will behave identically, a natural law about systems at the point of transition between orderly and turbulent" (1987: 180).

Margaret Wheatley, a professor and management consultant, has explored the implications of chaos theory for her field. The same principles are relevant to organizations, she believes, because they are entities, "possessing many of the properties of living systems" (1992: 13). She states:

> If capacity to deal with information, communicate, defines a system as conscious, then ... organizations qualify as conscious entities.... They have capacities for generating and absorbing information, for feedback, for self-regulation. In fact, information is an organization's primary source of nourishment; it is so vital to survival that its absence creates a strong vacuum. If information is not available, people make it up. Rumors proliferate. (106–7)

Wheatley's key conclusion after applying the principles of chaos theory to her experience of organizations is that organizations reflect, at all levels, a simple set of "founding principles" and that organizational change follows

The Mandelbrot Set

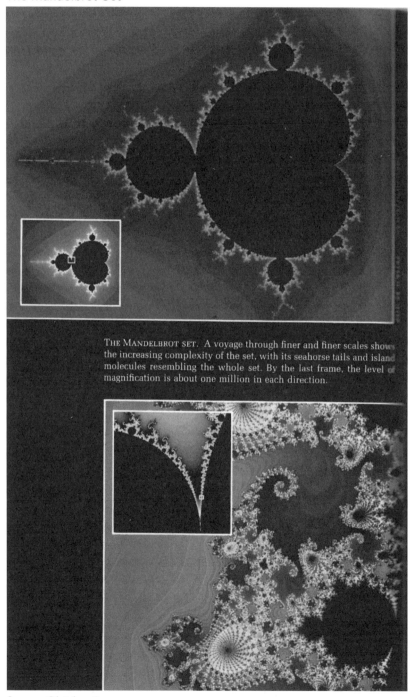

THE MANDELBROT SET. A voyage through finer and finer scales shows the increasing complexity of the set, with its seahorse tails and island molecules resembling the whole set. By the last frame, the level of magnification is about one million in each direction.

Source: Gleick 1987: 114–115

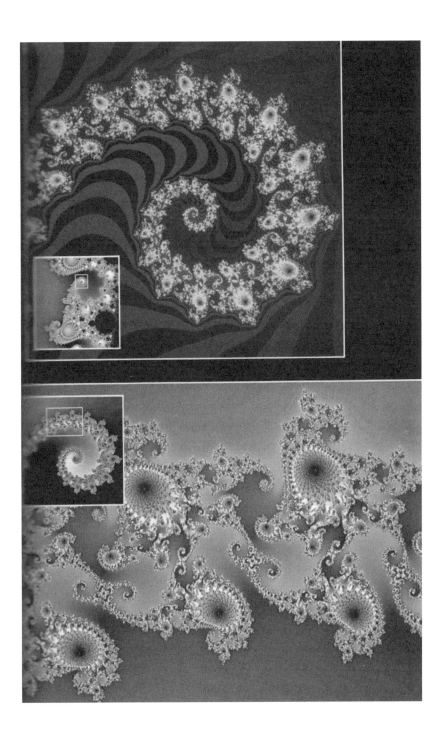

HEINZ-OTTO PEITGEN   PETER H. RICHTER

the rules of fractal geometry. She says:

> In spite of the vast complexity of our organizations, they are not held in place by a set of complex controls, but by a few guiding principles—key patterns with great autonomy for individual members of the system.... Fluctuations, randomness, and unpredictability at the local level, in the presence of guiding or self-referential principles, cohere over time into definite and predictable form. (1992: 11, 133)

Wheatley refers to the power of guiding principles to hold together a large, complex system as "the strange attractor of meaning" (134). The "strange attractor" as a feature of organizations, brings us back to the issue of free will and structural roles. How do institutional structures affect our behaviour even though we are free? The "strange attractor" of the institutional entity's movement through chaos and order is one possible explanation. As David Peat describes the action of a strange attractor: "[It] does not pull and trap things in a mechanical way; rather, it exerts a more subtle influence so that the system weaves and dances around it, always relatively free, yet never escaping from its influence" (1994: 203). Elsewhere, David Peat and John Briggs speak of "the wild, seductive pull of the strange chaotic attractor" (1989: 77).

Like Margaret Wheatley, I believe that chaos theory and fractal geometry apply to institutional entities going through change. I have come to these conclusions:

- an institution is a complex, non-linear system;
- the whole is more than the sum of the parts;
- the behaviour of the system over time is guided by a few simple rules;
- during change, you can expect to find chaos in order and order in chaos, simple behaviour from complex causes and complex behaviour from simple causes;
- the behaviour of individuals cannot be predicted but, over time, predictable patterns emerge in the system as a whole; and
- these patterns are repeated on all scales.

Predictability in a non-linear system is a non-linear process. We cannot say that this event will happen after that event. There is no mechanical relationship between cause and effect. We also cannot understand or predict the behaviour of institutional entities by examining the individuals involved. In organizations, as in physical materials, "it is no longer meaningful to talk of the constituent electrons' individual properties, as these continually change to meet the requirements of the whole" (Zohar 1990, quoted in Wheatley 1992: 117). If we look only at particular individuals and incidents, it is difficult to see the patterns. Or if we look at a pattern only in one location, we don't see how it is repeated in other locations and on other levels, because it is never exactly the same.

What we can do is look for patterns and expect them to be repeated in various forms over time and at all levels. From the patterns, we can deduce the guiding principles of the institution—the real guiding principles, which may or may not be related to the institution's stated guiding principles.

Anne Wilson Schaef's Concept of the Addictive System

A good example of this kind of analysis can be found in the work of Anne Wilson Schaef. Schaef's journey into the concept of patterns on all levels of a system began when she and other members of her extended family realized that one of their members was an alcoholic. As they learned more, they discovered that it was not just the one family member who needed to recover; the whole family was suffering because it had become entangled in an addictive system. Meanwhile, she had discovered that several clients in her counselling practice were also alcoholics or came from alcoholic families. She turned her attention to the study of addiction.

Schaef and co-author Diane Fassel describe the key characteristics of addicted individuals and families: denial, confusion, self-centredness, dishonesty—including putting up a good front to outsiders—perfectionism, a constant effort to get more of everything (or the "scarcity model"), attempting to maintain control—or at least the illusion of control—frozen feelings and ethical deterioration. They list many other characteristics beyond the key ones, including crisis orientation, depression, stress, abnormal thinking processes, forgetfulness, dependency, negativism, defensiveness, projection, tunnel vision and fear (1988: 62–68). They also describe the characteristic processes that take place in an addictive family. They include:

- "the process of the promise": the continual hope that things will get better;
- "the process of external referencing": where individuals learn to define themselves, their values and their behavioural norms by relying on outside authority;
- "the process of invalidation": where anything the individual or family can't understand or control simply does not exist;
- "the process of fabricating personality conflicts": a form of denial that resists acceptance of a person's input by saying that personalities are in conflict;
- "the process of dualism": where there are always just two choices, one right and one wrong, and other people are either for us or against us; and finally
- "the process of the pseudopodic ego": where the addictive system

absorbs everything that is different from itself and uses it to perpetuate the system (1988: 68–73).

Schaef and Fassel have come to see organizations and larger systems as entities: "By system we mean an entity that comprises both content ... and processes" (1988: 60). I quoted Schaef's definition of a system in Chapter Five, including her statement that a system is "larger than the sum of its parts. It has a life of its own, distinct from the lives of the individuals within it" (1987: 25). In *When Society Becomes an Addict* (1987) she outlines how society as a whole shares the characteristics of the addictive individual and family. She compares addiction to a hologram, a three-dimensional laser photograph described earlier in this chapter.

> The essential feature of a hologram is that each piece of the hologram contains the entire structure of the entire hologram; each piece is not just a part of the whole, it has the entire pattern and way of functioning of the whole embedded in it. This is a useful way to look at the Addictive System. The system is like the individual, and the individual is like the system. In other words, the Addictive System has all the characteristics of the individual alcoholic/addict. And because we live in this system, every one of us, unless recovering by means of a system shift, exhibits many of these same characteristics. (37)

In *The Addictive Organization* (1988), Schaef and Fassel include organizations in the picture as the link between individuals and systems:

> Organizations themselves function as addicts, and because they are not aware of this fact of their functioning, become key building blocks in an addictive society, even when this dramatically contradicts their espoused mission or reason for existence. Addictive organizations are the infrastructure of the addictive society. They are the "glue" that perpetuates addictive functioning on the society level. (54)

Schaef and Fassel also refer to a "generic addictive process that underlies all the various addictions" (51):

> It becomes obvious that the system functions as an addict and reflects the addictive characteristics of the individual, while the individual reflects the addictive process of the system. Actually, neither reflects the other, for they are not a mirror, they are the other. (53)

I think anyone familiar with systems of oppression—sexism, racism, heterosexism, and all the others, particularly class—will recognize Schaef's list of characteristics and processes. The typical dynamics of oppression demonstrate all of the patterns she describes—self-centredness, dishonesty, dualism, promises, control, confusion and ethical deterioration. Three of the processes Schaef has defined are particularly vivid illustrations of oppressive systems in action. These are invalidation, the pseudopodic ego and the scarcity model. According to Schaef and Fassel, the addictive system uses the process of invalidation to "define into nonexistence those ideas and experiences that the system cannot know, understand, or most importantly control.... It narrowly defines what is worth knowing and what is not worth knowing" (1988: 71). They define the pseudopodic ego as: "a process the addictive system uses to absorb and utilize for itself everything that is different from itself. It is a type of colonization. In this process, things that represent a different system become absorbed into the addictive system ... it owns these differences, and then uses them to perpetuate the system intact" (69–70). The scarcity model, as Schaef and Fassel define it, is "the abiding belief that there is simply not enough to go around" (65). "The system in which we live operates on the same scarcity principles," they say. "The addictive system is constantly in search of more armaments, a larger gross national product, or more international influence. At every shareholder meeting, the bottom line focus is measured by getting bigger in one way or another" (65).

When they dug down, beneath the patterns, to find the guiding principles, Schaef and Fassel found, on the individual level, the "fix," and on the systemic level, self-preservation. The individual addict will do anything, lie to anyone, including themselves, because "getting the 'fix' becomes the centre of an addict's life. Everything else is overshadowed" (1988: 63). The "fix" may be a substance, such as alcohol, or a process, such as spending money. Among those in the elite class, the "fix" can be wealth and power. Whatever it is, it becomes something worth sacrificing anything, even sanity or life itself. The addictive system sacrifices the processes that maintain life to preserve itself. In addictive organizations, "the spoken goal of the organization may be productivity, profit, or service; the unspoken goal is usually to preserve the system and the status quo" (1987: 132). The goals on the individual and organization/system level form a complementary circle in the picture presented by Schaef and Fassel:

> The society in which we live needs addictions, and its very essence
> fosters addictions. It fosters addictions because the best-adjusted
> person in the society is the person who is not dead and not alive,
> just numb, a zombie. When you are dead you are not able to do
> the work of the society. When you are fully alive, you are constantly
> saying no to many of the processes of the society: the racism, the

polluted environment, the nuclear threat, the arms race, drinking unsafe water, and eating carcinogenic foods. Thus, it is in the interest of the society to promote those things that "take the edge off," get us busy with our "fixes," and keep us slightly "numbed out" and zombielike. Consequently, the society itself not only encourages addictions, it functions as an addict. (1988: 59–60)

The work of Anne Wilson Schaef and Diane Fassel is a good example of organizational and systemic analysis based on the principles of quantum mechanics, chaos theory and fractal geometry. They seek out patterns, repeated on all levels and over time, and then deduce the real principles behind them. This does not give them the ability to predict specific events, in a linear fashion, but it does inform their analysis, allowing them to make "educated guesses" about the response they might expect to any intervention they make, at both individual and organizational levels. It improves their ability to diagnose systemic problems beyond the symptoms that show up in individual behaviour. An accurate diagnosis contributes a great deal to a strong strategy for healing.

I think Schaef and Fassel demonstrate the importance of going beyond the liberal tendency to look only at individual people and incidents. If there is inequity built into the founding principles of an institution, it will be repeated over space and time on all levels—consciously or not—through the logic of the structure. If we are going to learn to diagnose injustice and inequity in our institutions, and then build strategies for healing, we must discover the patterns at all levels and the determining principles that shape them.

Chapter Seven

The Road to Equity at North American Universities—Naming Patterns

Return to the Strategic Questions

Chapter Six discussed the question: Are the reactions of an institution predictable? The answer is yes, if predictability is understood, in the light of quantum mechanics, chaos theory and fractal geometry, as an analysis of repeating patterns on all levels, and the underlying principles that shape them. Returning to the events recounted in "The Story," is it possible to define some of the patterns that can be expected to emerge when a university is asked to accept as equals people that have been excluded before, in this case, women of colour with poverty in their class background, two of whom are in a lesbian relationship? If so, what can we deduce from these patterns about the real, underlying purpose of the university? Or, if we assume the underlying purpose of all institutions is self-preservation, what does the university as an institutional entity understand to be the true self-interest, the essence, which it must preserve?

Through reflection on my experience at Canadian University and the literature I have found on efforts to achieve equity in other Canadian universities, I have made a beginning at defining patterns.

A Ton of Feathers

Early in their history, Canadian universities were, for the most part, reserved for white, conservative, upper-class men. Gradually other white men entered the institution, men from the middle classes, then the working classes, then men with political perspectives other than conservative. Dividing lines based on gender and colour have been more resistant to change.

Men of colour are making slow inroads into Canadian universities, with major struggles along the way. Several well-publicized Ontario human rights cases provide a small window on the stories of men who are perceived as "different" by their colleagues. In 1976, the Ontario Human Rights Commission ruled that Dr Singh was denied a tenure-track position at Algoma University College on the basis of his national origin. Witnesses testified that the principal of the college expressed a concern about "too many Pakistanis in the department" and that hiring one more would undermine the "Canadianization" and "immaculate community image of the College" (Calliste 2000: 142).

In 2000, the same body ruled that Dr Kin-Yip Chun was denied a tenure-track appointment in the Physics Department at the University of Toronto because of discrimination. Dr Chun, an internationally acclaimed physicist, was denied access to the tenure track four times. When he complained to the administration of the university, he experienced harassment leading up to his dismissal from the department. The administration blamed his difficulties in the department on "personality problems" (Calliste 2000: 141). The few cases that follow the human rights process to the end give a tiny hint of the extent of such discrimination.

White women are also slowly making inroads into Canadian universities—very slowly. In the sixty-four years from 1931 to 1995, the proportion of women faculty in Canada increased from 19 to 21 percent (*Globe and Mail* 1995, quoted in Emberley 1996: 210).

The frustrating and painful experience of white women on Canadian campuses is well documented. White female faculty across Canada have adopted the phrase "chilly climate," a term coined by Americans Roberta Hall and Bernice Sandler in 1982 (Prentice 1996) to describe their experience with systemic discrimination in academe. Their point is that systemic discrimination is not experienced in immediately obvious ways, through undeniable acts of discrimination, but rather it accumulates day by day through constant demeaning incidents, mounting, eventually, to what Paula Caplan labelled "a ton of feathers" (Prentice 1996).

The Chilly Collective (1995) at the University of Western Ontario published a collection of essays that describe the "ton of feathers" weighing down women at Canadian universities. In the Introduction, Alison Wylie writes:

> Time and again, those documenting the chilly climate for women in academia observe that it is precisely because these practices are highly localized, and may seem trivial taken on their own that often they are "not seen as discriminat[ory] [either by those who perpetrate them or those who are victimized by them] even though they do make women uncomfortable and put them at a disadvantage" (Sandler 1986). It is the persistence and recurrence of such practices which ensure that they will have non-trivial consequences—that they will reinforce the cycle of progressively eroded confidence, lowered expectations, and compromised ambitions.... It is also precisely because of the relative invisibility of these practices that they are so widespread, and so insidious, both in eroding the confidence and capacity of individual women to participate fully in academic settings and in undermining the

institutional programs designed to promote equity for them. (40)

The authors of the collection leave no doubt about their view that the continuing barriers for women on Canadian campuses have structural causes. Alison Wylie continues:

> Our numbers have remained low long after overtly discriminatory policies have been struck down and, in some quarters, even after widely publicized employment equity or affirmative action programs have been initiated. Since at least the mid-1980s this situation has led many to argue that we face, to varying degrees and with differing consequences, persistent systemic discrimination which, precisely because of our elite status in other respects, throws into sharp relief the nature and depth of the mechanisms that continue to sustain gender inequity throughout North American society in all its myriad forms—constituted as racist, homophobic, classist, and ablist—to name a few of its variants. (29–30)

If white women, labelled as outsiders only on the basis of gender, face huge barriers to equality at Canadian universities, women of colour, with both gender and race counting against them, face even higher walls. Two of the essays in the Chilly Collective's publication are written by Patricia Monture-Angus, a Mohawk woman who studied law at three Canadian universities and taught at two others. She describes, in a powerful and painful way, how much more "chilly" the university climate is for a woman who is marginalized not only by sex, but by race as well. She writes about her experience of reading the first version of the Chilly Collective manuscript, as a reviewer:

> I sat with these women's words of their own pain and exclusion and I felt empowered by our common experiences. At the same time, I also began to feel invisible. Invisible because race and culture have such a significant impact on my experiences of university and this layer was almost totally absent from the women's storytelling. (Monture-Angus 1995a: 14)

Later in the same essay, Monture-Angus writes:

> It should be easy to recognize that women are under-represented in the academic fold. There are still fewer people of colour and Aboriginal people who hold faculty positions within Canadian universities. Aboriginal women and women of colour are dramatically under-represented in institutions of "higher learning." Universities remain a bastion of White male privilege. My

experience of the university, and in particular the demands of an academic career, are complicated by the fact I am both Mohawk and woman. Many times during the last six years of my teaching career, I have felt either confused about or uncomfortable with certain aspects of my job. This feeling is rooted in my difference either as a woman or as an "Indian" or some combination of the above. I have named these uncomfortable and confusing experiences contradictions. The experience of contradiction is my expression for a state of being that I often slam into head first and the experience leaves me overwhelmed and motionless. (Monture-Angus 1995a: 54)

Other Aboriginal women and women of colour who have studied and worked in a university setting have written about their experience. Some of these women are: Audre Lorde (1982), Wanda Thomas Bernard, Lydia Lucas-White (and Dorothy Moore) (1981), Agnes Calliste (2000), Patricia Hill Collins (1989), Patricia Williams (1991), Himani Bannerji (1991), Linda Carty (1991), Martha Tack and Carol Patitu (1992), Betty Jones (1993), Roxanna Ng (1993), bell hooks (1994), Terri Sabattis (1996), Jean Graveline (1996) and Patti Doyle-Bedwell (1997). These authors provide a catalogue of the demeaning experiences that drive women in this position to a painful choice: assimilate (to the extent that visible difference allows) or engage in a battle with the institution (Sabattis 1996, 31).

Some of the experiences described are particular to students. For example:

- exceptional economic hardship because of membership in a marginalized group (Sabattis 1996, 32);
- invisibility or negative stereotypes of Aboriginal people and people of colour in the curriculum and literature, and students being asked to fill the gaps themselves when they point them out, even though this is the professor's job (Collins 1989: 752; Carty 1991: 13–37; Bannerji 1991: 69, 74–100; hooks 1994: 32, 43–44; Calliste 2000: 149–152; Monture-Angus 1995b: 57, 60; Sabattis 1996: 34, 41; Williams 1991: 80–83; Graveline 1996: 354);
- faculty responses ranging from discomfort to ridicule when issues of gender or race are raised in class (hooks 1994: 30–31, 39; Sabattis 1996: 34);
- professors' assumption that their knowledge from the literature is always superior to students' knowledge from their experience (Carty 1991: 13–15, 20–21; Monture-Angus 1995b: 60);
- comments that if they are present in the university it must be because of affirmative action or other special programs rather than ability

(Sabattis 1996: 40);
- difficulty adjusting to the jargon of academic work or the particular profession they are studying (Carty 1991: 22; Sabattis 1996: 37);
- lack of appropriate field placements or supervisors (Sabattis 1996: 43);
- lack of appropriate high school preparation because of streaming and preconceived notions of Aboriginal and visible minority students' potential (Sabattis 1996: 66); and
- having professors assume they must have plagiarized others' work or had extra help because they couldn't possibly produce a paper as good as the one they wrote (Carty 1991: 14).

Other accounts apply to Aboriginal women and women of colour who enter the academy as faculty. The particular experiences include:

- disproportionate relegation to less secure, non-tenured and part-time academic positions (Bannerji 1991: 72; Tack and Patitu 1992: 1);
- being the only person of colour hired as a token (Calliste 2000: 150);
- complete lack of support from superiors, even to the point of deans and others backing white student complaints against them that would never be considered if made against other faculty (Tack and Patitu 1992: 1; Williams 1991: 21, 28–32, 97; Doyle-Bedwell 1997);
- public humiliation by colleagues or superiors (Calliste 2000: 146);
- negative, even hateful, student resistance in class and in teaching evaluations (Lorde 1982: 96; Bannerji 1991: 72–73; hooks 1994: 153–54; Williams 1991: 95–97; Graveline 1996: 328–36);
- white student complaints of bias, too much personal involvement, "pushing" political opinions, discriminating against them, making them feel unsafe or guilty, not teaching "real" law, or English, or whatever, even complaints about dress and jewellery (Ng 1993: 189, 191–193; Monture-Angus 1995b: 62, 66–67; Williams 1991: 21, 28; Doyle-Bedwell 1997);
- complaints from students that a minority professor did not teach a subject exactly the way a white professor did, assuming the white professor's approach to be correct (Monture-Angus 1995b: 61; Doyle-Bedwell 1997);
- physical and other threats from students (Ng 1993: 189; Williams 1991: 96);
- students' refusal to accept a low mark from an Aboriginal or visible minority professor (Monture-Angus 1995b: 66, 73; Doyle-Bedwell 1997);
- hostile comments in papers and on examinations (Monture-Angus 1995b: 62);
- an excessive workload because of being asked to represent a minority group on every committee, on every panel and in every collection of articles that come up, also because they are the only faculty member

with whom students from minority groups feel comfortable talking about their problems, or the only one who can supervise reading courses students want in order to fill the gaps in the curriculum (Monture-Angus 1995b: 55, 64);

• colleagues' resistance to including any perspective other than white ones in their teaching, and perceiving any suggestion that they do so as an attack on academic freedom (Monture-Angus 1995b: 63; Williams 1991: 84);

• having white students attack minority students because they are angry over what the professor is teaching (Monture-Angus 1995b: 63);

• seeing today's minority students experiencing the same problems they did as a student and realizing that there has been no progress (Carty 1991: 15; Monture-Angus 1995b: 65);

• discrimination in the promotion, re-appointment and tenure processes (Monture-Angus 1995b: 66);

• having a paper trail built of small or non-existent problems which is later used against them in evaluations, contract renewal or tenure and promotion applications (Calliste 2000: 154);

• being accused of putting ideas into minority students' heads, or coercing them to speak up about their experiences of racism (Graveline 1996: 314);

• and being told that students' respect for the school is reduced by your presence in a professor role (Williams 1991: 115).

Some experiences apply to women of colour and Aboriginal women in the university setting whether they are students or faculty. For example:

• racist social norms surrounding friendship and relationships (hooks 1994: 42; Sabattis 1996: 32);

• high community expectations of success and extensive service to the community (Sabattis 1996: 36);

• an expectation that written expression will be impersonal, analytic, and "objective" when many minority cultures value the opposite (Lorde 1982: 125–126; Williams 1991: 47–50, 92–95; Sabattis 1996: 37);

• research/writing in areas of concern to Aboriginal and visible minority people being seen as unimportant, not serious, biased or rhetorical rather than scholarly (Williams 1991: 47–50; Carty 1991: 14, 21; Bannerji 1991: 69; hooks 1994: 38; Sabattis 1996: 37; Doyle-Bedwell 1997);

• the expectation that all their opinions represent their group (hooks 1994: 42–43; Sabattis 1996: 41);

• the competition and individualism of academic work, which is sometimes in opposition to minority cultures (Sabattis 1996: 41);

• harassment by white students and faculty (Williams 1991: 21, 28–32, 97; Sabattis 1996: 43);

- racist slurs, jokes and stereotypes (Calliste 2000: 149, 151, 153);
- threats and assaults (Calliste 2000: 143);
- a classroom ethic that devalues experiential knowledge and the physical, spiritual and emotional aspects of life (Carty 1991: 36; Doyle-Bedwell 1997; hooks 1994: 7–8, 15–17, 135–138, 140–141, 145–146; Sabattis 1996: 45);
- lack of role models (Sabattis, 1996, 67);
- the loneliness of being the "only one" in a class, department, faculty, university (Bannerji 1991: 68–69; Carty 1991: 15; Jones 1993; Monture-Angus 1995b: 64; Sabattis 1996: 68; Williams 1991: 55);
- the pressure to become as similar as possible to white, middle-class people and support white, middle-class ideals (Bernard, Lucas-White and Moore 1981: 267; hooks 1994: 5);
- betrayal when some white allies discover the cost of real institutional change and withdraw their support (hooks 1994: 30; Calliste 2000: 146);
- constant realization that minority people's opinions are not taken seriously (Bannerji 1991: 69; Doyle-Bedwell 1997; hooks 1994: 39–40, 150; Calliste 2000: 143);
- facing other differences in perception because of working-class or low-income origins (hooks, 1994, 178, 182–185);
- the invisibility of racism to white faculty, students and administrators (Carty 1991: 14; Calliste 2000: 142; Monture-Angus 1995b: 62);
- being blamed for your own experiences of racism, labelled as "crazy" (Calliste 2000: 142, 145);
- the pain of encountering other members of minority groups who have chosen denial of racism and sexism as a survival mechanism (Monture-Angus 1995b: 58);
- characterization of minority people as angry, confrontative and tactless, even threatening and intimidating (Monture-Angus 1995b; 68; Williams 1991: 56–57);
- low expectations (Calliste 2000: 153);
- facing statements that the university would have to "lower its standards" to accept minority students or hire minority faculty (Williams 1991: 5, 155);
- tokenization; for example, "I wish our school could find more blacks like you" (Williams 1991: 9–10);
- having your ideas and voice stolen by white "experts" that suddenly emerge when funding is available to study minority communities (Calliste 2000: 156);
- the assumption that racism is just a matter of perception, or is "theoretical" or "abstract" (Williams 1991: 13);
- being told to laugh racism off, "you take it too seriously" (Williams 1991: 166);

- having everything you do noticed because you are visible (Williams 1991: 55–56);
- having to be excellent to be perceived as average (Sabattis 1996: 67);
- constant pain, fear, and anger (Doyle-Bedwell 1997; Lorde 1982: 124; Monture-Angus 1995b: 59, 68; Graveline 1996: 351); and
- being "perpetually tired from perpetual struggle" (Carty 1991: 16).

Patti Doyle-Bedwell vividly describes the struggle to resist internalizing the racist experience of the university:

> I do the Indian thing, I believe the pack of lies as the truth. The trauma of living in an oppressive society is believing the dominant society's image of who I am.
>
> Hearing the word Indian brings certain images to mind such as Squaw, drunk, stupid, savage, less than human. I have fought these images all my life. I am different but not less than others. These images shape the mainstream perception of my reality. I have internalized these images. I have learned that racism feels like being stabbed. The violence of racism feels like razor blade cuts all over my body. The bleeding continues and I feel so empty.
>
> It takes incredible courage to stand up in front of a class where no matter what I say, it is Mi'kmaq dribble. It takes incredible courage to say I am a law professor. Who do I think I am? That, I do not know. Why do I do the Indian thing and believe in their perception that I am incompetent as a teacher? I am frozen for many weeks. I am scared to even cry, for fear that I will never stop. (1997)

The Black and Native women at the centre of "The Story" expressed their experience of frequent small attacks on their right to participate in the institution. They carried their own "ton of feathers." Some examples of these undermining incidents were:

- the Community Specialty Coordinator's failing mark on Hannah's paper, despite her apparent approval of it when the class discussed it, approval of it by Hannah's classmates and tutor, and Hannah's re-writing of it in accordance with the Community Specialty Coordinator's criticisms;
- accusations of plagiarism and self-plagiarism, once against Laura, twice against Beth and a formal accusation against Hannah that went to the Senate Discipline Committee, only to be dismissed in five minutes;
- the Bachelor's Field Placement Coordinator's discussion of Beth's and Laura's field placements with their supervisors and placement of notes on these conferences in their files without telling them or their

supervisors, despite a policy that students should be included in such discussion and informed of notes placed in their files;
• the Chair of the Equality Committee's questioning of the honesty of the students who spoke in the Circle on Discriminatory Harassment and accusing Lillian of coercing the students, inciting them and putting words in their mouths;
• the rumours that the students "cried racism" to excuse a poor academic record.

In the struggle by women and people of colour to gain access to the university, there has been progress over the centuries. However, the evidence still points to powerful structural barriers and recognizable patterns in the institution's mechanisms for undermining the newcomers and their knowledge.

Progress and Backlash

The women at the centre of "The Story" were working to make their Department and University more open to people of Black and Native descent and culture. They were not the first to do this. Over the past few decades many pioneers from both groups had worked to make university education more accessible for their communities. As well, both Canadian University and the Department had invested time, energy and resources into increasing access for women and students from minority groups.

One of the things that makes "The Story" interesting to me is the number of women involved in the higher ranks of the University at the time. Canadian University has been the scene of a long, slow struggle for women seeking equal participation. This battle is by no means won, but just before the events in question white women had made some break-throughs in entering the hierarchy of the University above the level of professor. The first female dean was appointed the year before Lillian started teaching in the Department. The deans involved in this story were the first, second and third female deans at the University. The Academic Vice-President was the first woman to hold a position at that level in the institution as well. She had been in that position for only a year when she played her role in the events recounted in "The Story." As a result, all the key decision-makers below the level of the President were women, a very new and unusual situation at this University.

The central women in "The Story" were not alone in their efforts either. There were many others scattered across the campus—students, faculty and those in support roles, such as the Employment Equity Officer and the Black and Native Student Counsellors. There was also the history of the Department—twenty-five years of an affirmative action admittance policy and a series of programs aimed at increasing access for women and minority groups. Many in the Department, including those in decision-making roles, cared deeply about these efforts. It was this history that brought the Black, Native and immigrant players in "The Story" into the Department in the first place and made them feel that their viewpoint would be welcome. For some reason, however, their efforts to make change were different from previous ones. They triggered an institutional backlash while other change efforts had not. Why?

In Chapter Five I asked this question: What kinds of change will institutions tolerate, and what kinds of change do they find threatening? I proposed this answer: an institution's self-interest lies in the preservation of its own essence, which comes from its history and is expressed in its deepest values and structures, particularly its methods of granting, maintaining and regulating power. In a large and complex institution, there is great scope for change that is not threatening, change that helps individuals but does not touch the institution's essence. In other words, it is "token" change. When change does touch the institution's essence by challenging its deepest values and structure, the institution will defend itself.

If my propositions are correct, this group of students and faculty caused the University to react as if its essence were threatened—its essence as expressed in its values and structure, particularly its methods of granting, maintaining and regulating power. I suspect one of two things happened: either this particular group of students and faculty succeeded in challenging the way they were traditionally de-valued and shifted power just a little—enough to cross the line from reform to structural transformation, from token change to a real re-distribution of power and benefits—or the cumulative effect of all the past changes had made this institution ready to react to the slightest next step. In order to consider these two possible triggers of institutional response, I think it is important to consider the difference between reform and structural transformation, and examine the role of the token.

Tokens

Institutions do not change in a vacuum. Although the institution creates a "chilly climate" for those that have been excluded for centuries by reason of gender and race, it can go along for many years completely unconscious of the situation, just as individuals are often oblivious of their privilege. It is used to doing things in a certain way and sees no bias in these "normal" activities and attitudes. The voices of those who complain are easily written off because of their lack of legitimacy in the institution to begin with.

At some point, however, the pressures begin to accumulate. Sometimes the change is forced from the outside. For example, a regulatory or funding body or a court of law requires the institution to make room for those that have been excluded in the past. Sometimes people within the institution who come from once-excluded groups organize for further change. Sometimes, changing mores in the surrounding culture simply exert pressure.

By necessity, these changes are small to begin with—a statement of intent, promises to a pressure group or regulatory body, new policies, a change in the language of a vision statement, the hiring of the first member of the most recent group to challenge its exclusion. For some, these small steps are a start, and their expectation is that the process will continue. For others, including the institution itself, the "first steps" are token gestures, intended only to stop the critique without making real change. Once the reforms are in place, the institution tries to carry on as normally as possible. Life, however, has changed completely for the "tokens," those first members of the excluded group to be accepted into the institution.

When I attempted to track the sociological concept of the token to its source, I discovered the work of Rosabeth Moss Kanter, particularly the published version of her PhD thesis, *Men and Women of the Corporation* (1977). She uses these definitions: a "uniform" group is made up entirely of one social type (100:0); a "balanced" group is made up of two social groups in roughly equal numbers (50:50); a "tilted" group has a preponderance of one social group, that is, a "majority" and a "minority" (65:35); a "skewed" group is made up of one social group with a few representatives of a minority group (from 99:1 to about 85:15). The majority is the "dominant" group; the few representatives of the minority group are called "tokens" (209).

As we saw in Chapter Five, Kanter has a structural view of organizational dynamics. She believes that individual behaviour can never be understood without understanding the context, particularly the person's relationship to structures of power, influence, status and potential for movement up or down the "ladder of success," as defined by the person and the organization. She also believes that no individual action can be understood without its context in time, in relation to the past and the predicted future. Individuals' behaviour in organizations reflects what they can do to accomplish material comfort, satisfaction and dignity within the limits of their situation. These actions are strategic and rational in context. Behaviour is not mechanically inevitable but a response chosen within a certain latitude of freedom. Organizations do not control so much as they limit, define and reward with opportunity and power (250–53).

Kanter believes that organizational change cannot come about from analysis based on individual behaviour and change. In fact, such analysis frees organizations from taking responsibility for shaping the actions of individuals, and pits people against each other instead of pointing to their joint interest in change. In an individual behaviour model, people are encouraged to compete for scarce resources rather than change systems to benefit many more people. Organizational change, according to Kanter, comes from structural change models, particularly those that pay attention to opportunity, power and numbers (261–4).

According to Kanter, numerical relationships influence social interaction, and therefore, the implications for an individual of being in a token position are immense (207). In the first place, a token is visible; his or her strengths show up better, sometimes causing others to be jealous, even in some cases bringing on retaliation (217). Mistakes show up as well, creating strong performance pressure. The token is always a "test case," measured not only against work standards, but also against the stereotypes the dominant group holds of his or her group (214). The token is not allowed to be just an individual, but must become a symbol, representative and spokesperson. This can cause the token to become trapped in his or her role in a way that a member of the dominant group would never be. It can cause exhaustion, as the token tries to keep up with the pressures of visibility, along with the necessity of representing his or her group on every committee in the organization (210–11).

On the other side, the presence of the token makes the dominant group more aware of its commonalties as a group and anxious to preserve these features, causing a tendency to exaggerate them and heighten the cultural boundaries (234–36). The dominant group constantly tests the loyalty of the token, forcing him or her to laugh at derogatory jokes, accept harassment, refrain from expressing criticism or requests, turn against his or her own group and act in a manner that excludes others of his or her kind. This gives the dominant group the impression that members of the token group are always fighting each other (228–29).

According to Kanter, when there are two tokens, the dominant group prevents them from acting in solidarity. One is designated as superior, the other inferior; one a success, the other a failure; one a "good" token, and the other a "bad" token (237).

The advantages and disadvantages of the two groups become internalized and institutionalized. The tokens, punished for both success and failure, can develop behaviour that reflects their lack of power. This can increase their disadvantage, while members of the dominant group adopt behaviour in line with their aspirations and get promoted for it (158). People in a token position become less committed to the work, not because of their character but because of the structural nature of their position. Ironically, the organization sometimes decides not to bring in more of the token's group, because they aren't successful, when, in fact, more members of the group would solve the problem (172).

Rosabeth Moss Kanter has written and produced a video for diversity training, called *A Tale of 'O': On Being Different* (1993). In the film she expands on her earlier work. She defines the choices a token has for survival—overachievement (with the ensuing risk of exhaustion), imitation of the dominant group or hiding behind a member of the dominant group and giving this person credit for the token's work. She also expands her description of the two-token situation. After the dominant group labels one token "good" and the other "bad," it has a tendency to treat them in opposite, but equally destructive ways. The "good" token is overprotected, not allowed to take risks. Since risk is the basis of advancement in organizations, the "good" token is rarely allowed to advance or advances at an unusually slow pace. The "bad" token, on the other hand, is overexposed, put through extra tests. The dominant people wait for this person to fail, then punish him or her and conclude that he or she "just couldn't make it."

Kanter's analysis in *The Tale of 'O'* may describe Lillian's position in the Department. There were two faculty members in what Kanter would define as token positions, Lillian and the Department's one Black professor. I don't know the Black professor's story well enough to judge whether or not her treatment fits Kanter's description of the "good" token, and she was absent when "The Story" took place. However, when I encountered Kanter's description of the "good" token/"bad" token dynamic, I couldn't help comparing two incidents in "The Story." During the meeting of the Equality Committee following the Open Talking Circle on Discriminatory Harassment, Lillian reported that the committee chair accused her of inciting the Native and Black students, putting words in their mouths. In contrast, during the meeting to resolve the conflict in the Practice of Community Work course, the Department Head and the Dean of Health noted that the Department's Black professor would be returning the next fall and could sort the situation out.

The patterns that form around tokens make their life in the institution very uncomfortable. In an essay titled "Surviving the Contradictions: Personal Notes on Academia," in the Chilly Climate collection, Patricia Monture-Angus writes:

> When I considered my hesitation [to writing an Introduction for this book], I realized it was at least partially resistance to the "why ask me again" syndrome. I am offended by colleagues who would like to ask me to do something but they feel their asking puts an extraordinary burden on me. Not being involved can leave me feeling isolated or inadequate. Not being involved often means that there are no Aboriginal women involved, and that has particular consequences. This is only one of the contradictions where I can be caught. I know that this dilemma is not the creation of my colleagues but that it is the result of the systemic exclusion of Aboriginal Women (and other women of colour) from universities. The under-representation of members of equality-seeking communities within Canadian universities has particular consequences for the first few members of these groups to claim previously forbidden positions. This is even more disturbing

in institutions that have a commitment to equity. The demands on these few professors sends our quality of life into an irreversible tailspin. (1995b: 12)

Benjamin Bowser, Gale Auletta and Terry Jones (1993), speaking from Black male and white female perspectives in a United States context, describe their choices as tokens:

> There is nothing more degrading than feeling the bite of racial exclusion and put-downs made by even the most well-intended white colleagues. The victim of such behavior has three no-win choices. First, he or she can mention the offense in conversation, but this not only violates the middle-class European-American's social rule of politeness but also presents additional costs: Besides being considered rude and possibly maladjusted, the injured party usually will be ignored, excluded, or labeled a troublemaker from then on. Second, he or she can avoid speaking up. Say nothing long enough, however, and the victim is left to struggle with mounting internal anger, pain, doubt, and blame. Third, he or she can disassociate from other people of color and work toward being accepted as an individual apart from his or her race. This approach also has its price. The individual is never perceived simply as such. At best, this "honorary white" status lasts only as long as he or she is seen to be like a real white person and supports white interests. (16–17)

In spite of "violating the European-Americans' social rule of politeness" and the daunting "additional costs," some people in token positions make the choice to speak up and organize for change. Others who are part of the dominant group make the decision to support them as allies. The women at the centre of events in "The Story" were experienced and effective social change agents. They organized themselves and others, found and used all the existing channels of communication with those who held power and found out and used the institution's policies. For example, they re-organized the Equality Committee to be sure it had the representatives it was supposed to have on all the other committees. When the Committee's advocacy on behalf of students became part of the informal discipline procedure against Lillian, they re-organized the committee so student advocacy was carried out by members external to the University. They researched and wrote briefs proposing new policy and practice for Native students' field placements and a policy giving students the right to take a support person to meetings with professors and administrators. They rallied support from external organizations, external and internal allies and used every existing channel for complaints. Lillian relied on her

Faculty Association Representative as an advisor and advocate. Her peda-gogy also did not treat social change as a theory but engaged students in action.

Almost a decade after the events recounted in "The Story," "Beth" wrote to me that collective organization for structural change was second nature to the Native students. She said:

> I think that another factor in why we acted as a group is in part due to not being used to being "individuals," because Native communities are very organized around the Collective rights over individual ones. There is an intrinsic sense of community and taking action against things that affect others. There is a commit-ment to making things better for the next seven generations that people take very seriously in everything that they do. I think that this is what keeps me fighting for change. I was as angry that this could happen to any "non-mainstream" person as I was angry that it was happening to me personally. (Personal communication)

The institution had accommodated changes—growing numbers of women as both students and faculty, a smaller number of disabled people, openly gay/lesbian people and people of colour, affirmative action admission policies—but at this point, it suddenly increased its resistance. It responded with a backlash.

Backlash: Change has "Gone Too Far"

I have encountered definitions of "backlash" in both literature and conversation that imply it is simply a synonym for institutional resistance to change. I would argue that its meaning is more specific, that it happens when an institution makes a sudden, energetic effort to reverse change. It has always put up resistance but has also accepted change to a certain point. It then balks because it somehow perceives the change as having "gone too far."

The question is, what, in the perception of an institutional entity, is "going too far"? Backlash could be like the spring-back action of a stretched elastic. The change accumulates to a certain point—new policies are adopted and implemented, a formerly excluded group is admitted and its numbers increase until a critical mass is reached, the newly admitted group becomes less willing to behave as tokens and expectations of equality rise—until suddenly the institution hits the limit of its capacity to accept change and snaps back.

Another institutional definition of "going too far" could be the point where the institution grasps the cost involved in change. In an article exploring the reasons organizations avoid equity conflict, management professors and consultants Anne Donnellon and Deborah M. Kolb (1994) discuss the high cost of conflict over diversity issues, both emotional and financial. If the conflict is suppressed, the costs are borne by one side—the victims. If the conflict is dealt with openly and fairly and a resolution is found, the costs are borne by both sides.

My guess is that "going too far" is not just a matter of change accumulating to a certain point, numbers of formerly excluded people reaching a critical mass or a sudden realization of the cost, but rather the point where the change threatens to become structural in nature. An institution can handle a large number of individuals from a new group as long as they function as individuals, accommodating themselves to the institution's habitual way of doing things. However, when the newcomers and their allies become organized to the point where they are putting pressure on the institution's deep values and power-structure, that is a different matter. Many of the strategies listed above—researched policy proposals, activating the hollow shells of committees or other bodies with the potential to make change, using channels that have previously existed only in theory and mobilizing pressure from allies and external organizations—are all strategies with the potential for structural transformation. They can take token change—change of language, intent and public face, change at the individual level, reform—and turn it into a real transformation of the purpose, values and power structure of the institution. I suspect this is what happened when the Board of Governors of Canadian University drew a line on behalf of the institution by rejecting the proposed policy on discriminatory harassment. The next day, Lillian's class tried to create a safe setting for some of the people most affected by this policy decision to talk about their experiences. The setting turned out not to be safe. The Talking Circle became an institutional event as well. A line was crossed. Backlash was triggered.

Serious Misconception Number One: Oppression Is Either Present or It Is Not

On the level of the institutional entity, I believe that an important trigger for backlash is the point when change crosses the line from reform to transformation of the institution's deepest structure and values. On the individual level, an important trigger seems to be the perception on the part of those who hold power in the institution that they are being personally accused of moral wrong. This reaction, as far as I can see, comes from two assumptions: the dualistic notion that oppression is either present or it is not, and the idea that, when one is deciding whether or not oppression is present, intention counts more than impact.

I think the assumption that oppression is either present or not was expressed several times during the events of "The Story." During the meeting to deal with the student complaints, the Dean of Health called the Department "the flagship of affirmative action in the Faculty," and asked why the students weren't complaining about other departments that had not even begun to deal with issues of access for minority students. She seemed to be saying that the Department did not deserve criticism because of the efforts it had already made and might even have been suggesting that a Department with an affirmative action admittance policy could not be the site of discriminatory treatment.

During the hearing to consider whether or not Lillian's grievance would go to arbitration, it seemed to me that the Board of Governor's lawyer made an even clearer statement of this assumption. He argued that it was impossible for the Department to discriminate because they had taken steps against racism, such as the affirmative action admittance policy and the hiring of a Black faculty member. He referred to "the ridiculous allegations that this [Department], which is the opposite of racist, be accused of these things." In her testimony during the same hearing, the Department Head said: "I don't think [these allegations] have any relevance to the [Department]. I would argue instead that the [Department] has had a long record of affirmative action, staff training in regard to minority groups and has tried to develop its curriculum to include women and minorities. I would argue that we have a long list of accomplishments. I don't think this has any relevance to the [Department]." In these statements, I heard the dualistic assumption that an equitable institution is the opposite of a discriminatory one. There seemed to be no understanding of the slow, complex, difficult and uneven process of achieving equity.

Dualistic assumptions run deep in Western culture. The twentieth-century physicists who explored quantum theory found that the English language was not adequate to describe their discoveries because it is too committed to dualism. We tend to think in mutually exclusive categories: bad or good, subjective or objective. We also thought an electron had to be either a wave or a particle, but quantum physics showed that it could be a wave and a particle. Physicist Neils Bohr remarked that English forces us to use concepts that simply do not work in the new paradigm of science. In order to talk about the quantum world, we have to use "complementary, mutually contradictory, accounts" (quoted in Peat 1994: 233). David Bohm said that to describe a reality that was not made up of objects in interaction, but continuous movement, unfolding and enfolding, we had to lose our dichotomies between "inner and outer, mental and physical, subjective and objective, for all are aspects of one underlying movement" (quoted in Peat 1994: 237). Bohm speculated that we need a new sort of language, based on verbs, to describe processes, activity, transformation and change. He called his hypothetical language the "rheomode."

Physicist David Peat has spent many years comparing the new worldview of twentieth-century physics with the traditional Aboriginal worldview. A few months before Bohm's death, Peat arranged for him to meet with several speakers of the Algonkian family of languages (Blackfoot, Mi'kmaq, Cree and Anishnabe). Bohm discovered that the language he had imagined already exists, for these languages are verb-based (Peat 1994: 238). The reason the Algonkian languages, along with other First Nations languages, are verb-based is because the Indigenous peoples of the Americas see the world as constantly in transformation.

The nature of our English language bears testimony to our Western commitment to dualistic thinking and a worldview that involves only interactions among objects or individuals. No wonder we have trouble grasping the process of movement toward equity. We continually slip back into thinking that we, and our institutions, are either oppressive (bad) or equitable (good).

Serious Misconception Number Two: Intent Counts More than Impact

A related assumption concerns how one can tell whether or not oppression is present. It says that oppression cannot be present where people do not intend to discriminate. Kate Kirkham, a professor at Brigham Young University, calls this response "over-personalization." In an article on classroom discussion of racism and sexism, she says:

> When asked to respond to the question of who really is racist and/ or sexist, many majority group individuals, in my research and teaching experience, assume: "If I didn't intend something as racist or sexist then it is not racist/sexist." In other words, the general criteria they use in testing for racism/sexism is an overpersonalized one. They believe that personal motive deter-mines the presence of racism or sexism in interactions. (1988–89: 51)

Jennifer Bankier, former chair of the Status of Women Committee of the Canadian Association of University Teachers, has written about the important role this assumption plays in triggering backlash. In a 1996 article she describes the destructive cycle of reactions triggered by an equity complaint in a university setting. She names the central cause as the failure of academics to understand that discrimination is a matter of impact, not intent.

Bankier's description of the cycle consists of five steps. In Step 1, the members of an equity-seeking group (Group X) name their experience of discrimination in good faith. In Step 2, the members of the dominant group (Group Z) react with "surprise, shock, pain and sometimes fear." If they have forgotten, or never knew, that discrimination can be uninten-tional, they equate an accusation of "X-ism" with moral evil. Step 3 is divided into two possibilities: Step 3a, Group Z listens to and accepts that their practices are unintentionally harming Group X and proceed to work out a solution together; or Step 3b, "demonization." Bankier describes Group Z's demonization logic like this:

> I didn't want to hurt anyone, therefore I didn't hurt anyone. The complainant(s) are making this up! They're covering up their own inferiority at my expense! We never had any trouble until these particular member(s) of Group X came here. There isn't any general problem of discrimination against Group X. It's just that these particular members of Group X are bad people. I'm dealing with an evil monster, a demon. Therefore, I'm justified in taking any defensive measures I can think of. If we could get rid of these particular, destructive member(s) of Group X then we could all live happily ever after. Now, what's the most effective way to defend myself and perform an X-orcism? (1996: 4–5)

In Step 4, the members of Group X, who may have originally understood that the discrimination they experienced was unintentional, are now being persecuted by Group Z. They decide that everything is intentional after all and take action to defend themselves, including further complaints of intentional persecution. Bankier names Step 5 the "Tornado of Fire" and describes how each group seeks outside allies, with Group Z usually having more powerful and influential allies than Group X, including the university's administration. If the administration joins in the "X-orcism," as they may if they have no understanding of equity dynamics, they will, according to Bankier, make a terrible mistake. Whether they succeed or fail, they will inflame the situation further, and once Group X is outside of the institution, they will have nothing more to lose and may take legal action or involve their communities outside of the university.

As Bankier points out, the liberal notion that intent counts more than impact seems to play a major role in the outrage and betrayal experienced by institutional power-holders when those who experience discrimination in their institutions speak out. There may have been specific incidents of abuse of institutional power, but even if this is not the case, they seem to hear the stories of those who experience institutional discrimination as a personal accusation, aimed at them. Believing that discrimination cannot take place where there is no intention to discriminate, combined with the dualistic notion that oppression is either present or it is not, makes them prone to turn blame on those who make the issue visible. They are likely to, in Marie Fortune's words, "misname the problem," "blame the victim" and "shoot the messenger" (Fortune 1989: 120–22).

Earlier in this chapter, I recalled the meeting to deal with the student complaints, where the Dean of Health called the Department "the flag-ship of affirmative action in the Faculty" and asked why the students weren't complaining about other departments that had not even begun to deal with issues of access for minority students. I speculated that she may have been assuming the dualistic notion that discrimination had either to be present in the Department or not. The same comment could have come from the assumption that discrimination cannot be present where there is a clear demonstration of good intentions to eradicate it.

The Department Head's repeated allegation that Lillian was "too negative" may have come from the same assumption—that good intentions (that is, the Department's efforts to be accessible) count more than impact (that is, the minority students' experience of structural inequality in the Department). In my work as an adult educator, I frequently engage students in role-plays. In my experience, whenever I include a character with a structural view of the issue under consideration, my students, almost all of whom see the world through the lens of liberal ideology, label that character's viewpoint as "negative." I have come to see the word as a linguistic mechanism used by those with a liberal view to blame structural injustice on the individual who points it out.

A related term is "over-sensitive." The thinking seems to be that social ills cannot be present when there are well-intentioned people involved, so the person pointing them out must be "over-sensitive" or looking at the world from a particularly "negative" viewpoint. The irony in this is that those who are using the terms in this way could be said to demonstrate "over-sensitivity" and a "negative" viewpoint by hearing structural analysis as personal accusation. Kate Kirkham says this about her classroom discussions of racism and sexism:

> Many of the majority group members, who had been quick to label a minority group member as over-sensitive, became more aware of how their own version of over-sensitivity was showing up with just as much emotional conviction behind it. (1988–89: 51)

As I will show later in this chapter, I think these two related assumptions, that oppression is either present or it is not and that oppression is judged by intent rather than impact, play an important role in the triggering of institutional backlash. In this belief I am agreeing with Jennifer Bankier's analysis of the manner in which a "Tornado of Fire" comes about.

"Second Stage" Anti-Racism

The assumption that oppression cannot be present where there are good intentions to eliminate it completely denies the real process of institutional change. According to chaos theory, as discussed in Chapter Six, the boundaries crossed during change processes are not linear, but fractal. Steady progress cannot be expected, but rather wild fluctuations.

One could also say that when the first steps toward change are taken, by an institution or an individual, the deeper levels of structural oppression come to the fore; when the deliberate forms of discrimination are cleared away, the structural roots become more visible.

Robert Wright, former Race Relations Officer for the Dartmouth, Nova Scotia, School Board, says that, in his experience, the teachers who worked to learn anti-racist practice were the most likely to be accused of racism. This is because they grasped anti-racist principles enough to take risks; for example, teaching controversial material and encouraging open discussion of racism among students. The process of teaching about racism inevitably raised strong feelings among the students and usually conflict as well. As a result, these teachers were more likely than their colleagues to be accused of racism by Black students, their parents and communities. The teachers would reject the allegation, because they had clearly progressed farther than other teachers in their anti-racist practice. Their reaction—of hurt, betrayal and defensiveness—created an opening for the school board and the media to react against the students and parents with the full force of institutionalized racism. The students, their parents and community members were portrayed as irrational, "over-sensitive" and "negative," and were punished for it.

Even if the individual faced with the accusation did not become defensive, the institution would often do it on his or her behalf. The assumption was that the parents and students were "biting the hand that fed them," proving their irrationality and extremism by attacking the very teacher who had been working against racism in the school. Wright referred to this as the "second stage" of anti-racist practice, that is, learning about the nature of backlash. He feels that anti-racism educators need to better prepare white allies for this stage when it comes. By introducing them only to the first stage of anti-racist practice, without warning them about the second stage, we betray them (Personal communication, 1998).

In my opinion, there is a strong parallel between Wright's description of what happens to anti-racist teachers and the events recounted in "The Story." I think it is precisely because the Department had so clearly demonstrated its desire to challenge oppression, over a long period of time, that the Native and Black students went beyond gratitude for being accepted as tokens and assumed that, if they pointed out how they could be made more equal with other students, the Department would want to act on the information. It is because of the Department's challenging of discrimination that so many Native and Black students, along with the two pioneering professors, were present in the Department in the first place. I think the great irony of the situation is that it was because they criticized this Department, a leader in anti-oppressive practice in the University, that the rest of the institution saw backlash as a legitimate response.

Serious Misconception Number Three:
An Oppressed Group Does Not Oppress

There is another serious misconception about discrimination that seemed to play a role in triggering backlash at Canadian University; that is, the assumption that one oppressed group will not oppress another. In "The Story," the dynamics of race (as opposed to gender) are fairly clear because many of those that implemented the institution's strategies for resistance to change, at least on the front lines, were women. Not only were they women, but they were, for the most part, self-declared feminists who participated in white women's struggles for access to the University.

A number of visible minority and Aboriginal women comment on the lack of sensitivity they experienced from feminists in relation to issues of race; for example, Monture-Angus (1995a and b), Calliste (2000) and Carty (1991). Himani Bannerji tells of her deep disappointment when she realized most feminists did not see racism as an issue (1991: 71). Her whole chapter, "Who Speaks For Us?" is about the absence of women of colour from feminist academic work (1991: 67–108). bell hooks dedicates three chapters of *Teaching to Transgress* (1994), and two other volumes, *Ain't I a Woman? Black Women and Feminism* (1981) and *Feminist Theory: From Margin to Center* (1984), to the struggle between women of colour drawn to feminism and white feminists. Patricia Monture-Angus points out (1995b) that her experience results from both of her marginalizations—as a woman and as a First Nations person. These two aspects of experience, she says, are often inseparable. Linda Carty also writes:

> As many Black, South Asian, Native and Asian feminists have long stated, we do not share any common experience of oppression with white women from which it could be possible to theorize 'a feminist standpoint' and assume a unity of social relations in feminism. As a Black woman, my sisters and I continually ... find it ludicrous that seemingly well-intentioned feminists ... cannot (or are unwilling to) understand that we cannot be female or Black, we are female and Black. For us the two are one and the same, we do not have a choice. As Black women we experience our femaleness and Blackness together, always at the same time, and we challenge whether it is possible for white women to be white or female because we see them as white and female. (Carty 1991: 31)

Why are white women, including those who intellectually grasp the parallels among different forms of oppression, sometimes closed to understanding racism when confronted with it directly? I think part of the reason is that our understanding of the relationship between sexism and racism is often shallow. These are not just two entities, which can be added together for women of colour and taken apart again when we want to make common cause. Sexism and racism have developed together in a specific historical context. Both people of colour and white women have been exploited to the benefit of capitalism and white men, particularly elite-class white men, but in different ways. In the process, we have been played off against each other. For example, in various times and places, white women have been frightened into accepting white men as their protectors, to the point of losing their own independence, by the myth that men of colour are sexual predators. Another example is the relationship between upper-class white women and people of colour in the role of servants. Although both were once legally the property of white men, they experienced extremely different types of treatment. The white woman in such a situation was often completely dependent on the servants, even to raise her children, and yet was the one who gave the orders in the house.

As a result of the complex inter-twining of gender and race through the last few centuries, racism is experienced differently by men and women of colour because of sexism, and sexism is experienced differently by white women and women of colour because of race. Women of colour are far ahead of white women in their analysis of these relationships. Until white women catch up, we will continue to trip over our too-simplistic analysis when we encounter issues of race.

Another part of the answer to the question of why white women, including feminists, are unable to grasp our racism lies, I believe, in a general belief that those who are themselves oppressed know better than to oppress others. In fact, it is the opposite that seems to be true: we learn to oppress others through our own experience of oppression. In *Becoming an Ally*, I explored the work of Alice Miller and Arno Gruen, both psychotherapists who searched for the origin of cruelty in the conventions of Western child rearing. They propose that we learn the oppressor role through our own experience of oppression, especially when we are children. The pain of childhood experiences of powerlessness, if left unhealed, they argue, can lead to loss of feeling and empathy, and a quest for self-protection by using power to control others (Bishop 2002: 60–75).

Margaret Green (1993) goes even further in her analysis of the relationship of women's oppressed and oppressor roles. She writes about her experience as a therapist leading anti-racism workshops with white women. She concludes that our experience of oppression in childhood provides "fertile ground in which the unconscious roots of racism develop and are allowed to flourish" (179). When childhood curiosity brings improbable responses, such as "they're no different from us," or "he's black because he's covered in chocolate," accompanied by tension or anger, our curiosity is discouraged, and we experience the pain of lies from adults we love and trust. Many children also experience pain and powerlessness when they try to stand up to injustice. Later, when we are adults, this pain can result in projection of fears or idealization onto people of colour.

Green explains that when white women are accused of racism, we become guilty and defensive, but underneath that is rage at what we perceive to be an unjustified attack. Any perceived attack raises feelings from past unjustified attacks experienced because as women we are also targets of oppression. When white women work on ourselves as oppressors in racism, Green notes that we must go back again and again to our experience of oppression as women. She even finds that specific forms of oppression are connected; for example, during her workshops, a woman having trouble when her job involved welcoming new immigrants discovered the pain of never feeling welcome in her own family, where she had been "an accident"; women who admitted feeling that Black people are stupid discovered their own feeling of stupidity as a result of their oppression; and women who felt that Black people are more sexual than white people discovered their own sexual repression and self-hatred.

According to Green, our repressed pain emerges as re-enactment, either seeking re-victimization for ourselves or passing on the hurt to someone less powerful. Society's major oppressions provide a socially acceptable way of projecting negative self-esteem and channelling hurtful behaviour. As white women, it takes much more than an intellectual understanding of racism to overcome it, we have to successfully see, take responsibility for, and heal our own pain before we will truly be able to function successfully as allies and stop perpetuating racism.

The Cornwall Collective (1980) thinks that feminists fail to grasp racism because we do not understand its structural nature. We hold to our liberal assumptions about individual effort and good intentions, while continuing to reproduce oppressive structures. Even though the women's theological programs they examine in their book are race-conscious and have the best of intentions, the authors give multiple examples of how the women's programs continue to "mirror the dominant system," including incorporating the dominant system's racism. We fail to realize, they say, that individual "repentance" does not bring about societal change:

> A theology of individual sin and individual salvation prevents us from addressing systemic issues because it implies that if we "repent" (recognize the evils caused by racism and sincerely want change), we can claim to be non-racist (individual salvation results from individual repentance). To make such a claim denies the systemic reality (which, theologically speaking, involves corporate sin and corporate salvation), and in so doing short-circuits any steps we might make toward lasting change. (43)

Elsewhere in the chapter they say: "Only if we can say the 'I' — 'I am a racist' — will we be able to move beyond a liberalism that adopts the language of equality but maintains the structure of oppression" (41). In other words, we must accept our responsibility for changing our structural context. Most of the institutional power-holders in "The Story" were women, pioneers in advancing the participation of women at Canadian University. They also grasped the parallels among oppressions well enough to be pioneers in establishing affirmative action policies for minorities on campus. This may have played a role in the way they interpreted and acted upon allegations of racism. As I observed the events, it seemed that the female decision-makers' history of fighting against sexism and racism contributed to their reluctance to see allegations of structural injustice as valid.

Tactics of Backlash

There are a variety of institutional tactics involved in backlash. Susan Prentice (1996) took on a research project for the Canadian Women's Studies Association comparing incidents of backlash against the women in various Canadian universities who drew public attention to the "chilly climate" issues. She listed some of the institutional tactics: critiques of the methodology of the "chilly climate" reports, denial of the problem, appeals to proceduralism, subversion of equity procedures to de-legitimize the complainants, re-attribution of the problem from the institution to those making the complaint and demonization of those who raise the issues.

The writers of the essays in the Chilly Collective collection (1995) expand upon this list. Their stories include accounts of their universities:

- opening employment equity or sexual harassment offices and hiring officers with the purpose of directing the discontent into safe channels (Wylie 1995: 46; Michell and Backhouse 1995: 137);
- issuing public relations statements listing everything the university has ever done for women, touting the progress that has been made (Wylie 1995: 46);
- claiming that the discrimination is a thing of the past or the doing of people who are now gone (Wylie 1995: 47);
- ignoring reports and briefs (Wylie 1995: 47);
- attacking the methodology of the reports, particularly the fact that the complainants are anonymous and the sample is small (Wylie 1995: 50; Michell and Backhouse 1995: 137);
- accusing the writers of the "chilly climate" reports of looking for attention or trying to create a "media event" (Wylie 1995: 50; Michell and Backhouse 1995: 140);
- blaming those who point out the tension for causing it in the first place (Michell and Backhouse 1995: 138; McIntyre 1995: 216);
- reducing discrimination to a matter of perception (Backhouse 1995: 75);
- putting the onus on the victims to prove the discrimination with "hard

evidence" (Backhouse 1995: 76);

- claiming that nothing can be done because of shrinking budgets (Backhouse 1995: 77);
- attacking verbally, in private and in public (Michell and Backhouse 1995: 140);
- crying out about the implications for male faculty reputations (Michell and Backhouse 1995: 138, 148);
- quoting women who disagree with the reports (Michell and Backhouse 1995: 150–51);
- isolating and vilifying those publicly associated with "chilly climate" reports (Michell and Backhouse 1995: 152–153);
- claiming that the university's traditions are inviolable (President's Advisory Committee on the Status of Women, University of Saskatchewan 1995: 180);
- attempting to distinguish feminists, that is "extremists," from other women (President's Advisory Committee on the Status of Women, University of Saskatchewan 1995: 192);

They also experienced attacks from colleagues in the form of public and private verbal attacks (Michell and Backhouse 1995:140), threats (MacIntyre 1995:236) and hate mail (McIntyre 1995:213).

A female scholar in the United States, Athena Theodore, carried out more than ten years of research on academic women who brought complaints against the administrations of their universities to external agencies or the courts. Between 1970 and 1983 she surveyed 470 such women. Even though their experiences took place twenty years earlier than the events recounted in "The Story" and the issue was sexism rather than the mix of sexism, racism, heterosexism and class we encountered, their accounts provide strong parallels to Lillian's experience.

Theodore reports that all of the women she surveyed experienced harassment as a result of making their complaints public. Some were "irritating … actions that may or may not appear to bear directly on the sex discrimination issue" (1986: 152). I think a similar incident in Lillian's story is the memo she received after using the computer in the Department office. The women in Theodore's study were accused of being "assertive and unladylike … abrasive, aggressive, demanding and contentious" (153). Lillian's parallel experience, in my opinion, was being called "negative," "not constructive" and "undermining." Theodore found it common that the women she studied were accused of being "non-collegial" and had this label used against them in disciplinary, tenure and promotion procedures (169–75), an experience Lillian shared.

The women in Theodore's study were "scolded, chided, and berated as being irresponsible." For example, administrators make remarks like "I regret this action on your part," or "I expect that you, as one with administrative experience, would automatically discuss with me any event that has an impact on the department and the college." One respondent received a letter from an administrator saying: "I have told you before (and it's a matter of record) to stay in channels. This allows me to keep track of you and your needs and to help you rectify, or better yet, prevent the time-consuming situations in which you manage to involve yourself, me, and other departmental personnel"(153). The tone of several of the letters Lillian received strikes me as similar to these quotes. For example: "This is disappointing, especially when I hoped and many of us hoped, that your appointment to faculty would help us build on what has been accomplished and move forward in the area of cross-cultural and anti-discriminatory theory and practice. We have talked about most of these issues on more than one occasion and I am willing to do so again. If, however, I cannot soon see progress, then I will have [to] consider referring these matters to the Dean for disciplinary action," and "I have asked many times to talk with you, [Lillian], about the student feedback on your teaching and I ask again in this letter. As you know, I have a right and a duty to talk with faculty members about their teaching and all aspects of their work as faculty members in this [Department]. I must insist that you and I meet in the normal Department Head and faculty member way."

Theodore's subjects describe harassment in relation to their contract renewal, promotion and tenure applications (154) similar to what happened around the deadline for Lillian's re-appointment application, their salary increases were withheld (156), as the Dean threatened to withhold Lillian's, and their work was arranged into very inconvenient and inappropriate schedules without consultation (155), as was Lillian's during her final year.

Many women in Theodore's study report having their classes closely monitored "to find evidence of poor teaching ability for a forthcoming showdown at a committee hearing or court testimony"(157). Here is a testimony from a physics professor:

> I was called in to the office of the department head, and was told that there had been numerous complaints about my teaching in one of my classes of well over a hundred students. Students of physics are chronic complainers, especially when the course is required and not elected. However, I felt that communication was good between the students and myself, and I felt comfortable with the class. When I asked who filed the complaints and what the complaint was about, I was told that the names couldn't be revealed because it would violate the confidence of the students. I suggested that someone from the department meet my class and try to resolve the problem. The assistant dean met with my students (about 110 of them) and asked for their complaints. One student raised his hand and said that he did not like to recite at

the blackboard. When asked if they would like to have me replaced with another teacher, they replied "no" unanimously. The
'numerous complaints' turned out to be a possible one. (157)

This account has a parallel in the Department Head and Dean's attempt to
use four anonymous negative student comments out of all of Lillian's many
above-average evaluations to change the focus of Lillian's informal
disciplinary meetings. These were also central to the process that led to
her dismissal. The women in Theodore's study were "accused of disloyalty
in engineering or 'orchestrating' student demonstrations and strikes" (157),
in a similar way to the accusations that Lillian coerced and incited students,
putting words in their mouths.

The advocacy work carried out by Theodore's subjects on behalf of
other women at their universities came under particular attack. Theodore
says: "In their roles as advocates they discover all too soon that they are, as
one woman describes it, 'the scapegoats for the insecurities, fears, and
hostilities' of their employers towards all women"(163). This echoes Lillian's
experience of being subjected to an informal disciplinary process primarily
because of her advocacy for Native and Black students.

The women in Theodore's study received very little support from
their faculty unions and associations (202). In the early stages, Lillian
received major support from hers, with strong action on her behalf by
several individuals, in particular her Faculty Association Representative.
In the end, however, the union betrayed her by settling her case with the
Board of Governors against her will.

Theodore comments on the heavy emotional toll on the women she
studied. "The women complain about nightmares, nervousness, and even
mental breakdowns along with fright and self-doubt about their abilities
and their capacity to continue fighting" (167). "The effects of protest are
echoed throughout their statements: 'It was a nightmare!' 'The whole
experience was torture!' 'I am desolated!'" (233). The focus of my account
in "The Story" is more on what happened than its effect on Lillian, but the
personal toll was great. The poem Lillian wrote after the cancellation of
the arbitration expresses a tiny bit of the emotional price she paid.

Theodore described other mechanisms of institutional backlash and
organized them into categories. Under the heading "The First Line of
Defense," she lists: "ideological pronouncements," "stalling," "secrecy,"
"distortions, lies and deceit," "divisive tactics" and "power games with
government." Under the heading "Taking Care of 'Troublemakers,'" she
lists: "punishment to fit the crime," "harassment," "character assassination," "blacklisting" and "guilt by association." Under the heading, "The
Myth of Collegiality," she lists: "alienation and the deep freeze," "sacred
cows of academia," "the hostile head" and "the fragmented department"
(1986: Table of Contents).

In fact, Theodore's book would almost serve as a catalogue of institutional patterns in relation to equity. Anyone involved in these struggles would recognize such chapter titles as: "The Revolving Door," "In Search of Academic Freedom," "The Unwritten Rules," "Exhausting the Channels," "Committees as Obstructions," "The Double Standard," "Shifting the Criteria," "Competency Under Question," "The Quagmire of Due Process," "Apathy and Fear," "The Token Woman," "The Reluctant Unions," "The Costs of Fighting" and "With the Deliberate Speed of a Turtle" (1986: Table of Contents).

Athena Theodore's study provides a catalogue of the tactics used by a university engaged in resistance and backlash. An article by Somer Brodribb, Sylvia Bardon, Theresa Newhouse, Jennifer Spenser and Nadia Kyba, all members of the University of Victoria Chilly Climate Committee, focuses attention on a specific set of backlash responses, all associated with the University's Employment Equity Office (Brodribb et al. 1996). The authors describe their experience of the University attempting to force them to break their anonymity and prove their case through the Employment Equity Office. Beyond describing what happened, the authors go on to name the institutional dynamics involved, outlining six successive stages: 1) "confidence tricks," which encourage those with complaints to trust the Equity staff and share all their information, thus sharing it with the administration; 2) "circling" by the Equity Office in order to figure out the relative political leverage of both sides; 3) "reconciliation/co-option," where the complainants were encouraged to enter mediation with the direct perpetrators of sexual harassment as a substitute for the university taking any responsibility for the situation; 4) "delay/suspension" by means of two contradictory reports, internal and external; 5) "distancing/unavailability," when the Equity Office began to block the complainants, and finally, 6) "doorslam/disappearance/denunciation," when the Equity Office abandoned the complainants altogether.

The authors conclude that their Equity Office reflects a professionalization of equity work that is deliberately designed to "manage dissent and reclaim authority" (13) by making equity issues the sole property of the Equity Office and convincing women to trust the process, as well as provide jobs for anti-feminist women on campus (20). As a result of their experiences, the women say they "remembered how systemic, organized and sustained discrimination really is" (20).

Other authors give accounts of backlash at United States and Canadian universities. Graveline (1996), Carty (1991: 26), hooks (1994: 5), Williams (1991: 80–82) and Sabattis (1996: 63) all speak out about their experiences of racism at their universities and describe responses that echo the list above. After even their mildest efforts to name the racism they saw, they describe being labelled as "troublemakers" and having all of their subsequent actions interpreted in the light of that designation. Their supposed reason for "making trouble" was an attempt to mask their mediocrity as a student or teacher.

Graveline (1996) describes the first step in the backlash she experienced as "personal assassination" (350). She paraphrases and quotes Chandra Talpade Mohanty's description of this dynamic. Mohanty suggests that in order to maintain "business as usual" in the face of challenges from visible minority people, system-wide conflicts are interpreted in "narrow, interpersonal terms," so that conflict resolution can be applied to differences between individuals. She calls the process "personalization" (Mohanty 1994, reported in Graveline 1996, 350).

Leela Madhava Rau (1995) provides further description of this dynamic, which she calls "demonization." She held the position of Race Relations Officer at the University of Western Ontario for two years. During that time, a professor was accused of making a racist statement in class. She was cleared of the charge by an adjudicator but also criticized for lacking "the hallmark of a caring and sensitive member of the teaching profession" (Rau quoting from the written judgement of the adjudicator, 323). The professor proceeded to demand an apology, payment of all her legal costs and a year's salary in compensation from the university. This action triggered media portrayals of the professor as a victim, demands by the faculty association that the race relations policy be scrapped and replaced, and demands from the student newspaper that the Race Relations Officer resign.

During the incident, many misrepresentations of what happened were circulated by the accused professor and others, but the Race Relations Officer could not give out corrected versions of the story because of the confidentiality required of her office. Specific demands concerning the Race Relations Policy and Officer led to a discussion of free speech and academic freedom on campus in which the Race Relations Officer was accused of being the powerful "thought police" in a totalitarian regime.

In the end, the professor accused of racial harassment received the apology, her legal costs and a year off with pay. The Race Relations Policy was re-written by a panel selected for their "neutrality" on race relations issues—the Race Relations Officer and any other visible minority members of the campus community were automatically considered biased. Rau resigned in complete discouragement and describes the personal cost of her experience in strong words:

> For some time I have been trying to think of an analogy which would convey graphically my feelings during these years. When the image first came, I rejected it in disbelief but the feelings engendered in me at Western have been a part of my life only once before, following a sexual assault on a deserted Montreal street in 1985. I do not make this comparison lightly; it has taken

me some courage and time to write these words. They may not be popular—the trial by media of a Race Relations Officer will be seen by some as reducing the tragedy of sexual assault on women. However, for me the two experiences were alike. In both instances, there was a sense of loss of control, whether it is being dragged across a street, screams stifled by an unknown attacker or waiting day after day for letters and editorials of hatred, intimidation, and vitriol. The sense of being wrong, although intellectually you know you did the right thing, was very similar. But perhaps what remains with me from both instances is the fear and violation. In one case the violation was physical, in the other, a more subtle form of mental or intellectual attack. But in both instances, I was exposed and there seemed to be no escape.

The only event which prevented the last two years from becoming unbearable was the birth of my son in April 1993. However, the time before his birth was an unremitting nightmare. Through the worst moments on campus, with the denunciations and calls for my dismissal, what saved me was protecting and nurturing this being. Try to eat, try to relax, don't just sit there and weep, think of the child—these injunctions from friends, family, and midwives kept me going and gave me the courage to continue. Yet at the same time, this led to the development of a public persona.... I knew people didn't really want to hear that I felt I was balancing on the edge of an abyss so I strove to make others comfortable. What is surprising, on reflection, is that so many people did not delve deeper, despite their innate knowledge that my life must be hellish. So I fought to maintain my composure, never knowing what might be thrown at me from one day to the next, worried that at some time the armor would crack, and my anger and pain would be revealed to a university which had rendered me guilty without trial. During these bleak days I was told, on more than one occasion, "You should expect this, it is a part of your job," as if nearly a year's worth of persecution based on misinformation should be a minor irritant....

What allowed much of the feeding frenzy to occur was the demonization of Leela Madhava Rau, woman. After a while, I doubt that those spreading their slanderous letters around the campus ever thought about me as a human being. (339–40)

From my experience at Canadian University and the accounts in the literature, I think the heart of backlash is this dynamic—named "personal assassination" by Graveline (1996: 350), "personalization" by Mohanty (Graveline 1996: 350) and "demonization" by Rau (1995: 340). Prentice (1996) describes it as the "re-attribution of the problem from the institution to those making the complaint and demonization of those who raise the issues." Fortune calls it "shooting the messenger" (1989: xiv). An older term for this process is "scapegoating."

Scapegoat

In Chapter Five, I told the story of my dream and the beginning of my attempts to draw "The Story" in chart form, and I included the completed drawing, after seven rounds of simplification. However, it is easier to understand if it is broken down into steps.

In the first step, the chart is reduced to only the players. The horizontal scale at the top of the drawing is the timeline. Each player is placed where he or she became involved. The vertical scale is the hierarchy of Canadian University, with each player placed on his or her level. Before leaving the portrayal of the players involved in "The Story," I added markings to distinguish the males and females, and filled in the circles for the five women of colour. As I explained earlier in this chapter, an interesting aspect of "The Story" is the number of white women in fairly powerful positions (dean and above) in Canadian University at the time. The drawing of the players is portrayed in Figure 2.

The next drawing (Figure 3) shows appeals for help (the solid arrows). The students, and later Lillian, asked for help, at level after level, right to the top of the Canadian University hierarchy.

The next drawing (Figure 4) shows the supportive responses (broken arrows) that resulted from some of the appeals for help. Two faculty members, including Lillian, gave support to the students. The students also received supportive responses from the Dean of Graduate Studies, the Vice-President of Student Services and the Employment Equity Officer. Later, when Lillian came under attack, she received support from the Vice-President of Student Services and the Employment Equity Officer.

The final drawing (Figure 5) shows the blaming and punishing responses (dotted arrows). One arrow travels from a group of five faculty in the Department to the students. The remaining arrows, from the Department Head, the Deans, the Academic Vice-President and the President, are all directed at Lillian.

My most emotional moment in the creation of this chart came when I saw the forest of blaming, punishing arrows pointing at Lillian. The students originated the actions aimed at making the Department more open to their participation, resisted their treatment by the Community Specialty Coordinator and later criticized the Department, including allegations of racism. Lillian entered the fray as their support person and ally. Yet, in the end, most of the institutional backlash landed on her. I remembered the comments my informants told me were made about Lillian by the former chair of the Equality Committee—that she coerced the students into saying what they did in the Talking Circle on Discriminatory Harassment

Figure 2: The Players

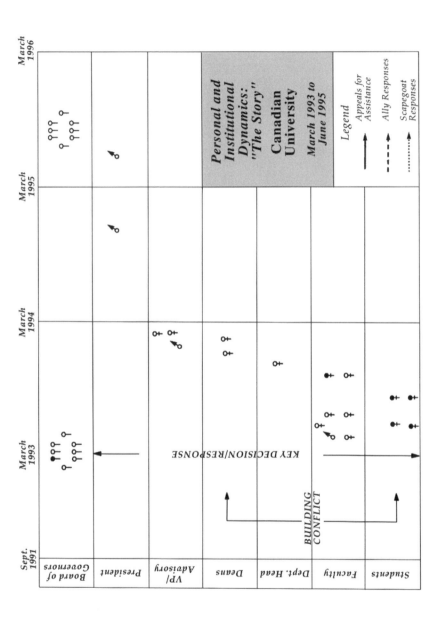

Figure 3: Appeals for Help

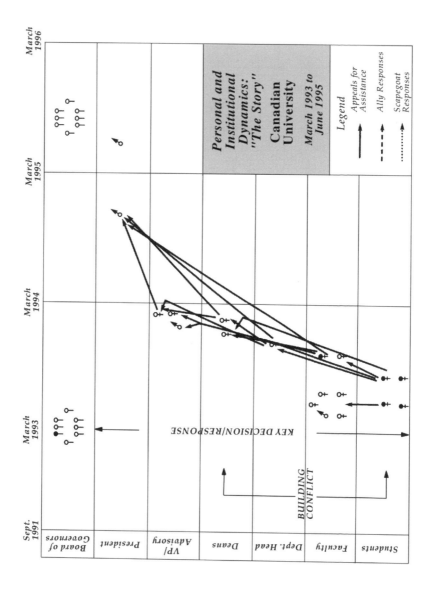

Figure 4: Supportive Responses

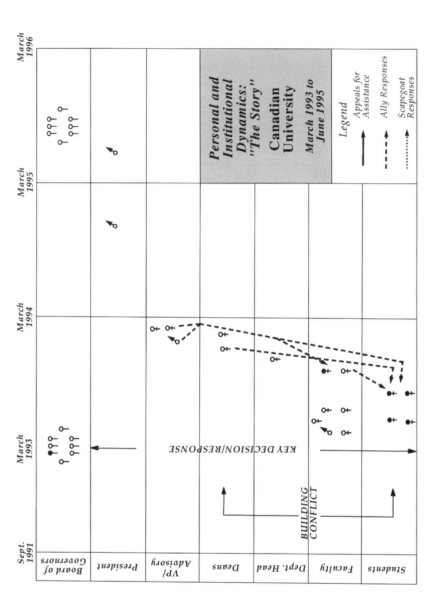

Figure 5: Blaming and Punishing Responses

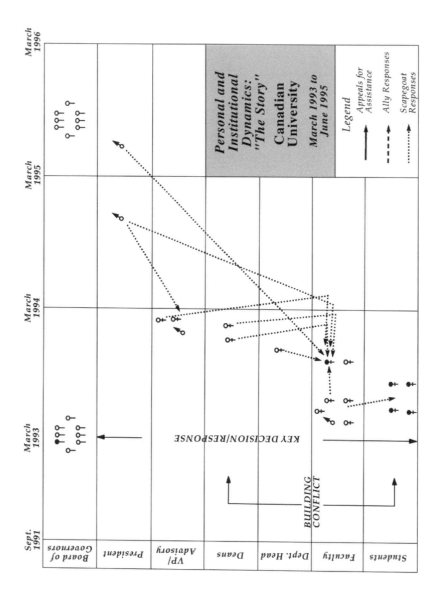

and that the Department didn't have any trouble with Black and Native students before she came. I began to see Lillian as a scapegoat. This led to an exploration of the concept of the scapegoat.

The original scapegoat was literally a goat. It appears in the Bible, in Leviticus 16:20–22:

> He shall bring forward the live goat. He shall lay both his hands on his head and confess over it all the iniquities of the Israelites and all their acts of rebellion, that is, all their sins; he shall lay them on the head of the goat and send it away into the wilderness in charge of a man who is waiting ready. The goat shall carry all their iniquities upon itself into some barren waste and the man shall let it go, there in the wilderness. (*New English Bible* 1970)

Collective "sins," including "acts of rebellion," are projected onto the goat, and the goat carries them away, "into the wilderness." The image became a powerful one for me in light of the fact that Lillian was forced to leave Canadian University.

There is a disagreement about scapegoats in theological literature. A discussion of both sides of the debate can be found in the work of Walter Wink (1992). He gives a summary of the arguments made by Rene Girard (1977), who argued that the scapegoat is a positive social mechanism that permits reconciliation in situations of conflict; it pays a small price in violence to avoid much larger violence. Wink disagrees with this analysis, pointing out that there are many non-violent mechanisms for reconciling conflict, such as apologies, gifts, agreement to cooperate, submission and third-party mediation. He also criticizes Girard's belief that conflict comes from scarcity and is therefore simply a function of nature. In his own analysis, conflict comes from the unequal distribution of power in society. In Wink's view, what the scapegoating mechanism does is project the anger that results from systemic injustice onto one person, or group, always choosing those who have the least power to defend themselves. They can then be blamed and destroyed. The anger is vented for the moment; the systemic injustice is preserved and made invisible once again. Those who hold and benefit from power, along with the institutions that grant that power, are off the hook (144–53).

Wink's analysis made sense to me. Although the Department had been working for years at the task of eradicating sexism, racism, ableism and discrimination based on language and religion, these forms of oppression still lingered. It is very difficult to change such things within the context of academic freedom and free speech. The dominant liberal ideology resists asking questions about whose academic freedom and free speech. Also, as discussed earlier, in the context of a liberal ideology, intention is the primary factor. From this perspective, the Department deserved credit for what it had done. In the Western dualistic way of thinking, good intentions had eradicated the oppression. There is little room in liberalism for understanding backlash and the difference between token change, or reform, and structural transformation.

From a structural viewpoint, no matter what the intent, impact is primary. The Black and Native students were not yet experiencing equity. They were proposing further changes, believing that their suggestions would be welcome. By doing this, they made the remaining inequity clearly visible. To those who saw the situation through a liberal lens, this may have appeared to be an unjustified attack. For reasons that I think have to do with her status as a token (possibly the "bad" token), they may have perceived it as coming from Lillian more than from the students. Because of this, it seems, they labelled her a "negative" and "uncollegial" colleague, someone who didn't fit in the faculty, the cause of their undeserved discomfort.

The letters written by the Department Head to Lillian from the beginning of her quasi-disciplinary action until the end of her grievance, to my mind, demonstrate this liberal tendency to see the structural critique, coming from the collective analysis of the Equality Committee and Native Support Circle, as an attack on the Department coming from Lillian personally. The Department Head accused Lillian of "putting a negative spin ... on every issue" and "badmouthing" the Department. She seems to have ignored Lillian's structural position, as an oppressed person under attack, and perceived Lillian's refusal to meet with her alone as a personal lack of collegiality when she wrote: "I have asked many times to talk with you, [Lillian].... I must insist that you and I meet in the normal [Department Head] and faculty member way" and "I have to conclude that you refuse to meet with me to discuss in a collegial fashion."

From the viewpoint of the institutional entity and its interests, first the students and later Lillian made injustice visible, a dangerous situation for an institution with a major funder (the Federal Government) actively interested in its stated values of justice, accessibility and equality. It made sense to me that the institution would react as Wink described, by projecting the blame on a highly visible token and then expelling that person.

When Marie Fortune (1989) wrote about the scapegoating process, it was not on a university campus but rather in a major church in the United States. She was assigned by the national office of her church to serve as advocate and pastor for six women who made public their sexual abuse by their minister. She describes the terrible price paid by the women for speaking out, parallel to that paid by the women confronting "chilly climates" in the academic world.

What I call "scapegoating," she calls: "shooting the messenger," "misnaming the problem" and "blaming the victim" (120–22). As she describes these dynamics, "shooting the messenger" involves the institution turning on the bearer of the bad news, usually the victims, and attacking their credibility, ethics and motives. "Misnaming the problem" appears to be the same dynamic Susan Prentice (1995) labels "reattribution of the problem"; that is, turning the situation around into concern for the perpetrator in the face of the "terrible attack" made on him (or her). "Blaming the victim" involves portraying the victims as the cause of their own problems. I think an example from "The Story" would be the campus rumours suggesting that the students at the centre of "The Story" "cried racism" to draw attention away from poor academic performance. "Blaming the victim," as I understand it, would also have been the result if the Department Head and Dean had successfully diverted attention from Lillian's student advocacy to the four negative evaluations of her teaching.

All of the women's stories referred to in the section on the tactics of backlash—the Chilly Collective (1995), Graveline (1996), Carty (1991), hooks (1994), Williams (1991), Mohanty (1994), Rau (1995), Sabattis (1996) and the women interviewed by Theodore (1986)—are stories of scapegoating. It is clear to me that this tactic is a central component of backlash.

I believe that scapegoating works, in part, because of the individualism of liberal ideology. When most people understand the world to be made up of individuals, how simple it becomes for an institution to draw attention away from the injustice inherent in its structure and project the conflict on those who made the inequity visible.

The Token Becomes the Scapegoat

In my discussion of scapegoating, I mentioned that I think Lillian's colleagues may have perceived the students' complaints as coming from her because of her high visibility as a token. The qualifications for a scapegoat are visibility and vulnerability. As Rosabeth Moss Kanter's analysis underlines repeatedly, two of the key features of tokens are those same two attributes. An ally of the newcomers can become a scapegoat, although this is a risky strategy for the institution because of the relative institutional power of an ally. Even a relative bystander can be a scapegoat, for example, a journalist who writes a story about the events in question. However, it seems to me the most common scapegoat is a token, simply because the visibility and vulnerability of the token position make blaming the token a safe and convenient strategy for the institution.

Clarification: "Personalization"

One of the readers of a draft of this book pointed out that I was creating confusion by using the word "personalization" in several different ways. This seems to be a good place to clarify. Part of the process of oppression is that the oppressed person is "de-personalized," in other words, objectified or stereotyped, portrayed as "other" or "not-human." This dehumanization justifies their treatment by the oppressor (Memmi 1990). During the process of scapegoating, the structural injustice is projected onto the victim, a process called "personalization" by Chandra Talpade Mohanty, who explains that system-wide conflicts are interpreted in "narrow, interpersonal terms," that is, attributed to differences between individuals (Mohanty 1994, in Graveline 1996: 350). It is the structural injustice and institutional conflict that are personalized in this process, not the scapegoat. In fact, the person chosen to be scapegoat probably qualifies as the "screen" for this projection because they have been de-personalized.

Another use of the word describes the reaction of people with privilege when they hear accounts of structural oppression and take it personally, thinking that they are being accused. This is the dynamic Kate Kirkham calls "over-personalization" (1988–89: 51). Here, again, it is not an oppressed person who is being personalized, but the process of reacting to an accusation of structural oppression.

I have tried to keep these terms as clear as possible by using "over-personalization" for a privileged person taking discussion of structural oppression personally, and "scapegoating" for the projection of conflict over structural injustice onto an oppressed person. I hope, in this way, to avoid confusion with the basic invalidating dynamic of "de-personalization."

Avoiding Backlash: The Plateau

In my practice as a workshop facilitator, I have had the privilege of working with two voluntary organizations that have avoided organizational backlash, even though they have been on the path toward equity for more than ten years and many of the conflicts that could trigger backlash are present. In both cases a small but determined group of staff, including one or two managers, has persistently pushed the process along from the beginning and significant changes have been made. In both organizations, however, I have observed a pattern I think of as "the plateau," where the process seems to be stalled and people are frustrated with the lack of progress. Members of the group that has traditionally lacked access and power continue to experience disrespectful and discriminatory treatment and find stubborn pockets of resistance and individual backlash. Some give up hope and resist putting in any more effort. Meanwhile, many members of the dominant group feel that they are doing their best and can't figure out why the less-powerful group isn't more patient and grateful. They feel they ought to have "arrived" as an equitable organization by now because their intentions are good and they've done what they are supposed to do. They, too, are tired of putting in effort.

At the YMCA in Halifax-Dartmouth, the Diversity Committee maintains a well-developed program of diversity training. Every person hired by the organization is required to take part in the training workshops. The committee also has an affirmative action hiring agreement with the Nova Scotia Human Rights Commission and is working on tools and procedures for recruitment, hiring and supervision. The YMCA wants to increase the number staff from minority communities and screens all potential employees for their level of diversity awareness. In spite of the years of work they have committed to these goals and the progress that has been made, members of the Diversity Committee say they feel as though they have hit a wall. Employees from minority communities are still concentrated in particular types of work, on the lower end of the staff hierarchy, and Diversity Committee members who are people of colour still experience degrading treatment when they and their children take part in Y activities. The Committee still fights an uphill battle against denial and resistance.

New Directions for Children, Youth, Adults and Families, in Winnipeg, Manitoba, founded in 1885, this organization has evolved from a shelter and orphanage to a dynamic organization with twenty programs providing job preparation, education, life-skills, therapy, counselling and residential care. These programs serve some distinct populations; for example, individuals who are mentally disabled, sexually exploited, transgendered or deaf. There is a high percentage of Aboriginal children, youth and families in many of the programs.

For the past ten years New Directions has worked to become more culturally proficient in its work with Aboriginal peoples. As staff resistance to this initiative became evident the management searched for a way to help people understand the importance of culture and of how their own value base impacts the work they do. This search led to the establishment of an ongoing three-day training program in culture and diversity for all staff to help them recognize the values they bring to their work places. There is also an anti-heterosexism training program, "Breaking Barriers," as well as ongoing workshops in colonization and decolonization. Initially all management were required to participate in these groups. Now to be more honouring of the Aboriginal value of "whoever is ready to learn will be there" participation is voluntary.

Hiring Aboriginal staff in programs where there is a high number of Aboriginal participants is a priority and is supported by an employment waiver with the provincial Human Rights Commission. The organization has an Aboriginal Cultural Advisor who provides ongoing teachings to managers as well as guidance and support to programs, staff and participants. An Aboriginal manager facilitates a group with all managers to explore racism.

Shirl Hauser coordinates the New Directions' program to prepare and support foster families. In a diversity workshop, she remarked that her organization's experience of moving toward diversity has many parallels with the process foster families go through, particularly when "the honeymoon is over." Foster families, she explained, often expect the foster child to be grateful, and the child doesn't feel that way. In a later e-mail, she explained further:

> Many of the challenges we face in order to reach across the barriers of prejudice and anger are mirrored in foster families' struggle. Foster parents must work through the multitude of layers of differences—cultural and family life customs and the harsh learnings and defences arising from trauma—in order to embrace the child who has joined their family. Ultimately they will create a new family. As will we.

Why have these agencies been able to avoid organizational backlash when others haven't? This is a question I am currently still exploring, but I can suggest a few reasons. Both organizations have made a clear policy commitment to the diversity process at the top level. Both have at least a small group of persistent and knowledgeable staff continually working out strategies for moving the diversity agenda forward. Both of these core groups are diverse themselves and are modelling healthy ally relationships in the way they work together. Both organizations have made a considerable commitment to education of their members at all levels over a long period of time, so there is at least a common language and everyone knows of the organization's commitment to its diversity policies. In both cases there are key leaders at the management level for whom this is their primary personal commitment. I do not know which of these common characteristics is crucial in avoiding organizational backlash, or if it is all in combination, but these are the important features I have observed in these two organizations.

What kind of support is helpful for those who are stuck on "the plateau"? My experience shows that it is useful for them to get an overview of other organizations working toward equity. They find out that they are not alone on the plateau, and that it is no surprise that their task is not accomplished yet, given the power of the interlocking institutions that maintain discrimination and injustice in the world. It helps when they make the distinction between strategies that are aimed at the level of individual change and those that have the goal of structural transformation, and to understand that changing a structure is more than changing the individuals who participate in it. Above all, it seems to help to understand that they, as members of an organization travelling the equity road for more than a decade, are pioneers. In some ways, they have "travelled beyond the edge of the map."

In Western culture we like processes to have an end point, neat and finished. We need to reach goals, see progress, accomplish something. The road toward equity is long, complicated, painful, frustrating, confusing and full of twists and turns. In short, it is "fractal." An individual travelling the path of becoming an ally must come to understand that as long as the whole society is founded on injustice and inequality, an individual cannot become non-oppressive. An organization on the path toward equity must understand the same thing. Like cleaning the house or washing the dishes, the task is never finished as long as there is dirt to be tracked in or meals to be eaten. As in the process of breaking an addiction, the organization is always "recovering."

I give great credit to these organizations, particularly the grassroots participants and key leaders who continue to push the process along. It is a difficult journey, but they have avoided organizational backlash and are still engaged in the struggle. They are pioneers, creating paths for others to follow.

Institutional Power-Holders: Ideology and Choices

In my observations of organizations in what I call the plateau stage of the struggle toward equity, the importance of institutional managers and other power-holders who committed to the cause cannot be underestimated. These are people whose scope of action is limited by their institutional role, but their scope is broader and they have more power and influence than others to move the process forward. When there is conflict over equity in the organization, these are the people most able to resolve it while avoiding organizational backlash and protecting those who are in vulnerable positions. Equity conflict always holds the possibility of structural transformation, and those who hold power granted by the institution face a choice: act on behalf of the institution's resistance to change, or act as an ally to members of groups seeking equity in the institution.

The choice made by institutional power-holders faced with an equity conflict is heavily influenced by their ideology. In fact, if their ideology is liberal, they may not even perceive themselves as making a choice. With assumptions from an individualistic, or liberal, worldview, the decision-maker may not see the histories of power and oppression working in the situation and may not even recognize or admit his or her own power-base in the institution. He or she may make no distinction between intent and impact, see conflict itself as a problem and perhaps even perceive the situation as an unjustified personal attack. The result of these assumptions can be a reaction of injured innocence and fear, leading to self-defence and a trigger for the kind of institutional backlash described by Bankier (1996) as "a Tornado of Fire." The action taken will usually be punishment and, if it is directed at an individual, the result will be scapegoating. This distracts attention from the systemic conditions that gave rise to the conflict in the first place, and the result is the perpetuation of oppression in the institution. Nothing changes at the systemic level and the pressures begin, almost immediately, to build toward a repeat of the same process with different individuals further down the road. The pattern of action and reaction can become a cycle, with a scapegoat (or more than one) ejected on each round. The institution tries to preserve its current form, although it cannot do so completely. If chaos theory holds true in matters of institutional transformation, every effort to make change has some effect.

If the institutional power-holder has structural assumptions, he or she will more likely perceive the situation as a group of people struggling to gain a toe-hold in an institution that has denied them and their knowledge legitimacy for centuries. They likely will expect the institution to resist the newcomers' presence beyond presenting an appearance, in other words, as tokens. They will be more likely to take responsibility for their privilege, use their sphere of institutional power to act as allies and believe the word of the traditionally excluded people about the inequity they experience in the institution. They will have a tendency to respond with curiosity rather than defensiveness and proceed to explore the situation, analyze it and engage in collective problem-solving, involving all parties. This process may lead to new solutions and learning at both the personal and institutional levels. The traditionally excluded group will continue to be included, and eventually the process will result in structural transformation of the institution.

What I have described above are *possible* responses based on worldview. I have also assumed good intentions, which might not always be the case. A person's worldview informs his or her range of responses, but there are still personal choices to be made. When I first discussed this analysis with my informants for "The Story," they quickly pointed out that some individuals who held institutional influence during those events held a structural worldview, but still responded by scapegoating, or at least did not take a stand against the scapegoating. In their opinion, these people acted as they did out of fear and vulnerability to possible punishment by the institution.

Their analysis underlines the risks involved when an institutional leader uses his or her power and influence on behalf of traditionally excluded groups, especially in a conflict situation. The institution has great power to punish and reward those within it and can both choose and shape those who play its designated roles and represent its interests. If the power-holder's efforts to act as an ally are successful, the traditionally excluded people can be protected and the equity process in the institution can be advanced. If not, the individual leader can be isolated and marginalized, labelled a "troublemaker" like those he or she has supported, and even removed from or driven out of leadership. At Canadian University, those I know of who chose to support Lillian and the students paid a price, personally and professionally, although much less than that paid by Lillian and the students.

Allies who hold positions of institutional leadership bear a heavy responsibility and walk many fine lines, but those that remain faithful to their vision of organizational equity can give crucial support to individuals in vulnerable positions and bring about some amazing transformations in their organizations. I salute those patient, skilful, persistent and courageous enough to walk this road.

The Essence of the University

According to chaos theory and fractal geometry, the behaviour of an entity is the result of repeating patterns on all scales, shaped by underlying principles. Using my experience at Canadian University and the literature on equity conflicts in other universities, I have made a start at defining some of the patterns. They are: oppression and invalidation of the newcomers and their knowledge, acceptance of tokens and token change, hitting the limits where the institution perceives change as "going too far" or "too expensive," backlash, scapegoating and the plateau. Athena Theodore defined many more (Theodore 1986, see Tactics of Backlash in this chapter). These patterns should point to some underlying principles.

My first question in Chapter Five was "What is the self-interest of the institution?" My answer was: "An institution's self-interest lies in the preservation of its own essence, which is expressed in its deepest values and structure, particularly its methods of granting, maintaining and regulating power." It is not within the scope of this book to delve deeply into the history of the university as an institution, but I think a brief reflection is appropriate.

The essence of a corporation is easy to define, as demonstrated in Jerry Mander's analysis in Chapter Five. It is profit. What is the self-interest of a university? A prominent historian of universities, Eric Ashby (1967), writes:

> A university is a mechanism for the inheritance of the Western style of civilization. It preserves, transmits and enriches learning, and it undergoes evolution as animals and plants do. In short, the university is the key institution devised by Western Civilization for the advancement of knowledge and the training of society's most highly skilled workers. Originating in the European Middle Ages, it has become the primary vehicle in all parts of the world for the preservation and transmission of the highest learning, the advancement of scholarship, the training of specialists in fields of endeavor vital to society, and the improvement of national life. (417)

As "a mechanism for the inheritance of the Western style of civiliza-tion," the university transmits both the strengths and the flaws of that civilization. It carries the energy, creativity, technological advancement and respect for the individual that have come out of Western civilization, along with its materialism, its mechanisms for constantly increasing the gap between rich and poor and its assumptions about who is at the centre of society and who is on the margins. Ashby speaks only of the positive aspects of the West and equates the whole world's highest status citizens with its most skilled and knowledgeable, defined as university-educated. He, like the university itself, makes a huge assumption about whose skills and knowledge are valuable and whose are not. The ability to use a telescope counts in this system; the ability to survive on what others throw away does not. The ability to develop new agricultural chemicals counts; the ability to work with nature in an ancient cooperation does not. The ability to perform an organ transplant counts; the ability to heal with spiritual energy does not.

According to Hastings Rashdall, "The earliest university statutes were primarily concerned with establishing rules for what should be taught, when, how, and by whom" (1936:4). The clergymen and teachers who established the first curriculum at the University of Paris in the early twelfth century had access to the work of a scholar often referred to as a genius. Hildegard was founder and abbess of the convent of St. Rupert, a major centre of learning near Bingen, in Germany. She had written three books on mysticism and philosophy, two scientific studies of nature and medicine, the earliest Western descriptions of the circulatory and nervous systems, the first known morality play and hundreds of sermons and letters. She was an artist, musician and composer of seventy-seven songs that are still performed and recorded today. She was an advisor to kings and popes (National Film Board of Canada 1984, Hoving 1994). In 1174, aware that higher learning was moving out of religious orders and into the new secular universities, she travelled to Paris to submit her work for consideration. Three months later, the founders of the university told her to take her books home; they were not worthy of inclusion in the curriculum (National Film Board of Canada 1984). Since they did include Aristotle, who wrote that women were deformed human beings, unworthy of education, I think one can assume that Hildegard's work was rejected at least in part because her sex made her knowledge illegitimate in the eyes of the new institution.

Although the university has other functions and has evolved, the centre of its essence seems to have remained unchanged for the whole eight hundred years or so of its existence—perpetrating "Western civilization" by legitimating the knowledge of some and not others. Those whose knowledge was not part of the canon of "Western civilization"—women, the poor, followers of religions other than Christianity or Christian heresies and people of colour—have slowly, over the centuries, trickled into the realm of legitimate participants in the university, some more quickly than others. They have done so by demonstrating a willingness to learn the acceptable knowledge of the West. Religious belief is not much of an issue now, unless believers make claims in opposition to science. Christian heresy is not an issue at all. Other bodies of knowledge, however, are still excluded. Agnes Calliste, a sociologist at St. Frances Xavier University in Nova Scotia, quotes Leith Mullings in saying: "Debates about anti-racism (or critical multiculturalism) and the intellectual canon are not simply about which books to read but 'about power and privilege and how they are to be distributed'" (2000: 107). She goes on to say:

> Anti-racism questions the devaluation of the knowledge and experiences of subordinate groups as well as the marginalization and silencing of certain voices in the university and in society. (145)

If defining the canon of Western knowledge is the essence of the university, this will be reflected in the patterns of its response to women, people of colour, and people with roots in the less-powerful classes, and their allies, particularly those that insist on giving value to the traditional knowledge of these groups.

Strategic Questions, Again

I have used my own experience and my reading to make a beginning at defining some patterns of institutional behaviour that emerge when a university faces a conflict over justice and equity. In my reflection on the essence of the university, I briefly speculated on the underlying principles that shape these patterns. Now it is time to return to the questions I asked in Chapter Five, in particular, those that are concerned with strategies for change: Which of our current equity tactics make change only at the individual level? Which are capable of making change at the institutional level? Which are capable only of reform? Which have the potential to bring about structural transformation? What new tactics do we need to develop, and what old ones can we revive, that would focus not just on individuals, but on the institution itself and its habitual, often unconscious, ways of doing things? Finally, I want to add one more question: What do the institutional behaviour patterns defined in this chapter have to do with strategies for change?

Part Three

Structural Transformation of Institutions

Chapter Eight

Changing the Patterns

Aiming Strategies at the Structure

If I, and the other writers I have quoted, are correct in our analysis that institutions are structural entities beyond the sum of the individuals within them, then there are profound implications for the strategies we use to seek social justice in institutional settings. The tactics we use that are aimed primarily at individuals—education, lobbying, pressure tactics, conflict resolution, legal mechanisms for human rights and harassment complaint procedures—do not lose their importance but must be used in conjunction with tactics aimed at transforming the structure of the institution. We must also understand the patterns of institutional response to change, as well as individual responses, and be prepared for them. We need to remember that change in an institutional entity does not follow the logic of a machine but the dynamics of an organic entity. When we hit a point of backlash, our strategies for dealing with the conflict must also take both the individuals and the institution itself into account. In this chapter, I comment on some of the tactics we are already using and propose a new one.

Thinking Structurally

The first step in all of our strategies, I think, has to be learning to think structurally. This means we must become more aware of the institution, its values, history, culture and "normal" ways of doing things. We must develop our understanding of how the norms of the institution affect the people who work, study or otherwise participate in it. Patricia Monture-Angus gives an example:

> The problem that all these examples describe is structural. It includes assumptions upon which educational institutions are based. It might be helpful to provide a clear example of the way structural assumptions operate within the institution. As a professor, I wield a certain amount of power. I do not deny this. It is true, I decide whether a student passes or fails; if an "A" or a "C" is earned. However, when I stand in front of a class, many of the individuals have more privilege and power than I can ever imagine

154

having. This power is carried as a result of their skin-privilege, or their gender, or their social status, or family income. The law school, however, functions solely on the view that I am the powerful one. Students are protected against "alleged" bias by a professor by the grade appeal process. However, I am not any professor. I am not male, White, and my family is not economically advantaged…. There is no protection available to me in any policy of either the law school or the university if the situation arises where I experience a student who discriminates against me based on my gender, culture, or race. The complexity of my involvement in the institution as a professor is not recognized in tenure and promotion processes. Although universities are attempting to diversify their faculties, few attempts are made to alter the policies and practices of the institution to reflect that diversity. There is only one outcome: I am forced to find ways to accommodate my own difference. (1995b: 21–22)

Because the institution's structure is "normal," it is almost invisible. Part of the challenge of learning to think structurally is to make our unconscious knowledge of the institution conscious. This involves a critical examination of ideas we have deeply internalized—an exciting, if sometimes painful, process. It is what the feminist movement of the 1960s and 1970s called "consciousness raising." It involves reading, discussion and reflection. It requires us to develop the skill of asking critical questions: Where did this way of doing things come from? Who benefits from it? Who pays a price?

When we are dealing with people who have the power to make decisions on behalf of the institution, we must be aware not only of their power but their limitations. If we can negotiate with them about how and when they can push the limits of the institution and help organize the support they need to challenge the institution's resistance, I think we have more chance of success than if we simply assume they are all-powerful and put pressure on them to do what we want them to do, now. I think it also gives us more potential for developing long-term allies in high places if we have a good analysis of their position within the "principalities and powers" of the institution itself. There are certainly times when we must put pressure on high-level decision-makers, but taking this route without understanding the constraints on their position can result in making unnecessary, and possibly dangerous, enemies.

Breaking Through the Denial

Thinking structurally involves breaking through the institution's denial of its unjust and inequitable structures. In Chapter Six, I described the work Anne Wilson Schaef has done on addictive behaviour patterns. After exploring the parallel process of addiction in individuals, organizations and North American society as a whole, she turned to questions of healing, or "recovery" as it is called in the twelve-step organizations. She finds the same parallels in the process of recovery at all levels. She says:

> We cannot recover from an addiction unless we first admit that we have it. Naming our reality is essential to recovery. Unless we admit that we are indeed functioning in an addictive process in an Addictive System, we shall never have the option of recovery. Once we name something ... it becomes ours, as does the power we formerly relinquished to it. Once we reclaim that personal power, we can begin to recover and not until then. Remember, to name the system as an addict is not to condemn it: it is to offer it the possibility of recovery. (1987: 144)

Schaef also sees the process of breaking through individual denial as essential to breaking through it at the organizational and societal levels. She and Diane Fassel say:

> When addiction is the "norm" for the society or when persons are addicts or come from addictive families, unless they are recovering, their denial systems tend to remain intact and they just do not "see" what is going on at a systemic level. In fact, sometimes seeing the pieces themselves serves to ... draw attention away from the larger systemic problem. In this way, the addictive process is supported and can continue. (1988: 83)

Schaef also draws hope for this process from the parallel she sees between the individual addiction process and the Addictive System:

> Can a whole system recover from its addictions? The idea is staggering. Yet alcoholism is one of the few fatal diseases for which the possibility of recovery is guaranteed. Why not recovery for a whole Addictive System? (1988: 143)

Breaking through denial, at both the individual and institutional levels, is a painful process, but essential.

Structural Assumptions about Equity Conflict

Thinking structurally involves understanding the specific concepts of equity conflict discussed in Chapters Six and Seven. First, progress toward justice and equity does not follow the logic of a machine but the patterns of chaos typical of an organic entity, a pattern better described by fractal geometry than by straight lines. The particular patterns you can see depend on the scale of observation, whether you are watching from a satellite or through a microscope. In institutional change terms, I think this means the patterns are visible in different ways to someone at the centre of a conflict, someone a step or two removed and someone outside altogether. The person a little farther from the centre (an ally to the central person or people perhaps?) and the person outside (a community member?) can take on a role of helping everyone to maintain a broader perspective.

Second, an institution moving toward more justice and equity is involved in a process. It may have changed for the better in some ways, but that does not mean the work is complete. An institution that has started to move has not necessarily arrived. We can never expect progress to be steady, either. It will fluctuate, like the edge of a fractal shape.

Third, good intentions are helpful on the level of individuals' feelings and relationships, but they are not a measure of progress toward equity. That is measured by impact on those who experience the oppression, whether it is intentional or not.

Fourth, as discussed in Chapter Five and my earlier book, *Becoming an Ally* (2002: 115–16), it is important to remember that privilege blocks vision. Those who experience inequity can usually see it much more clearly that those who benefit from it. It behooves members of a privileged group to take members of oppressed groups very seriously when they describe their experiences of discrimination. In "The Story," a white male Department faculty member was reported as saying that if he couldn't see racism, it didn't exist. This is a common response and comes from the perception-clouding effects of privilege.

Defensiveness

Defensiveness is a major stumbling block on the road to justice and equity. Defensiveness, at both the individual and institutional levels, preserves denial, increases resistance to change and, as seen in Chapter Seven, can trigger backlash. In my experience, learning to think structurally greatly reduces the potential for defensiveness. Those who understand that we are shaped by the structures around us, usually unconsciously, tend to be open to discovering more about how our roles in the structures affect us. Those who accept that "unlearning" oppression is a long process, for both individuals and organizations, tend to accept that there is still work to do. Those who understand that most discrimination is not intentional are less likely to react as if they have been personally accused of doing something wrong. Those who grasp the perception-clouding effects of privilege will understand that they must listen to those who experience the oppression in order to know what is going on. In summary, those with a structural view of organizations and society as a whole are less likely to react to equity issues with defensiveness.

Returning for a moment to the long process of "unlearning" oppression, white people who are committed to anti-racist activism have joked for decades about being "recovering racists." The Metro Coalition for a Non-Racist Society in Halifax, Nova Scotia, nick-named "The White Group," did a skit one year for African Heritage Month based on an Alcoholics Anonymous meeting.

When I first met this concept, I found it very liberating. The parallel between unlearning racism and recovering from addiction helped me accept that I had committed myself to a long process, one that would be very rewarding, but would also require work, humility and self-discipline. I accepted as well that the process would last my whole life. This allowed me to drop my expectation of being perfect. I could leave behind the understanding that anti-racism is a state and accept it as a process. Above all, it allowed me to stop being defensive and put that energy instead into learning and working for change. This was the beginning of my work on the concept of becoming an ally (Bishop 2002: 114–15).

Later, when I began reading Anne Wilson Schaef's books about addictive organizations and the addictive society, I saw that the parallel between recovering from addiction and healing from internalized oppression and privilege can apply to our collective structures as well. There are some implications of this insight for strategy, which I will discuss later, but for now, I want to make the point that the abandonment of denial, the understanding that most oppression is unconscious and the acceptance of equity as a lengthy process are essential for reducing the dangerous defensiveness that can trigger and feed backlash.

Roles

As I said above, part of thinking structurally is understanding that we have roles in institutions and society, roles beyond our own making. We who want justice and equity must be clear about where we stand in terms of class and the decision-making structure in the institution. In particular, we must understand our degree of power. At all levels, change requires us to reflect, ask critical questions, form networks and alliances, organize collectively and take action. For those who are the "newcomers" to the institutions, strategies for institutional change must also include strategies for survival. These include mutual support organizing, attention to physical, emotional and spiritual health, and cultivation of relationships with committed allies.

For allies in powerful positions, it is particularly important to think structurally. People with power in an organization have much more latitude to make change than those with less power, although always within limits set by the institution. By reflecting critically on the possibilities and limitations, people in powerful positions in organizations have great potential to move the organization toward justice and equity. It is also particularly important for people in powerful positions to avoid dualistic thinking, confusion between intent and impact, denial and defensiveness.

Every action and reaction at the decision-making level of an institution has far-reaching effects on those with less power.

People somewhere in the middle, not powerful decision-makers but not "newcomers" either, have a particular ally role in the struggle for justice and equity. Allies in the middle can support the survival of those who are targets of institutional oppression and can try to educate those in powerful positions. While paying attention to their limits within the institution and the requirements of personal survival, middle-level allies can often use the relative power of their voice in the institution to help those with less power be heard. They can also use their relative security to "take the heat" away from those who are the direct targets of oppression. Working in close consultation with "newcomers" and never taking over leadership from them, it is possible to take on particularly visible tasks; for example, serving as the contact person on a press release or presenting a brief. When allies take on these visible roles, it can increase the safety of those whose voices are really speaking through the press release or brief. Middle-level allies walk many fine lines. A complete discussion of this role is beyond the scope of this book. I refer those who want to know more to my earlier book, *Becoming an Ally* (2002).

At all levels, it is important to be clear on institutional roles, ally roles and differing levels of power and influence in the organization. This is also part of thinking structurally.

Taking Responsibility for Privilege

For those with some degree of power and security at different levels of the institution, becoming clear on our roles as allies means taking responsibility for privilege. Typically, institutions and individuals with a liberal viewpoint see the oppressed group as responsible for its own "advancement." When allies take responsibility for privilege, this belief is turned on its head. It sees the eradication of oppression as a task that belongs to those that derive privilege from it. Peggy McIntosh's oft-quoted article "White Privilege: Unpacking the Invisible Knapsack" is a classic expression of taking responsibility for privilege. McIntosh says:

> Through work to bring materials from women's studies into the rest of the curriculum, I have often noticed men's unwillingness to grant they are overprivileged, even though they may grant that women are disadvantaged. They may say that they will work to improve women's status, in the society, the university, or the curriculum, but they can't or won't support the idea of lessening men's. Denials that amount to taboos surround the subject of advantages that men gain from women's disadvantages. These denials protect male privilege from being fully acknowledged, lessened, or ended.

Thinking through unacknowledged male privilege as a phenomenon, I realized that, since hierarchies in our society are interlocking, there was most likely a phenomenon of white privilege that was similarly denied and protected. As a white person, I realized I had been taught about racism as something that puts others at a disadvantage, but had been taught not to see one of its corollary aspects, white privilege, which puts me at an advantage. I think whites are carefully taught not to recognize white privilege, as males are taught not to recognize male privilege. So I have begun in an untutored way to ask what it is like to have white privilege. I have come to see white privilege as an invisible package of unearned assets that I can count on cashing in each day, but about which I was "meant" to remain oblivious. White privilege is like an invisible weightless knapsack of special provisions, maps, passports, code books, visas, clothes, tools and blank checks.

As noted previously, the Cornwall Collective (1980) expresses a similar analysis this way: "Only if we can say the 'I' — 'I am racist'—will we be able to move beyond a liberalism that adopts the language of equality but maintains the structure of oppression."

It is clear to me that taking responsibility for privilege is a key turning point in the process of becoming an ally. When it comes up in introductory "ally" workshops, I can reliably expect an explosion. Participants are angry with me because they feel I have "accused" them of racism, sexism, heterosexism and all the other "isms," although I don't accuse anyone. I simply model the process. As an adult educator I look for emotional responses in workshop participants. They show me where the learning is taking place. As an ally-in-progress myself, I feel those same emotional responses show me exactly where internalized dominance has its hold on me. Taking responsibility for privilege is definitely one of those points.

I become even more convinced that taking responsibility for privilege is at the centre of the process of becoming an ally when I see the extreme response of individuals and institutions that believe they have been accused of oppression. This applies particularly, at this point in history, to perceived accusations of racism. I think "The Story" includes several examples. Another is the response of police associations to police officials who recognize systemic racism. At a conference and later in a media interview, Larry Hill, Deputy Chief of the Ottawa Police Department, said that systemic forms of racism exist throughout society and police are not exempt. "Our members are not racist," he said, "but we are no different than any other organization. Do stereotypes exist? Yes. So if we're going to call that racial profiling, then yes, certainly it occurs in our police force as well as other police services." The president of the Ottawa Police

Association responded that his membership felt the Deputy Chief had unfairly branded them as racists (*Toronto Star* 2003: A1).

After a human rights inquiry ruled that a Halifax police officer stopped African-Nova Scotian boxer Kirk Johnson and impounded his car because of his race, Halifax Police Chief Frank Beazley apologized to Johnson and his family. He did not force the officer involved in the incident to apologize, because "it may have been an unconscious stereotype. How do you punish someone for something they did unconsciously?" He did require the officer to take diversity training and committed the police force to "rooting out racial discrimination in its ranks." The police association objected, saying: "[Our members] stand behind Mike's decision that he stopped [the car] because of experience and training and that's all. Not because of racism, not by profiling, not by stereotyping. No apologies" (CBC 2004).

The most dramatic illustration I have seen of the "sore point" of taking responsibility for privilege happened in a defamation suit brought by Carol Campbell, a Halifax police officer, against Anne Derrick and Rocky Jones, two prominent Halifax lawyers. During the investigation of a $10 theft at a school, Campbell conducted a personal search of three twelve-year-old Black girls in a publicly visible place, including looking inside their underwear. Media coverage of the event named Constable Campbell and used the term "strip search." The girls' parents took action against the Police Department and School Board, hiring Derrick and Jones to represent them. At one point, Derrick and Jones held a press conference where they expressed their opinion that the treatment of the three girls would probably not have happened if not for their age, socio-economic status and race. Constable Campbell sued the two lawyers for defamation. The judge and jury at the trial, six years later, found the two lawyers guilty and awarded general damages of $240,000 plus $75,000 in court costs to Constable Campbell. Two years after that, the Nova Scotia Appeal Court reversed the judgement (*Campbell vs Jones* 2002). Constable Campbell went to extreme lengths to defend her reputation against Derrick and Jones' references to systemic discrimination, keeping the case going for eight years. The judge and jury at the first level apparently felt that Constable Campbell suffered more damage from the lawyer's comments than she would have if she had been completely paralyzed in an accident, since the amount of money they awarded was far higher than it would have been in a case of complete loss of physical function. This example, and the others I have described, say to me that the issue of taking responsibility for structural privilege is a central one for allies to grasp.

It is extremely important to understand that we all carry with us the injustices done in our people's name. We inherit these injustices along with the privilege passed on to us by previous generations. It is especially important to remember this when we feel we are being accused of oppression, whether directly or by implication, when someone who experiences oppression tells their story. The point is not to hear such an accusation as an indictment of individual moral evil but as an opportunity to take responsibility for privilege.

Guilt and Responsibility

Taking on responsibility for privilege, personally and as a member of an oppressor group, involves making some distinctions: between responsibility and accountability; and between responsibility and guilt.

As I use the term accountability, it refers only to that which is within our individual realm of power and influence. If we have certain resources and decision-making powers included in an institutional role we hold, for example, we are accountable for the decisions we make and our use of those resources. If we have power and resources generally because of our class position, that is something for which we are accountable.

When we are speaking of privilege that comes to us uninvited, because we belong to a group with a history of oppressing another group, that is not something that is within our control. It began as a system or structure long before we were born. Responsibility applies to this situation. It means what it says—the ability to respond. This includes acceptance of our role as the present generation, with the opportunity to change the injustices we have inherited from the past. It also includes the ability to avoid defensiveness. Defensiveness tends to freeze our ability to respond, diverting energy into saving face.

Resisting the freezing effects of defensiveness involves making a distinction between taking responsibility and feeling guilt. In earlier drafts of this book and in the workshops I facilitate for allies, I used to write off guilt as a useless waste of energy. However, Michael Hart, a member of the Cree Nation and Professor of Social Work, challenged me on this. He pointed out that guilt takes place in a relationship. When one party has wronged the other, or abused power over the other, two things are required from the offender or oppressor for the relationship to heal. First, the offender or oppressor must become aware, on a feeling level, of the experience for the person or people who have been hurt. This is the difference between an apology that is heart-felt and one that is not. Second, the offender/oppressor must do something about it. Without either, the ability of both parties to move forward is limited. By writing off guilt, I was leaving out the feeling level of the healing process. Michael wrote:

> I think the issue is not whether to experience [guilt] or not, it is how it is taken on. It has to be in context. One person cannot take on the guilt for all of the oppression. However, this does not mean that they shouldn't take on guilt at all. I think the measuring stick is whether someone is immobilized or whether the guilt becomes a destructive force either internally or externally. When either or

both of these occur, then the guilt has gone much too far.
Guilt is also a way for a person to continue what they are
doing. In terms of oppression, I think a lot of the reactions e.g.
those tied to what has been called "white guilt," are about actions
that allow individuals to remain the same while, at the most, they
tinker with structures or provide a token act to alleviate the guilt.
This type of guilt and action is for the oppressor. (Personal
communication)

Michael's point is well taken. Feelings of guilt, and its relatives, remorse,
regret and shame, are essential to the process of healing damaged
relationships between individuals and between peoples. These are feelings
that connect the past with the present and can motivate our ability to
respond. What we must leave behind, as Michael points out, are the type
of guilty feelings that freeze our ability to respond. These, it seems to me,
are connected with the past only and tell us nothing can be done.

Audrey Thompson has written an article about some of the unhelpful
things white anti-racist people do to escape our own discomfort about
racism (2003). She tells a story about the effects of immobilizing guilt. In
the incident she relates, she stayed at a friends' house and cared for their
children for two weeks while they went on vacation. Shortly after arriving,
she discovered that they had taken the car key with them. She left a
message at their hotel asking them to send the key by overnight courier.
Her friends decided it would not be practical to send the key. However,
they called daily bemoaning their stupidity in forgetting to leave the key
and suggesting solutions such as asking the neighbours for rides to the
grocery store. During one phone call, the husband of the couple said: "Be
sure when you talk to Janet that you make her feel better; tell her it doesn't
matter. She feels so guilty, and it's just ruining our vacation" (16). As a
result, Thompson spent her time during the phone calls reassuring them
that it was all right, that the children were enjoying the adventure of using
the bus and bicycles to get everywhere. She says:

> Once I knew that there was no question of doing anything about
> the key, I focused on making our conversations as comfortable as
> possible. But I did wonder why alleviating their guilt was the issue.
> Recently it occurred to me that there was an analogy here to white
> guilt about racism. It is not a perfect analogy, by any means—
> putting up with racism for a lifetime is not exactly like having to
> take the bus for a couple of weeks—but there's one point I think
> the two situations may have in common. People of color are not
> really interested in daily phone calls about how bad we feel. They
> just want us to send the key. (17)

Thompson points out the past orientation of immobilizing guilt:

> Although they genuinely felt bad because the kids and I were
> inconvenienced, it seemed to them that, "realistically," there was
> nothing that they could do. Accordingly, they stressed their
> stupidity in having forgotten to leave the key. Whereas a sense of
> responsibility might have led them to take some definite action to
> change the situation, their sense of guilt concentrated their
> attention on themselves and their need to feel better.... Covertly,
> their guilt also served to exonerate them. Guilt mourns a past that
> cannot be changed; since clearly it would have been wrong for me
> to blame them for something that was merely an oversight, their
> guilt carried the seeds of their absolution. (25)

Avoiding action is not the only problematic response to past-oriented
guilt. Another is, as Michael points out, token change to relieve the guilt. I
would add a third: defensiveness. Defensiveness wastes energy that could
otherwise be put into strategies for change and, as we saw in Chapter
Seven, can trigger institutional backlash.

The more I reflect on what Michael has said, the more I think that,
consistent with his Aboriginal way of seeing things, he has defined the
difference between static, dualistic guilt and guilt that is part of a healing
process. Static guilt comes from the Western system of "justice." It poses
a dualism between guilt and innocence, and guilt is connected to
punishment. The appropriate response to static guilt is self-defence, saving
face or deflection of the accusation by making some kind of visible but
shallow change. Guilt that is part of a process of healing connects us with a
living relationship of past, present and future. It understands that wanting
the situation to be right is important, but in order to make it right, we
must engage in a long struggle, in relationship. Joining in this process is
what it means to take responsibility for privilege.

Speaking on a personal note, as someone very accomplished at Western,
dualistic guilt and sometimes immobilized by it, guilt is not an easy
response to un-learn. I felt much better when I could just write it off! Now
I see that, like so many other aspects of internalized dominance,
immobilizing guilt requires a process of recovery.

Degrees of Power, Circles of Influence

Another liberal tendency that must be overcome in order to take responsibility for our privilege relates to another dualistic concept: our habit of
thinking we either have power or not. On one hand, our dominant liberal
ideology tends to make us think that everything is in our control and we
should be able to do something about it. This is part of our confusion over
accountability and responsibility. The fact that we haven't fixed the situa-

tion must mean that we are terrible people. This is an illusion, an over-estimation of our individual power, a form of perfectionism. It has the same effect as past-oriented guilt: it can freeze us, inspire token changes or cause us to misdirect our energy into defensiveness.

The other side of the liberal concept of personal power is to see ourselves as completely powerless. Oppression and injustice are too big for us. What can we possibly do that will make any difference? This is connected closely with the past-oriented guilt that causes us to feel miserable but still decide, like Audrey Thompson's friends, not to send the key.

Powerlessness is also an illusion. Each of us has a circle of influence, small or large, depending on our class and our position in relation to other forms of oppression. As described in Chapter Six, chaos theory tells us that institutions and cultures are not machines but complex, non-linear systems. During change in such a system, simple behaviour results from complex causes and complex behaviour from simple causes. I will return to this discussion of individual circle of influence and chaos theory in the next chapter. For now I want to make the point that I think it is only possible to take responsibility for our privilege and the oppression carried out in our name if we accept whatever sphere of influence we have, knowing that in a complex non-linear system we can never predict how large or small that circle will be at any given moment.

Building Strategy

Building strategy for change is a process of action and reflection, what popular educator Paulo Freire (1970) calls "praxis." My favourite image for this process is the spiral. In the centre, at the beginning of the process, those who wish to work together toward justice and equity reflect on themselves in terms of class, position in the institution, values, assumptions and in relation to different forms of oppression (race, sex, sexual orientation, language, ethnicity, etc.). This step is called "Placing Ourselves," and the question is: "Who are we?"

The next step is called "Reflection." The question is: "What is happening?" We name events and consider how we react to them, our hopes and fears.

The third step is "Analysis," and its key question is: "Why is it happening?" Here we examine the structure of the institution, its history, culture, values, trends over time, the actors and their interests. A very important component of analysis is "leverage points." These are the opportunities where those with less power could potentially influence events as if they had far more power. A leverage point could be good timing for an action, for example, when an ally on a committee or board informs you that a certain issue will be under discussion on a certain day. A leverage point could be an opportunity to make an important contact with a powerful player, perhaps on an informal level, or influence policy when it is

The Spiral

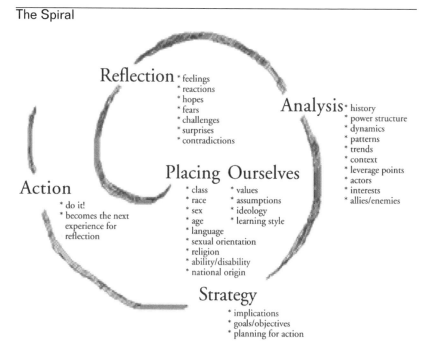

Reflection * feelings
* reactions
* hopes
* fears
* challenges
* surprises
* contradictions

Analysis * history
* power structure
* dynamics
* patterns
* trends
* context
* leverage points
* actors
* interests
* allies/enemies

Placing Ourselves
* class   * values
* race   * assumptions
* sex   * ideology
* age   * learning style
* language
* sexual orientation
* religion
* ability/disability
* national origin

Action
* do it!
* becomes the next experience for reflection

Strategy
* implications
* goals/objectives
* planning for action

being reviewed. A leverage point could be something like a review by a major funding body of the institution's progress toward equity. The analysis stage of building strategy includes looking for those opportunities when "the small can move the large."

The fourth step of the spiral is "Strategy," or planning some steps to take to move the cause forward. The question here is: "What are we going to do about it?" At the fifth step, we carry out our plans. The step is called, simply, "Action."

After taking action, the group starts around the spiral again, asking: "What happened as a result of our action?" "Why did it happen?" and "What are we going to do next?"

The spiral is a continuous form of strategy building. It is described in more depth in other sources (CUSO 1988, Bishop 2002 and 2004). More important here are the strategic implications of thinking structurally about our institutions.

Tactics for Reform

Many of the tactics we currently use for moving our institutions toward equity are aimed primarily at individuals. These include education, lobbying, pressure tactics, conflict resolution, legal mechanisms for human rights and harassment complaint procedures. I will discuss legal mechanisms for human rights and harassment complaint procedures in more detail later.

For now, the point I wish to make is that these tactics are valid, but it is important that they be used in conjunction with strategies aimed at the institution itself. Education of individuals is always necessary, but if it is divorced from structural transformation of the institution, it can act as a "vaccine," teaching the institution how to resist change. Individuals can say they've "done that." Institutional bodies can "cross it off their list." For example they may claim: "We've already had sensitivity training." Education can, in other words, be used as an excuse not to work at changing the deeper structural barriers in the institution.

Pressure on individual decision-makers can be an important part of changing structures. As noted earlier, if we have a sound analysis of the relative power of the decision-maker and the institutional limits within which he or she works, our pressure tactics can be much more effective, even result in the development of a high-level ally. Sometimes when we put pressure on an individual decision-maker about a case involving a newcomer to the institution, the result can be special treatment for that one person. This is a dangerous tactic that can work against collective strategies for change by planting the seeds of division among the oppressed.

Likewise, conflict resolution between or among individuals can be used to make differences in power invisible by assuming that all parties to the process have an equal voice. Later, the institution can claim that the conflict was fairly resolved and should not come up again. On the other hand, conflict resolution processes such as mediation and conflict facilitation can be very useful in resolving certain equity conflict situations before they have the opportunity to escalate into a situation of potential backlash.

Another tactic that is primarily aimed at individuals is the acceptance of token members of oppressed groups into the institution. On one hand, given the slow pace of institutional change and limits in institutional budgets, this is an unavoidable first step in the eventual transformation of the structure. On the other hand, as we have already seen in Chapter Seven, institutions are skilled at using tokens to prevent structural transformation. Tokens can be used to claim that there is no longer discrimination in the institution. Their presence can strengthen the belief that giving oppressed people a representative in the institutional structure can make change without the institution or those in more privileged positions taking any responsibility. Tokens can be played off against each other or used against their own people. When those with power in an institution want to defuse a demonstration about equity issues, a common tactic is to send out an employee who is a member of the oppressed group in question to deal with the demonstrators. When the purpose is to discredit a public allegation of inequity, institutional leaders know the best person for the job is a member of an oppressed group. Occasionally, individual members of oppressed groups come to prefer and benefit from the token role and can become impediments to change. Groups building strategies for institutional equity have to remember that any strategy involving pressure to hire or admit members of a "newcomer" group must be very carefully handled. It is particularly important to reflect on the structural nature of tokens, for better or worse.

Allies in powerful institutional positions have a particular opportunity and responsibility to ensure that token strategies are used well. The best time to press the institution to design token positions that lead to further structural change instead of blocking it is before the "newcomers" enter the institution. Fair employment practices, sound affirmative action policies, communication, education and effective complaint channels should be in place before any action is taken to include people who have been excluded in the past. After there are people inside the institution in token positions, allies in powerful roles can do more than people at other levels to protect them from abuse and continue the process so that the tokens do not remain token any longer than necessary.

The key in using each of these strategies is to remember that their primary purpose involves individuals. They were invented for reform. They can be useful. In fact, they are unavoidable. However, each must be used with care and consciousness to avoid harming the cause of structural transformation.

Tactics for Structural Transformation

There are many tactics for structural change. The students in "The Story" used some of them—organizing work and study groups, finding and using all the existing channels of communication with those who hold power, finding and using the institution's policies, exchanging support as allies on different issues, researching and writing briefs on policy, and engaging the support of internal and external organizations and allies. Lillian used her position as a teacher to communicate structural thinking and engage students in systemic transformation of the institution.

The Cornwall Collective, a group of women associated with theological colleges in the United States, provides a "catalogue" of the strategies and choices available for changing institutional structures and the power on which they are based. They name a range of tactics from less to more confrontational, including: using the regular channels for change, organizational development, data feedback, going by the book, building an internal power base, forming coalitions with external groups, using legislation to pressure those in power and seizing power to confront the administration (1980: 87–90).

Walter Wink (1992), whose powerful analysis of institutions as entities and the dynamics of scapegoating appear in chapters Five and Seven, argues that the predominant spirituality of the modern world's institutions is violence (13). He describes in detail how the "principalities and powers" act to perpetuate violence using such strategies as addiction (73), threat of punishment or death (92), scapegoating (144–53) and lies (99). The humans within institutions support the perpetration of violence, he says, through numbing ourselves (42), preferring to neutralize facts rather than change our beliefs (94), and above all, silent tolerance of injustice and lies (98).

Therefore in order to fight for justice, he says, we must break the silence (99), abandon our fear of punishment and death by "dying to the internalized bondage of the system" (157), create ways to resist non-violently (185–86, 207, 227, 233, 244), let go of hatred because we become what we hate (195–205), and "believe the future into being"; that is, we must act as if the future we hope for is already here (299). The "Powers," that is, institutional entities, are mortal, Wink explains. They become vicious when they see that their days are numbered, but when enough people withdraw the consent they need to survive, they will fall (313).

Donnellon and Kolb also suggest strategies: increasing the scope of diagnosis of problems to include social diversity issues, legitimating the diversity "lens" for examining organizational conflict, supporting collective action by internal groups who share the same social diversity issues and examining the consequences of power distribution so as to prepare for resistance, for example, by clearly linking loss of personal power to organizational well-being (1994).

The authors of *Gender at Work* describe structural change strategies in this way:

> Our work is organizational transformation, not simply tinkering with organizational margins to suit funding cultures, address the needs of political correctness, or appease organized constituencies. We believe that gender equality can be achieved by organizations only as they transcend the patriarchal and bureaucratic modes of organizing that perpetuate gender inequality. This implies tackling the gendered deep structure—that is, changing inequitable power relations, devaluing heroic individualism in favor of crisis prevention and team work, better work-family balance, and focussing on broad goals rather than narrow targets, both as means and as ends. (Rao, Stuart and Kelleher 1999: 221)

None of these structural transformation tactics is new. This is simply a list and a reminder that we must continue to use and develop them if we are going to be successful in transforming our institutions so that they are just and equitable.

Preventing, Delaying and Moderating Backlash

Along with our strategies to bring about transformation in our institutions, it is important to think about measures for preventing, delaying and moderating backlash. I am not suggesting conflict-avoidance on principle or by compromising the deep structural nature of the changes we aim to make. I am suggesting that we consider tactics for moderating backlash if we can, because its cruel effects fall most directly on those who have already suffered the persecution of being "newcomers" in the institution. Their allies suffer less directly, and the institutional entity is not able to suffer. As Donnellon and Kolb point out, if the conflict is suppressed in one way or another, the costs are borne by one side—the victims. If the conflict is dealt with openly and fairly, and a resolution is found, the costs are borne by both sides (1994).

Communication and education are part of backlash moderation. Our concepts of what needs to be changed and how are much easier to hear before the deep emotions of a conflict are brought into play. Strategies to bring more people from previously excluded groups into the institution and build understanding among them are helpful. Then when conflict arises, the tokens are less visible and vulnerable because that role is spread out among more people. A third and very important preventive strategy is the building of alliances with supportive individuals and organizations, both within and outside of the institution.

A few years ago I had the privilege of working with the skilled and committed diversity committee of Girl Guides of Nova Scotia. The diversity committee of Girl Guides of Ontario had encountered problems in their efforts to open their organization to those that had previously been excluded. They offered this excellent advice to the Nova Scotia group: go slowly, involve all levels (especially the top) and start with yourselves. The "go slowly" part was used by at least one person in the organization as an excuse not to move forward; I am not advocating that interpretation. Most saw it as I think it was intended: that is, don't rush to involve newcomers in the organization before you have done some learning and organizational preparation. These three points provide excellent advice to any group seeking equity in an institution.

Equity Conflict Procedures

When conflict does strike our efforts to create equity in institutions, we have a range of tactics we are currently using to deal with it. These are very important but limited by the fact that most are based on a liberal concept of institutions as a sum of their parts; that is, a collection of individuals. These tactics include mediation, formal complaint procedures (including investigations and hearings), procedures governed by human rights legislation (such as investigation and tribunals), procedures governed by labour legislation (such as grievances and arbitration) and civil suits.

Mediation is a useful way to sort out problems between individuals before they become large enough to engage the institution and perhaps trigger backlash. On the other hand, mediation assumes that the individuals involved are equal. It can be a dangerous tactic when one party has more institutional power than the other. The less powerful party may "agree" to solutions that are not adequate for them because they have no alternative.

Likewise, formal complaint procedures are valuable, particularly when they include an investigation conducted by a trained investigator and the possibility of negotiating a solution without going to a hearing. I took a basic level course in harassment investigation and was impressed by the degree of skill, knowledge and discipline involved in doing such work. It gave me respect for and faith in professional harassment investigation.

However, formal complaint procedures have great limitations. Anne Donnellon and Deborah M. Kolb (1994) give as an example the fact that very few disputes actually find their way into the process because the complainants fear the consequences. This is particularly true when the process includes punishment for complaints brought "in bad faith," like the complaints procedure included in the settlement agreement Lillian refused to sign. Systems such as negotiation and formal complaint procedures, say Donnellon and Kolb, are designed to deal with only individual complaints, not collective conditions, thus putting the onus on the individuals to resolve the conflict rather than on the organization to change the culture and practices that caused the problem in the first place (143). Chandra Talpade Mohanty agrees with this analysis. She describes the effect of negotiation and formal complaint systems as "erosion of the politics of collectivity through the reformulation of race and difference in individualistic terms" (Mohanty 1994, quoted in Graveline 1996: 350).

Formal complaint systems and institutional conflict resolution mechanisms based on human rights and labour legislation involve judicial or quasi-judicial procedures. These procedures are seeking a different kind of outcome from criminal trials (remedy instead of punishment) and the standard of proof is different (in formal complaint mechanisms and human rights cases, proof is based on a "balance of probabilities"). I do not want to belittle the importance of these procedures and the legislation behind them, particularly in cases where the problem is the deliberate misuse of power by an individual. However, they can take years to resolve, if they are resolved at all. Lillian's case dragged through various legal processes for more than eight years and still had no satisfying resolution. Cases like this can cost thousands of dollars and can wear people down, particularly those with less institutional backing and fewer resources. Because these procedures are based in our Western judicial system, their framework is adversarial and our general cultural approach to them contains many dualities—guilt or innocence, this "side" or that "side" "wins." They reduce all equity conflict to something that occurs among individuals. There is little room in them to treat equity conflict as part of a process of change in an institution. An adjudicator or negotiated agreement can call for institutional actions as part of a remedy, but these requirements are difficult to define and monitor. As our adversarial procedures create "sides" and widen the gap between them, the institutional entity quietly slips out the back door.

Adverse Effect and Systemic Discrimination

There are many examples of cases under human rights and labour legislation where institutional dynamics have been considered. I am not knowledgeable in the field of law, but as I read the judgements in these cases, I get the feeling that many people are trying to stretch the conceptual framework of judicial and quasi-judicial procedures to fit conflict that involves an institution as an entity. For example, human rights procedures use the concept of "adverse effect discrimination." This refers to laws, policies or procedures that are applied to everyone but affect some people differently from others. For example, in one human rights case a retail store required all employees to work Saturdays. An employee who was a member of the Seventh Day Adventist Church was forced to change from full-time to part-time work, losing most of her employment benefits, because her religion required that she observe the Sabbath and not work on Saturdays (*Ontario Human Rights Commission v. Simpsons-Sears* 1985).

Going one step further, those involved in the human rights field use the concept of "systemic discrimination." Michael Dunphy, who taught me human rights investigation, defined it this way: "Systemic discrimination is present when discrimination is practiced against a whole group of people, or when there are many repeated instances against one person" (Dunphy and Associates 1996: 5).

The lawyer who argued the Faculty Association case in the preliminary hearing concerning Lillian's arbitration used several different definitions of "systemic discrimination." One came from the Abella Report on Equality in Employment, which defined systemic discrimination as "discrimination that results from the simple operation of established procedures of recruitment, hiring and promotion, none of which is necessarily designed to promote discrimination" (*Public Service Alliance of Canada v. Canada (Department of National Defence)* 1996: 800).

Another definition used by the Faculty Association's lawyer came from Weiner and Gunderson, authors of *Pay Equity: Issues, Options and Experiences*. They defined systemic discrimination as: "an unintended byproduct of seemingly neutral policies and practices. However, these policies and practices may well result in an adverse or disparate impact on one group vis-à-vis another (1990: 5).

A third definition presented by the Faculty Association's lawyer came from an arbitration decision by M.G. Mitchnick. He made the following comments on systemic discrimination: "Ms Webb (Maureen Webb, a senior lawyer for the Canadian Association of University Teachers) in her submissions for the Association stresses in particular the fact that 'discrimination' complaints, as compared to more typical grievances alleging breach of a collective agreement, rarely have the benefit of an overt act on the part of an employer, but rather have to depend more often on an amalgam of evidentiary indicia, or patterns of conduct, in the nature of circumstantial evidence. This is particularly true in the case of allegations of 'systemic' discrimination, and arbitrators have recognized this" (Mitchnick 1995: 12).

These definitions, it seems to me, make little distinction between "systemic discrimination" and "adverse effect discrimination." They allow for the unintentional nature of it, but do not quite make room for the dynamics of an institutional entity engaged in a process of change. Maureen Webb came closest to a structural view when she advocated using "patterns of conduct" to prove the existence of structural inequality in an institution.

There is no doubt room for judicial and quasi-judicial procedures to move further in understanding and taking into account the dynamics of an institutional entity in specific cases of equity conflict. However, it seems to me there is still a gap here. I think we need something else, a process that will allow us to examine the "symptoms" (the individual conflicts) in the context of the "disease" (the inequity built into the history, values and power structure of the institution).

Roxanna Ng (1993) describes an equity conflict in a university setting:

> The dynamics that partly shaped the interactions described in the incident (I have chosen) involve relations of gender, race and class. These relations, which I call "sexism" and "racism," are not peculiar to this incident but are rather relations that have developed over time in Canada and elsewhere as groups of people have interacted. They have become systemic, that is, they are taken for granted and not ordinarily open to interrogation. In examining the incident, my intention is not to attribute blame or to identify victims, but to explicate the systemic character of sexism and racism as they are manifested in interactional settings. I maintain that in so doing, we move away from treating these incidents as idiosyncratic, isolated "wrong doing" perpetrated by a few individuals with attitudinal problems. Instead, we aim at a fundamental re-examination of the structures and relations of universities, which have marginalized and excluded certain groups of people historically, and continue to do so despite equity measures implemented in the last ten years or so. (191)

I agree; but how? What kind of procedure would allow us to "move away from treating these incidents as ... isolated 'wrong doing'" and "aim at a fundamental re-examination of the structures and relations of universities" or any other institution?

A Proposal

Employment equity professionals use a process called an "employment systems review" to make recommendations for equity in the employment practices of an institution. This involves a series of interviews with the organization's personnel to explore the formal and informal ways things are done and the impact they have on different groups within the institution. The employment systems reviews I am familiar with were carried out by a single professional investigator and reported to senior administration. By definition their mandate was limited to employment practices.

I believe we could develop a just and accurate method for investigating structural inequality in institutions by building on the concept and process of an employment systems review. I envision a panel, broadly representative of the institution but mandated at the highest level, with the task of examining the institution in a process similar to an employment systems review.

Unlike some past investigations of equity conflicts, this panel would not be formed in accordance with the liberal notion of "objective." In the story of Leela Madhava Rau, former Race Relations Officer at Western University, summarized in Chapter Eight, the university's Race Relations Policy was re-written by a panel selected for their "neutrality" on race relations issues. The Race Relations Officer and any other visible minority members of the campus community were automatically considered biased. This is a totally faulty approach because, as I explained in the Introduction, there is no such thing as objectivity or neutrality. In cases involving equity conflict, "objective" usually refers to people whose biases are less visible because they hold the views of the dominant group and the institution itself. Also, as explained in the Introduction to this book and at length in *Becoming an Ally* (Bishop 2002: 155–56), it is those who experience oppression that can see it most clearly.

The research methods used by a panel such as the one I am proposing would be as participatory as possible. As far as possible, facilitated group processes would replace individual interviews and collective analysis would replace that of individuals. Ideally such a panel would carry out investigation and analysis before being called upon to deal with a specific conflict or situation of backlash.

Whether before, during or after an equity conflict, the task of the panel would be to look for certain patterns that we know result from institutionalized injustice and exclusion. It would have to have the blessing of the highest level of the institution so that it would have a mandate to negotiate strategies of institutional change backed by the power to impose them if necessary.

A requirement for panels such as the one I am proposing would be a collection of literature on typical patterns displayed by an institution in various stages of encounter with the struggle for equity, similar to Athena

Theodore's survey (1986) or Chapter Seven of this book. It might even be possible to develop a reference "catalogue" of such patterns. This document could be used to identify the presence of well-known organizational behaviour associated with equity struggles at different stages. In other words, it would be possible to put the institution, instead of the individuals within it, "on trial" and propose remedies based on structural analysis. A guide to institutional patterns of change would also be a useful tool for anyone developing policies and strategies to move an institution toward equity.

Structural Thinking and Strategies for Change

The purpose of this Chapter has been to begin evaluating the strategies we are using to bring about equity in our institutions in the light of the structural analysis presented in the earlier chapters. Many of our current strategies assume that institutions are made up of individuals and the conflicts within them are solely among individuals. As a result, much of our attention has been given to the symptoms rather than the root cause of inequity.

I am not suggesting that we abandon any of our current strategies. They are important for dealing with situations when discrimination is intentional or institutional power is deliberately misused by an individual. However, it is also important to recognize their limitations. Equity conflict involves institutional entities beyond the individuals within them, and we need tactics and tools for dealing with this level as well. I think we need to learn to think structurally and apply this view to our strategies. This will help us stretch the limits of some of the tactics we already use and keep them firmly embedded within a larger structural context. I am also proposing that we develop new methods of challenging injustice at the institutional level. In particular, I suggest that we expand the methods and mandate of the employment systems review and develop a catalogue of institutional behaviour patterns associated with various stages in the struggle toward equity.

Chapter Nine

Hope

A Few Lights in the Tunnel

As the experiences recounted in "The Story" dragged on, with no satisfying conclusion, my hope for justice and equity in institutions like Canadian University was at a low ebb. There have been times when the institution seemed too entrenched and powerful, and the costs too high. I am particularly discouraged by the way the costs of change continually fall on the least powerful players.

However, the experience of studying what happened, analyzing the underlying forces, comparing the experience of "The Story" with that of others seeking institutional justice and making at least beginning proposals for how we might deal better with similar situations has given me a few new reasons for hope, a few lights along the sides of the tunnel.

Companions Along the Way

The first light in the tunnel is the network of social justice activists I have met along the way, in person or through their writing. They are passionate and courageous people who are bringing all their knowledge, strength, skill and determination to the cause of equity in institutions and society. Many have been knocked down for a period of time, but have gone back to the struggle later. Many felt alone, but then became connected into this huge circle of people who have experienced discrimination and are determined that future generations will not have to. There is energy, friendship and support available in this network.

Sheila McIntyre, in her essay in the Chilly Collective volume, speaks about the power of breaking the silence for connecting the sufferers and the fighters:

> The act of naming misogyny ... led literally hundreds of people—
> overwhelmingly women—to write or phone or drop by my office
> or introduce themselves on the street. Most supported me and
> most disclosed comparable experiences from their own lives.
> Women faculty from some 30 American and Canadian universi-
> ties and virtually every academic discipline wrote offering support
> or corroboration. I heard also from department-store saleswomen,

my students' parents, prison guards, clergy, colleagues' wives, journalists, homemakers, therapists, artisans—in short women whose lives connected with mine through the sharing of the daily lived experience of sexism....

Whenever I spoke, women's faces gripped me: faces hungry for validation, faces devastated to acknowledge the privatized damage normally kept buried. It was these faces I locked onto when I spoke, not those of the skeptics or the hostile. After each address, women of the hungry, devastated faces would approach me privately and ask me, nearly inaudibly, "You mean I am not crazy?" dreading I would not take them seriously. I think I needed them as much as they needed me. The contact allowed us all to exorcise and externalize the damage we are done by male legal institutions. (1995: 213, 219, 255–56)

Chaos and Hope

The brightest light in the tunnel, however, has been my exploration of chaos theory. I have always been inspired to keep going by the thought that one action or one voice could make a difference. As Australian singer Judy Small says in her song "One Voice in the Crowd":

> One brick in the wall
> You may be one voice in the crowd
> But without you we are weaker
> And our song may not be heard
> One drop in the ocean
> But each drop will swell the tide
> So be your one brick in the wall
> Be one voice in the crowd. (Small 1985)

However, I was still thinking of a steady accumulation until a certain point is reached—the one drop that would make the water spill over the side of the bucket or "the straw that broke the camel's back." I was still thinking in terms of a machine.

Now, I have come to see institutions not as machines, but as entities. As I read what chaos theory has to say about change in entities, I realized that there is no steady progress. Rather, there are wild fluctuations and shifting instability. In this context, a tiny movement can have vast consequences. When Edward Lorenz was playing with the computer model of the weather that resulted in his creation of the Lorenz Attractor, he made another discovery, what he called the "Butterfly Effect."

Before chaos theory, scientists assumed that measurements in experiments did not have to be perfect because small errors have small effects (Gleick 1987: 15). They also assumed that large, complex systems like the weather cannot be accurately predicted simply because no one could possibly do all the measurements and calculations (14). James Gleick quotes a scientist telling his students: "The basic idea of Western science is that you don't have to take into account the falling of a leaf on some planet in another galaxy when you're trying to account for the motion of a billiard ball on a pool table on earth" (15). Edward Lorenz discovered otherwise with his computer model of the weather.

One day he wanted to re-run a section of his model weather system. He typed in the numbers from the point where he wanted to pick it up and left it to print out the repeated patterns. When he came back an hour later, there was a surprise. At first the original patterns and new patterns matched. Then they began to diverge. Then they diverged further and further until it was completely different weather that was appearing on the page. After checking out every possible cause for this surprising result, Lorenz realized that because he had rounded off the numbers when he typed them in again, the whole system had changed over time. His system was so sensitive that a tiny difference, one part in one thousand, was not, as he had assumed, too small to matter. As the computer calculated its twelve equations over and over again, using the results of the last calculation as the beginning of the next, a tiny difference had been magnified until the weather was unrecognizable from the original (16).

Lorenz came to a conclusion from this experience: we can predict periodic systems, like the tides and eclipses, with a fair degree of accuracy, but when any non-periodic element is added, the system becomes unpredictable in a linear sense. The reason is the system's extreme sensitivity to small influences. A tiny disturbance grows when it is part of an operation that repeats and repeats endlessly. He dubbed this discovery the Butterfly Effect, defined by the now well-known sentence, "A butterfly beating its wings today in Peking can cause a storm in New York next month" (8). James Gleick points out that the Butterfly Effect appears in folk literature in the form of an old poem:

> For want of a nail, the shoe was lost;
> For want of a shoe, the horse was lost;
> For want of a horse, the rider was lost;
> For want of a rider, the battle was lost;
> For want of a battle, the kingdom was lost;
> And all for the want of a horseshoe nail. (23)

Before chaos theory, scientists believed they could ignore small influences because they would have correspondingly small effects. Lorenz proved them wrong. Margaret Wheatley applies this insight to institutions. She says:

Structures take in new information causing a small fluctuation. The information grows in strength as it interacts with the system and is fed back on itself. The disruption grows until the system can no longer ignore it. Far from equilibrium, the system falls apart. In most cases it can then re-configure itself at a higher level of complexity, better able to deal with the new environment.

Under certain conditions, when the system is far from equilibrium, creative individuals can have enormous impact. It is not the law of large numbers, of favorable averages, that creates change, but the presence of a lone fluctuation that gets amplified by the system ... where a small disturbance is fed back on itself, changing and growing, exponential effects can result....

Changes in small places create large system change through the wholeness that has united them all along. (1992: 19–20, 42, 95–96)

Anne Wilson Schaef also takes hope from a quantum perception of the world. Schaef's comparison of a hologram with an Addictive System bears repeating:

The essential feature of a hologram is that each piece of the hologram contains the entire structure of the entire hologram; each piece is not just a part of the whole, it has the entire pattern and way of functioning of the whole embedded in it. This is a useful way to look at the Addictive System. The system is like the individual, and the individual is like the system. In other words, the Addictive System has all the characteristics of the individual alcoholic/addict. (1987: 37)

Schaef goes on to describe the ramifications of small changes within such systems:

As people start shifting into a process system that is free of addictions and addictive behaviors, the system itself is making a similar shift. As the system changes to support that shift, individuals have still more options for change. The part is like the whole, the whole is like the part, and in some very basic ways they are the same. Changes in one are changes in the other and are reflected in both directions. What an exciting possibility! (1987: 149)

Another example of the quantum nature of change is the "hundredth monkey," a biological research project that has given hope to social justice advocates for decades. Ken Keyes Jr. (1984) describes what happened:

The Japanese monkey, Macaca fuscata, has been observed in the wild for a period of 30 years. In 1952, on the island of Koshima, scientists were providing monkeys with sweet potatoes dropped in the sand. The monkeys liked the taste of the raw sweet potatoes, but they found the dirt unpleasant. An 18-month-old female named Imo found she could solve the problem by washing the potatoes in a nearby stream. She taught this trick to her mother. Her playmates also learned this new way and they taught their mothers too. This cultural innovation was gradually picked up by various monkeys before the eyes of the scientists.

Between 1952 and 1958, all the young monkeys learned to wash the sandy sweet potatoes to make them more palatable. Only the adults who imitated their children learned this social improvement. Other adults kept eating the dirty sweet potatoes.

Then something startling took place. In the autumn of 1958, a certain number of Koshima monkeys were washing sweet potatoes—the exact number is not known. Let us suppose that when the sun rose one morning there were 99 monkeys on Koshima Island who had learned to wash their sweet potatoes. Let's further suppose that later that morning, the hundredth monkey learned to wash potatoes. Then it happened! By that evening, almost everyone in the tribe was washing sweet potatoes before eating them. The added energy of this hundredth monkey somehow created an ideological breakthrough. But notice, a most surprising thing observed by these scientists was that the habit of washing sweet potatoes then jumped over the sea. Colonies of monkeys on other islands and the mainland troop of monkeys at Takasakiyama began washing their sweet potatoes.

Thus, when a certain critical number achieves an awareness, this new awareness may be communicated from mind to mind. Although the exact number may vary, the Hundredth Monkey Phenomenon means that when only a limited number of people know of a new way, it may remain the conscious property of these people. But there is a point at which if only one more person tunes in to a new awareness, a field is strengthened so that this awareness is picked up by almost everyone. (11–16, with an internal reference to Watson 1980: 147–48))

As I said in the final chapter of *Becoming an Ally* (2002), hope is not a static state, not a "bet" on something that will happen in the future. It is a process, a way of being, a calling, a belief system. To me, the message of the "Butterfly Effect," the hologram and the hundredth monkey phenomenon is that we never know when some small action may change a whole system. Nothing we do is ever too small to count, even if, in the short term, institutional backlash seems to reverse our efforts. A change on any level is a change on all levels. David Peat says:

> A human being is a "model" or representation of the entire cosmos. But this should not be taken to mean that a human being is a model of the cosmos in the sense that a plastic toy is a model of an airplane. Rather, the human being enfolds the cosmos and within the order of body and mind can be found the cosmic order. Likewise, as human beings work at transformation ... they are affecting the entire universe. (258)

This is my reason to keep working and to keep hoping.

Notes for Educators

The Implication of Institutional Patterns for Adult Educators

In *Becoming an Ally* I wrote an extensive chapter for people who are interested in "educating allies" in a classroom or workshop setting. I would strongly recommend that anyone who plans to work with students or participants on their understanding of oppression read it.

Following the analysis of institutional oppression I have presented in this book, I wish to make three further points for educators: First, I feel our key task as educators is to understand and communicate the structural nature of oppression (Chapter Five). In that context, our second challenge is to change the emphasis from oppression to privilege and from personal defensiveness to responsibility for our role in oppressive structures (Chapter Eight). Third, we must prepare students/participants for backlash, what Robert Wright calls "the second stage" of anti-oppression work (Chapter Seven).

Teaching Structural Thinking

In North America, the vast majority of people who enter a classroom or workshop are looking at the issues from a liberal perspective—as a matter of individual acts and attitudes, a matter of "guilt or innocence." Part of our challenge as educators is to help them make the shift to understanding oppression as structural.

A talk about the difference between viewing a situation personally and structurally is useful, particularly if it is filled with examples such as the ones found in Chapter Five of this book, but talking rarely takes learning very far. Humans learn much better, and retain the lessons much longer, if they are challenged to figure out or at least apply the learning for themselves. This can be done through case studies and work in small groups to present an individual and structural perspective. General case studies work, but the best case studies are based directly on the concerns of the people in the room. For example, if the participants are all teachers, a case study involving a teacher accused of racism for failing a Black student will bring out the issues the group needs to talk about. The group can practise distinguishing between a personal and structural view by working out how the teacher would analyze the situation through each of these lenses.

If the setting is an experiential workshop, this discussion can be stimulated by a set of buttons or stickers with such slogans as "I am racist," "I am heterosexist," or "I am sexist" on them. Presented with such a collection of slogans and asked to wear them pinned to their clothing, a group will quickly come up with their deepest responses. This can set the context for a talk about what "I am racist" or "I am sexist" or "I am heterosexist" means when interpreted personally or structurally. It is not a good idea for the participants to actually wear the labels. Just being asked how they would respond to being asked to wear them is usually enough to bring out the feelings and the issues. Seeing people wearing the buttons or stickers can be very confusing to observers outside of the context of the workshop discussion.

Separating Accountability and Guilt from Responsibility

After helping students or participants understand a structural view of oppression, the next step is to distinguish between accountability and responsibility, and to separate personal guilt from responsibility. I am referring here to past-oriented guilt as discussed in Chapter Eight, the kind that causes immobility and defensiveness. If you have done an experiential exercise such as the one with the buttons or stickers, you will already be talking about guilt and responsibility along with the structural view. Anyone who can put on a button that says "I am sexist" or "I am racist" has already begun to accept responsibility for privilege (unless they have put it on to please someone else, for example you, the facilitator!). It helps students make the distinction if they can separate the impact of oppression in the present from its development in the past. For example, talking about the history of residential schools often leaves liberal white Canadians defensive and immobilized. If the presentation or discussion continues on into the current struggles to right the wrongs of the residential schools, there is an opportunity to take responsibility, because these struggles are taking place now, with many tasks available to be carried out by people who want to see that grave injustice corrected for the future.

Preparing Students and Participants for Future Backlash

Another feature of liberal ideology is the belief in steady progress toward better conditions. In Chapter Seven, I discussed the ideas of Robert Wright, former Race Relations Officer for the School Board in Dartmouth, Nova Scotia. His observation was that teachers who apply anti-racist principles in their classrooms are more likely than their colleagues to be accused of racism. His concern is that by giving people well-meaning anti-racist training in a liberal context, we betray them. We don't warn them that the path is not a steady upwards climb.

Referring back to the discussion of chaos theory in Chapter Six, work toward institutional equity is more likely to trigger a set of wild fluctuations, not steady progress towards improvement. When a teacher or anyone else tries to introduce anti-oppressive principles into an institution or situation, they may well trigger a backlash, which will strike out at them, but even more at the people they were trying to help in the first place. Backlash scapegoats the most vulnerable people. It is important that we prepare those we teach for the unstable process of institutional change, and particularly the possibility of backlash, right from the beginning.

Three Key Concepts

These are just a few suggestions. There are many ways for educators to help people see and act on institutional injustice. I feel that at the centre of this work should be these three key concepts: a structural view, taking responsibility for privilege and preparation for the ups and downs, and also the risks, of progress toward institutional justice. Education should never be done in a vacuum, but as part of a larger strategy for institutional change. In the overall strategy the principles suggested to the Girl Guides of Nova Scotia Diversity Committee by Girl Guides of Ontario are the key ones: go slow, involve all levels and start with yourself (Chapter Eight).

References

Aisenberg, Nadya, and Mona Harrington. 1988. *Women of Academe: Outsiders in the Sacred Grove*. Amherst, MA: University of Massachusetts Press.

Arendt, Hannah. 1963. *Eichmann in Jerusalem: A Report on the Banality of Evil*. New York, NY: Viking.

Ashby, Eric. 1967. "Ivory Towers in Tomorrow's World." *Journal of Higher Education* 38 (Nov.). Quoted in Rudy Willis, *The Universities of Europe 100–1914: A History*. London, Toronto: Associated University Presses.

Backhouse, Constance. 1995. "An Historical Perspective: Reflections on the Western Employment Equity Award." In Chilly Collective.

Bankier, Jennifer. 1996. "Trapped Inside the Circle: The Myth of Intent and the Resolution of Equity Disputes." *CAUT Bulletin, Status of Women Supplement* 43 (4) (April).

Bannerji, Himani. 1991. "But Who Speaks for Us? Experience and Agency in Conventional Feminist Paradigms." In Himani Bannerji et al. (eds.), *Unsettling Relations: The University as a Site of Feminist Struggles*. Toronto: Women's Press.

Bernard, Wanda Thomas, Lydia Lucas-White and Dorothy Moore. 1981. "Triple Jeopardy: Assessing Life Experiences of Black Nova Scotian Women from a Social Work Perspective." *Canadian Social Work Review* 10 (2) (Summer).

Bishop, Anne. 2002. *Becoming an Ally: Breaking the Cycle of Oppression in People*. Halifax, NS: Fernwood.

Bishop, Anne, with Jeanne Fay. 2004. *Grassroots Leaders Building Skills: A Course in Community Leadership*. Halifax, NS: Fernwood.

Bok, Sissela. 1982. *Secrets: On the Ethics of Concealment and Revelation*. New York: Pantheon.

Bowser, Benjamin P., Gale S. Auletta and Terry Jones. 1993. *Confronting Diversity Issues on Campus*. Newbury Park, CA: Sage.

Briggs, John, and F. David Peat. 1989. *Turbulent Mirror: An Illustrated Guide to Chaos Theory and the Science of Wholeness*. New York: Harper and Row.

Brodribb, Somer, with Sylvia Bardon, Theresa Newhouse, Jennifer Spencer and the assistance of Nadia Kyba. 1996. "The Equity Franchise." *Women's Education des femmes* 12 (1) (Spring).

Butler, John Sibley. 1978. "Institutional Racism: Viable Perspective or Intellectual Bogey." *The Black Sociologist* 7 (3/4) (Spring/Summer).

CBC. 2004. "Johnson gets apology from police." Available on-line at [http://novascotia.cbc.ca/regional/servlet/PrintStory?filename=ns kirkapology20040119&region=novascotia]. Last checked January 19, 2004.

Calliste, Agnes. 2000. "Anti-Racist Organizing and Resistance in Academia." In George J. Sefa Dei and Agnes Calliste (eds.), *Power, Knowledge and Anti-Racism*

Education: A Critical Reader. Halifax, NS: Fernwood.

Campbell v. Jones. 2002, 209 N.S.R. (2d) 81 (CA).

Carniol, Ben. 1995. *Case Critical: Challenging Social Services in Canada.* Third Edition. Toronto, ON: Between the Lines.

Carty, Linda. 1991. "Black Women in Academia: A Statement from the Periphery." In *Unsettling Relations: The University as a Site of Feminist Struggles.* Toronto: Women's Press.

Chilly Collective (eds.). 1995. *Breaking Anonymity: The Chilly Climate for Women Faculty.* Waterloo, ON: Wilfred Laurier University Press.

Collins, Patricia Hill. 1989. "The Social Construction of Black Feminist Thought." *Signs* 14 (4).

Cornwall Collective. 1980. *Your Daughters Shall Prophesy: Feminist Alternatives in Theological Education.* New York: Pilgrim.

Coser, Rose Laub. 1963. "Alienation and the Social Structure: Case Analysis of a Hospital." In Eliot Freidson (ed.), *The Hospital in Modern Society.* London: Collier-Macmillan.

CUSO Education Department. 1988. *Basics and Tools: A Collection of Popular Education Resources and Activities.* Ottawa, ON: CUSO.

Donham, Parker Barss. 1997. "A Classic Case of Obedience Over Conscience: Don't Be So Sure You or I Would Have Blown the Whistle on Shelburne Abusers." *Sunday Daily News,* April 27.

Donnellon, Anne, and Deborah M. Kolb. 1994. "Constructive for Whom? The Fate of Diversity Disputes in Organizations." *Journal of Social Issues* 50 (1).

Doyle-Bedwell, Patti. 1997. "Justice and Healing: A Teaching Journal." *Status of Women Supplement, CAUT Bulletin* April.

Dunphy and Associates. 1996. *Introduction to Human Rights Investigation: Workshop Manual.* Halifax, NS: Dunphy and Associates.

Emberley, Peter. C. 1996. *Zero Tolerance: Hot Button Politics in Canada's Universities.* Toronto, London: Penguin.

Fortune, Marie. 1989. *Is Nothing Sacred? When Sex Invades the Pastoral Relationship.* San Francisco: Harper and Row.

Franklin, Karen. 1998. "Inside the Mind of People Who Hate Gays." Available online at [http://www.pbs.org/wgbh/pages/frontline/shows/assault/roots/franklin.html]. Last checked February 7, 2001. It is an excerpt from "Unassuming Motivations: Contextualizing the Narrative of Antigay Assailants," in Gregory M Herek (ed.), *Stigma and Sexual Orientation: Understanding Prejudice Against Lesbians, Gay Men and Bisexuals* (1997). Thousand Oaks, CA: Sage.

Freidson, Eliot. 1970. *The Profession of Medicine: A Study of the Sociology of Applied Knowledge.* New York: Dodd, Mead.

Freire, Paulo. 1970. *Pedagogy of the Oppressed.* New York: Seabury.

Girard, Rene. 1977. *Violence and the Sacred.* Baltimore: Johns Hopkins University Press.

Gleick, James. 1987. *Chaos: Making a New Science.* New York, London: Penguin.

Globe and Mail. 1995. "The Progress of Women." 11 August, A18. Quoted in Emberley (1996).

Graveline, Jean. 1996. *Circle as Pedagogy: Aboriginal Tradition Enacted in a University Classroom.* Doctor of Philosophy Thesis, Dalhousie University.

Green, Margaret. 1993. "Women in the Oppressor Role: White Racism." In Sheila Ernst and Maggie McGuire, *Living with the Sphynx: Papers from the Women's*

Therapy Centre. London, UK: Women's Press

hooks, bell. 1981. *Ain't I a Woman? Black Women and Feminism.* Boston: South End.

_____. 1984. *Feminist Theory: From Margin to Centre.* Boston: South End.

_____. 1994. *Teaching to Transgress: Education as the Practice of Freedom.* New York: Routledge.

Hoving, Tom. 1994. Program notes for *Vision: The Music of Hildegard von Bingen.* Toronto: Angel Records.

Janigan, Mary, Ruth Atherley, Michelle Harries, Brenda Branswell and John Demont. 2000. "The Wealth Gap." *Macleans Magazine* August 28. Available on-line at [http://csf.colorado.edu/pen-1/2000III/msg03291.html]. Last checked March 13, 2004.

Jones, Betty B. 1993. "Working with the 'Only One' in the Division." Paper presented at the Annual International Conference for Community College Chairs, Deans, and Other Instructional Leaders, Phoenix, Arizona, February 17–20.

Kanter, Rosabeth Moss. 1977. *Men and Women of the Corporation.* New York: Basic Books.

_____. 1983. *The Change Masters: Innovation and Entrepreneurship in the American Corporation.* New York: Simon and Schuster. The quotes I used from this book were taken from Kanter's website [http://www.goodmeasure.com/frameset/library/articles/article2.htm]. Last checked August 19, 2001.

_____. 1993. *A Tale of 'O': On Being Different.* Video produced by Barry M. Stein. Available on Kanter's website, URL as above.

Kerstetter, Steven. 2002. *Rags and Riches: Wealth Inequality in Canada.* Ottawa: Centre for Policy Alternatives. Available on-line at [http://www.policyalternatives.ca/publications/ragsandrichessummary.html]. Last checked March 13, 1004.

Keyes, Ken Jr. 1984. *The Hundredth Monkey.* Second Edition. Coos Bay, OR: Vision Books.

Keynes, John Maynard. 1935. *The General Theory of Employment, Interest and Money.* Current edition: Amherst, NY: Prometheus Books, 1997.

Kingsolver, Barbara. 1988. *The Bean Trees.* New York: Harper.

Kirkham, Kate. 1988–89. "Teaching About Diversity: Navigating the Emotional Undercurrents." *The Organizational Behavior Teaching Review* 13 (4).

Lebacqz, Karen. 1985. *Professional Ethics: Power and Paradox.* Nashville: Abingdon.

Lorde, Audre. 1982. *Zami: A New Spelling of my Name.* Freedom, CA: Crossing Press.

Mander, Jerry. 1991. *In the Absence of the Sacred: The Failure of Technology and the Survival of the Indian Nations.* San Francisco, CA: Sierra Club.

McIntosh, Peggy. 1990. "White Privilege: Unpacking the Invisible Knapsack." *Independent School* Winter.

McIntyre, Sheila. 1995. "Gender Bias Within the Law School: '"The Memo' and its Impact." In Chilly Collective.

McQuaig, Linda. 1987. *Behind Closed Doors: How the Rich Won Control of Canada's Tax System and Ended Up Richer.* Markham, ON: Viking.

_____. 1993. *The Wealthy Banker's Wife: The Assault on Equality in Canada.* Toronto: Penguin.

Memmi, Albert. 1990. *The Colonizer and the Colonized.* London: Earthscan.

Michell, Gillian, and Constance Backhouse. 1995. "Epilogue: The Remarkable Response to the Release of the Chilly Climate Report." In Chilly Collective.

Milgram, Stanley. 1973. "The Perils of Obedience." *Harper's* 247 (1483) (December).
_____. 1974. *Obedience to Authority*. San Francisco, CA: Harper and Row.
Mitchnick, M.G., Arbitrator. 1995. *In the Matter of an Arbitration between University of Windsor Faculty Association v. University of Windsor*. Unpublished decision.
Mohanty, Chandra Talpade. 1994. "On Race and Voice: Challenges for Liberal Education in the 90s." In Henry A. Giroux and Peter McLaren (eds.), *Between Borders: Pedagogy and the Politics of Cultural Studies*. New York: Routledge.
Monture-Angus, Patricia. 1995a. *Thunder in my Soul*. Halifax: Fernwood.
_____. 1995b. "Introduction—Surviving the Contradictions: Personal Notes on Academia." In Chilly Collective.
National Film Board of Canada. 1984. *Behind the Veil: Nuns, Part 2*. Directed by Margaret Wescott. Produced by Signe Johansson.
New English Bible. 1970. Oxford and Cambridge, UK: Oxford University Press, Cambridge University Press.
Ng, Roxanna. 1993. "A Woman Out of Control: Deconstructing Sexism and Racism in the University." *Canadian Journal of Education* 18 (3).
Ontario Human Rights Commission v. Simpsons-Sears [1985] 2 S.C.R. 536. 23 D.L.R. (4th) 321. 7 C.H.R.R. D/3102 sub nom. *O'Malley v. Simpsons-Sears*.
Peat, F. David. 1994. *Blackfoot Physics: A Journey into the Native American Universe*. London: Fourth Estate.
Postman, Neil. 1992. *Technopoly*. New York: Knopf.
Prentice, Susan. 1996. "Addressing and Redressing Chilly Climates in Higher Education." *CAUT Bulletin, Status of Women Supplement* 43 (4) (April).
President's Advisory Committee on the Status of Women, University of Saskatchewan. 1995. "Reinventing our Legacy: The Chills Which Affect Women." In Chilly Collective.
Public Service Alliance of Canada v. Canada (Department of National Defence (CA) 1996.
Rao, Aruna, Rieky Stuart and David Kelleher. 1999. *Gender at Work: Organizational Change for Equality*. West Hartford, CT: Kumarian Press.
Rashdall, Hastings. 1936. *The Universities of Europe in the Middle Ages*. London: Oxford University Press.
Rau, Leela Madhava. 1995. "'Race Relations' Policy Brought to Life: A Case Study of One Anti-harassment Protocol." In Chilly Collective.
Richardson, Boyce. 1997. "Corporations: How do we Curb their Obscene Power?" Available on-line at [http://www.geocities.com/athens/3565/cancorp1.html]. Lasted checked February 27, 2001.
Sabattis, Terri. 1996. *Tutelage and Resistance: The Native Post-secondary Experience*. Master of Social Work Thesis, Dalhousie University.
Sandler, Bernice R. 1986. *The Campus Climate Revisited: Chilly Climate for Women Faculty, Administrators, and Graduate Students*. Washington, DC: Project on the Status and Education of Women, AAC.
Schaef, Anne Wilson. 1987. *When Society Becomes an Addict*. San Francisco: Harper and Row.
Schaef, Anne Wilson, and Diane Fassel. 1988. *The Addictive Organization*. San Francisco: Harper and Row.
Small, Judy. 1985. "One Voice in the Crowd." On *One Voice in the Crowd*. Penrith City, Australia: Plaza Records.
Smith, Adam. 1776. *An Inquiry into the Nature and Causes of the Wealth of Nations*. Current edition: Amherst, NY: Prometheus Books, 1991. Also available on-line

[http://www.online-literature.com/adam_smith/wealth_nations]. Last checked March 13, 2004.

Tack, Martha W., and Carol L. Patitu. 1992. "Faculty Job Satisfaction: Women and Minorities in Peril." *ERIC Clearinghouse on Higher Education*. George Washington University School of Education and Human Development, Washington, DC.

Theodore, Athena. 1986. *The Campus Troublemakers: Academic Women in Protest*. Houston, TX: Cap and Gown.

Thompson, Audrey. 2003. "Tiffany, Friend of People of Color: White Investments in Antiracism." *Qualitative Studies in Education* 16 (1).

Toronto Star. 2003. "Ottawa police, deputy chief at odds over racial profiling." March 2.

Tuchman, Gaye. 1979. "Women's Depiction by the Mass Media" *Signs* 4 (3) (Spring).

Watson, Lyall. 1980. *Lifetide*. New York: Bantam.

Weiner, Nan, and Morley Gunderson. 1990. *Pay Equity: Issues, Options and Experience*. Toronto: Butterworths.

Wheatley, Margaret J. 1992. *Leadership and the New Science: Learning About Organization from an Orderly Universe*. San Francisco, CA: Berrett Kochler.

Williams, Patricia. 1991. *The Alchemy of Race and Rights*. Cambridge, MA: Harvard University Press.

Wink, Walter. 1984. *Naming the Powers: The Language of Power in the New Testament*. Minneapolis: Fortress.

_____. 1992. *Engaging the Powers: Discernment and Resistance in a World of Domination*. Minneapolis: Fortress.

Wylie, Alison. 1995. "The Contexts of Activism on 'Climate' Issues." In Chilly Collective.

Wylie-Kellerman, Bill. 1998. "Exorcising an American Demon: Racism is a Principality." *Sojourners* March-April.

Yalnizyan, Armine. 1998. *The Growing Gap: A Report on Growing Inequality between the Rich and Poor in Canada*. Toronto: Centre for Social Justice.

Young, Iris Marion. 1990. *Justice and the Politics of Difference*. Princeton, NJ: Princeton University Press.

Zohar, Danah. 1990. *The Quantum Self: Human Nature and Consciousness Defined by the New Physics*. New York: William Morrow.

Index